Bi America
Myths, Truths, and Struggles
of an Invisible Community

HARRINGTON PARK PRESS
Bisexuality
Fritz Klein, MD
Senior Editor

Bisexual and Gay Husbands: Their Stories, Their Words edited by Fritz Klein and Tom Schwartz

Bi America: Myths, Truths, and Struggles of an Invisible Community by William E. Burleson

Eros: A Bi/Cultural Journey by Serena Anderlini-D'Onofrio

Bi America
Myths, Truths, and Struggles of an Invisible Community

William E. Burleson

Routledge
Taylor & Francis Group

NEW YORK AND LONDON

First published 2005 by
Harrington Park Press®

Published 2014 by Routledge
711 Third Avenue, New York, NY, 10017, USA
2 Park Square, Milton Park, Abingdon, Oxon OX14 4RN

Routledge is an imprint of the Taylor & Francis Group, an informa business

Cover design by Jennifer M. Gaska.

Library of Congress Cataloging-in-Publication Data

Burleson, William E.
    Bi America : myths, truths, and struggles of an invisible community / William E. Burleson.
       p. cm.
    Includes bibliographical references and index.
    1. Bisexuals—United States—Social conditions. I. Title.

HQ74.2.U5B87 2004
306.76'5'0973—dc22

                                           2004012047

ISBN 13: 978-1-560-23478-4 (hbk)
ISBN 13: 978-1-560-23479-1 (pbk)

To Mariann

ABOUT THE AUTHOR

William Burleson is a Twin Cities HIV-prevention educator, activist, and writer. He is one of the founders of the Bisexual Organizing Project in Minneapolis and is a past coordinator of BECAUSE, the Midwest conference on bisexuality. Burleson is a regular speaker and workshop facilitator discussing the bisexual community and the nature of sexuality at conferences and on college campuses. In addition he is a columnist for the *GLBT Press* in Minneapolis. Current and recent projects include producing a weekly Minneapolis cable access television show, *Bi Cities!,* and helping to plan the Eighth International Conference on Bisexuality, held in the Twin Cities in August 2004.

CONTENTS

Foreword

I first met Bill when I came to Minneapolis to keynote the 1999 BECAUSE conference. I was being shuttled around town by a long-time activist and mutual friend, Victor Raymond, who took me to meet Bill. Bill was the coordinator of the conference that year, and we were able to spend quite a bit of time getting to know each other. Since then, we've been colleagues as well as friends. I find him to be a caring and intelligent man who is a bi activist in the best sense of the word. Therefore, when Bill told me he was planning to write a book about bisexuality, I was excited to introduce him to my publisher, The Haworth Press.

When I started research in the 1970s, almost nothing was written about bisexuality. I remember going into the main New York Public Library on Fifth Avenue and finding only two cards in the catalog pertaining to the subject. In 1978 I published *The Bisexual Option,* which I updated in 1993. The book explored the many facets of this authentic sexual orientation and was the first in-depth look at the subject.

A good deal has happened in the world since 1978, even since 1993, and the bisexual community's ups and downs have reflected those changes. AIDS, the increasing trend away from liberalism toward a more conservative country, yet increasing success for gay and lesbian people in their fight for acceptance, have all helped shape what is now a small but vocal bisexual community.

In the mid-1970s when I started a bisexual support group in New York, it was one of a handful in existence in the United States. There I found people looking for answers, looking for support for being, what they thought, the only ones who felt this way. Now in 2005, I am sure it is still common for a bisexual support group to be the only one in existence, comprised of relatively few people in any of the larger cities of the country. Most of the country's smaller cities and towns still do not have these small support groups where people come looking to find out what this all means. However, in those cities that do have one, an individual can, with a minimum of research, find and join it. Even if people don't join, they know it exists and is out there if they ever decide they need it.

Although this change is important, even more dramatic has been the effect of the Internet on the bisexual community. All anyone has to do is type <www.bisexual.org> into a Web browser to be connected to a world of international, national, and local resources, offering support and information. In the twenty-first century this is indeed a valid community. A bisexual person, no matter where he or she lives, need not be completely isolated any longer.

Since my trip to the library in the 1970s, a number of books about bisexuality have been published (including several of my own). Of these books, several are of an academic nature, reflecting a newfound validity of bisexuality as a research topic. Several books of essays have also been compiled by bisexual editors. It is good news that the community is finding its own voice, as well as reflecting the growth and increased influence of the greater lesbian, gay, transgender, and bisexual communities. These general books, plus a few more about specific topics regarding bisexuality, are a small but decent start in creating a bisexual section in a bookstore.

Yet, despite all these changes, since the *Bisexual Option* came out no other mass-audience book looking at bisexuality in American culture has been available. Now there is with the publication of Bill's book. We know subcultures such as the bisexual community face great societal pressures and are usually in a constant state of change. What the bisexual community is at the present time is neither what it was in the past nor what it will be in the future. It is too easy even in this age of rich information to lose a segment of people, to forget to document their unique history and culture, and to have them disappear into history, forgotten. This book effectively addresses that issue. People will be able to see and understand this unique group, and when someone in the future wants to understand how bisexuality and bisexuals came to mean whatever it will mean then, he or she will have this in-depth book.

The more immediate use of this book is just as important. As people consider or come out as bisexual and want to understand what that means, they now have a new resource in that journey. When bisexual people want a parent or friend to better understand their lives, there is now a good book to recommend. Anyone interested in the richness of what it means to be human and wanting to understand a different subculture will be able to learn about the bisexual community.

I hope this book makes you question your assumptions about bisexuality and broaden your world to include people from a diversity of sexual expressions. But most of all I hope this book makes you feel comfortable with yourself, whatever your sexuality or gender expression.

Fritz Klein, MD

Preface

Some Notes About Language

Throughout this book and in doing the survey, I fought a losing battle between the fluidity of gender and the rigidity of the English language. With great trepidation I have chosen to accept *they* and *their* as newly crowned singular pronouns. I would rather suffer the slings and arrows of language purists than use *him or her* or *he or she* and leave out the transgender community and many good friends. Harder was avoiding the use of *opposite sex* and *same sex* to describe forms of partner relationships. The duality of sexual orientation that makes bisexuals invisible has a parallel in gender orientation (as I discuss in Chapter 6), erasing many transgender people. Also, the dance between *sex* and *gender* can be more complex than the language easily allows. I apologize.

I switch freely between LGBT (lesbian, gay, bisexual, and transgender) and GLBT. Both are in common usage, but depending on where one lives in the United States, one or the other predominates. I decided to use both. When I quote people, I might also use GLBTI ("I" for *intersex*). In addition, in the world, if not in this book, one may hear GLBTQ ("Q" for either *queer* or *questioning*) or GLBTA ("A" for *allies*). Indeed, I once spoke at a BTLGIQQA conference.

Also, I generally use *gay* to mean homosexual men and *lesbian* to mean homosexual women. Some may argue *gay* simply means homosexual, so if I mean homosexual men, I should say *gay men.* Perhaps so, but *gay and lesbian* is in common usage, whereas *gay men and lesbians* is a bit awkward and, I think, wordy.

I also indiscriminately flip between usage of *bi* and *bisexual.* I do so for poetic reasons only; I intend for both words to mean the same thing. I acknowledge a small number of people in the bisexual community don't like "bi." I guess I do. The argument has been made that "bi" is trivializing. The 1993 March on Washington for Lesbian, Gay, and Bi Equal Rights used bi so as to erase "sexual" from the title in an attempt to desexualize the image of the event. This abbreviated identity offended many bisexuals who maintain we are bisexuals and we should be proud of that name. I agree. On the other hand, I like bi too, especially when it makes for a better read (and for that matter, book title). Again, I apologize if I have offended.

Last, using *America* is asking for it. I know. At one time I might have resisted using it to refer to the United States. It seems so jingoistic, so U.S.-centric. That is all true, but its use is also very common, especially in other countries. People the world over refer to the United States as "America," and when referring to the countries of North and South America, it is typical to use "the Americas." The point of writing is communication, and I think when "America" is used it is clear what is meant.

None of these matters are trivial. Language is important, particularly when language has the power to intellectually delegitimize a whole community. I hope I have reached a good balance between understandability and politics.

Acknowledgments

This book is the collective wisdom of many, many people—certainly those people quoted in the book, but numerous others as well who did not make it onto these pages. My journey as a bisexual has been informed along the way by many good, kind, smart people who taught me through words and deeds what it means to be bisexual and what it means to be part of a community. I thank everyone who guided me and informed me, even though I usually pretended I already knew what they were talking about.

A special thank you to Dr. Fritz Klein for his guidance, patience, and wisdom.

Thank you to my partner of thirteen years who saved my behind with her skills in copyediting and help in making the book readable.

Thank you to Michael Ronn, Bob Grams, PhD, Anne Phibbs, PhD, Scott Bartell, MSW, as well as Dr. Klein for reading my rough draft and pointing out the many times I made little or no sense.

Thanks to Steve Parker for making me look thinner than I really am in the book-jacket photo—truly an extraordinary photographer!

And a big thanks to Anissa Harper, my copy editor at The Haworth Press. How she managed to make this book legible is beyond me. May we someday meet in person now that we've exchanged about a thousand e-mails.

Thank you to all who contributed to the online bisexual support group: Ravenmajel, Ronald, Eric, Happy, Tezza, Nancy, Julz, Valia, Glenn, Jennifer, Erika, Cool, Dominique, Paul, Jessie, Juli, Mike, Kimberly, Ron, Lori, Stephanie, Maria, Juliet, Areusa, and Diana, plus all those who contributed but are not quoted directly. I didn't realize how important the group would be when I started. Your input, whether you were directly quoted or not, was incredible.

Thank you to Sean Kinlin, Mark Schuller, and Dawn Pankonien for all their hard work on the Bisexual History Project, as well as to the Bisexual Organizing Project for their permission to reprint it. Last, but certainly not least, thanks to the participants of the Bisexual History Project: Scott, Magenta, Carey, Brian, Alix, Kevin, Rob,

Jodi, Elizabeth, Anita, Kathleen, and David, plus all those others who provided their stories. Your input was the start of everything, and if not for your heartfelt testimonies about your lives as bisexuals, this book could not exist.

Introduction

MY OWN STORY

I came out to myself on the corner of Twenty-Fourth Street and Hennepin Avenue in Minneapolis while riding the number 17 bus. I thought, "That's it! I'm bisexual!" I was seventeen years old, and I was privileged to know something about bisexuality, as my high school sweetheart identified as bisexual. I had also spent most of my life in the inner city where gay people undeniably existed. My parents and friends may have stereotyped and disparaged them, but they were our neighbors and clearly part of the fabric of the community. Still, it was ten more years until I came out to my friends and family.

At the time I had this epiphany in 1977, the gay liberation movement was going strong and making rapid headway in securing basic civil rights. The gay community was in a golden age of nightclubs, discos, and bathhouses, with no idea of the plague already beginning. For me, it all seemed so simple. I was attracted to women and men, which I thought was okay. I saw that most other people didn't share that feeling; I thought that was okay, too. I always knew some people would hate people like me; got it. It turned out anything but simple. Being bisexual put me, and others like me, in the center of the storm over gay and lesbian rights and challenged many people's core beliefs about sexuality and gender. It turned out it was just not that easy for me to be a bi American.

As an adult, I practiced serial monogamy as I went from relationship to relationship. My relationships with females were public and longer lasting, and my relationships with men private and short. My awareness of my bisexuality was a simple one of desires, secrets, and theory.

Throughout the 1980s I knew no one who was bi, yet I thought I understood what it all meant. As the decade came to a close, my life began to change. I quit drinking. I quit fooling myself that it didn't matter that I was bi, that it wasn't important. I started coming out publicly, little by little. By 1990 I was fully involved in the gay community and its culture. I loved it. After living a secret for so long, it was liberating to finally begin to talk about it.

But I wasn't gay. It didn't take very long before I was reminded of that. When I met my present partner of thirteen years, a woman, my life took another left turn. My newfound community of lesbian and gay friends quickly disintegrated when confronted with my flagrant violation of cultural taboos and community norms. I found I could not continue to travel in the gay community with a woman partner. I found out the hard way that I had much to learn about what it means to be bisexual in our society.

Then, in 1993, I attended my first BECAUSE, the Midwest conference on bisexuality. There, in a room filled with 150 other bisexuals, I found my home. Since that time I have attended eight more BECAUSE conferences, plus a few others around the country, and had the honor of being the coordinator of the event twice. I have attended support groups, as well as facilitated and founded other bi groups from scratch. I have helped build a bi organization in the Twin Cites and now produce a bi cable-access television show. I have edited newsletters, published articles in the gay, lesbian, bisexual, and transgender press, and been a speaker about the issue throughout Minnesota. And now, I am writing this book.

I am telling my story because this book depends on stories. It would be disrespectful of me not to write about my own life when so many others have contributed their stories of strength, pain, hope, and redemption. Because they did tell their own very personal stories, we are able to see and better understand what it means to be bisexual in America.

SOURCES

Most of the quotes come from three sources: interviews, the Bi History Project, and an online bi support group. The people in this book are all real people. However, depending on the desires of the person, sometimes names have been changed and details may have been altered to maintain varying degrees of confidentiality.

The Bi History Project

In the spring of 2000, fellow volunteers Mark Schuller, Sean Kinlin, and I created the Bisexual History Project. The goal was to document the stories of real people, to capture this moment in history as a community, and to start to document our history as a people. We told the attendees at the conference what we had planned, set up a camera in a public area of the conference, and waited to see who would come by and tell their stories. An audience gathered. By the end, fourteen people took the time and challenged their shyness to sit down and tell the entire world their stories. That summer Dawn Pankonien, a student at a local liberal arts college, volunteered to spend uncounted hours transcribing the four hours of tape into what is now the Bi History Project. By the end of summer, we achieved our goal by donating the entire document to the Minnesota History Center as part of The GLBT Collection.

The people from this project are not necessarily representative of all bisexuals. As out bi's (some more than others), they certainly do not represent all those who are attracted to more than one gender. What they represent most is the established, visible bi community: those people who will go to community events, attend the local Pride festival, become involved in the politics of the community, and, of course, be interested in attending a bi conference.

Many of the participants I have known for several years, and others I have just met. They are diverse both in gender, including transgender people, and in age, from the mid-twenties to the mid-fifties. What they share in common is self-awareness—an intelligence born of years of hard, personal work.

I have included the complete transcript of the Bisexual History Project in Appendix B. Although I use parts of it to illustrate topics throughout the book, much can be gained by reading it in its entirety. In fact, it may be a helpful place to begin reading this book before turning to the several chapters.

The Online Support Group

I know many of the participants in the Bisexual History Project, but the online support group is the complete opposite. It is anonymous by design, a place on the Web where people can write frankly about themselves and their experiences.

I formed the group to help me write this book. To find members, I e-mailed all the groups listed at the bisexual.org Web site and asked whoever received it to take the survey, to consider joining my book advisory group, and to pass the request along to others. Ultimately,

270 surveys were completed, and at its peak the support group had ninety members from all around the United States.

I must admit, I created the Web site more for the survey data and the group was more of an afterthought. I obtained the data I was after, but it turned out the group was more interesting. I've often said, only half in jest, if you put a quarter in a bisexual they'll talk about bisexuality for hours; it is so seldom that anybody asks, we are bursting to tell everyone about it. The support group members shared tales of isolation, joy, fear, love, heartache, and redemption; each story was unique, very personal, and yet very familiar. A pattern, very clear, very sincere, ran through the stories. Those patterns, those commonalities, are what make up this book.

The Survey

No one hates junk data more than I do. My online survey is just that: junk data. (1) It is not a representative sample of the bi community or the population as a whole. (2) There is no way to guarantee that people didn't take the survey more than once. (3) The sample group necessarily includes only people who go online, leaving out about half the population. (4) I found the participants through their affiliation with bi groups throughout the country active enough to have their own Web sites and therefore probably left out the vast majority of online bi's who are not part of a group. This is not how sociologists and cultural anthropologists like to gather data.

The survey does provide a picture of those who responded. It tells about the people who made up the online support group and, to a lesser degree, about those who are actively involved in the bi community (a group that is a tiny subset of all bi's). The survey gives anecdotal data about this population. It is important, because many of these questions have not been asked before, especially regarding community affiliation and feelings of acceptance. It would be wonderful if an academic researcher could do a more thorough survey of bisexuals someday, but until that day, and for my purposes, these data will have to do.

All the survey data can be found in Appendix A. Some of it is interesting because it is surprising; some of it is interesting because it affirms what one might have guessed. Either way, an individual is not a survey, and all those data do not tell about any one person. What it does is reveal patterns that can be used to help get a wide-angle view of a community.

The survey data are not very important in the scheme of the book. What *is* important are the stories of real people, living their lives. That is what I set out to do with this project: tell our story. Data are great, academia is wonderful, and I give the reader a good dose of both. But I believe what really matters are the people and their stories. No matter what readers' sexual orientation, political beliefs, or religious convictions are, I hope some commonalities with the individuals speaking here will be identified, connecting us to the human struggle we all have in our lives. Bi people, as is true of many other groups, are often reduced to stereotypes. I hope to reduce bisexuality to its humanity.

WHO AND WHAT THIS BOOK IS ABOUT

The meaning of *bisexual* is elusive. In the *Stanford Law Review*, Kenji Yoshino argues in "The Epistemic Contract of Bisexual Erasure" that a person's orientation may be defined along three axes: behavior, attraction, and self-identity.[1] This is a very useful model for my purposes.

With that in mind, I will be talking about three groups. The largest group is composed of those who "behave" bisexually. *Behave* is an elusive term all on its own, and people who have had or do have sex with people of more than one gender may or may not identify as bisexual. However, I am less interested in this group than I am the second group: those who identify as bisexual. As discussed in Chapter 3, people who call themselves bisexual are a tiny subset of those who behave bisexually.

The third group, and a population of special interest in this book, is a yet tinier subset of those who identify as bisexual. That group is the bi community. Chapter 4 reveals the small communities of bisexuals that exist at least in some places in America. Living below the pop-culture radar, they hold support groups, social events, and conferences; publish Web sites and newsletters; and possess community norms, history, and culture. All this, yet they enjoy neither attention nor acknowledgment from the rest of society, the gay and lesbian communities, or even the vast majority of bisexuals.

This categorization raises several questions: First, why don't more people who have or have had sex with people of more than one gender call themselves bisexual? Second, since a good number of people do identify as bisexual, why is there little—or in most places no—sign of a bisexual community? Finally, given the scarcity of bisexual community, what is different about those who *have* found and joined the bi community, and what makes that community unique?

These are the questions I had when I first went looking for my community twelve years ago, and these are the questions I attempt to address in this book.

Before going any further, it will be helpful to start at the beginning, or my own beginning at least. In the Midwest, many people discover the bisexual community—as I did—at BECAUSE.

Chapter 1

BECAUSE

WELCOME TO BECAUSE

The hotel was pretty much like any other suburban hotel, perched on former swampland just off the interstate. It was pretty much in the middle of nowhere, but it would be just as correct to say it was pretty much anywhere. Standing in the vast parking lot, looking out over the traffic on the freeway, it could have been in any city in any state in the United States. That impression is reinforced inside the hotel: it would be impossible to tell what part of the country you were in unless you noticed the framed tourist pictures of the Twin Cities hanging by the check-in desk.

On this beautiful Friday afternoon in April, the hotel was getting busy. Families were checking in for the weekend so the kids could use the pool and the parents could have a good meal in peace. A wedding party, complete with several generations of relatives, checked in. Businesspeople, apparently in some unfortunate industry requiring them to travel on weekends, glumly rode the elevator. It was a large hotel, and two meetings were taking place at the same time this weekend. There was a Christian group sporting a three-by-four foot foamcore poster of their charismatic leader and selling books and tapes to a well-dressed group of followers. And then there was BECAUSE.

BECAUSE, the Bisexual Empowerment Conference: A Uniting Supportive Experience, is an annual meeting for bisexuals from throughout the Midwest. This was the second time BECAUSE was held at a hotel. Although hotels are the traditional venue for conferences, previously BECAUSE had been held on college campuses and hosted by college GLBT student groups. Colleges seemed to be, or at least to have been, more in keeping with the culture of the event. Borrowed classrooms in Coffman Union at the University of Minnesota had felt more apropos than well-appointed, modern hotel facilities with cut-glass water tumblers and elaborate flower arrangements. But times change, as has the "bisexual movement." Besides, if "poly cons" and "science fiction cons" can be held in hotels, why not the most successful bisexual conference in the country?

That was the thought among the new group of planners for BECAUSE. There have been several different generations of conference planners since BECAUSE began in 1992. Some years have seen very little change in the leadership; others, including 2003, meant almost completely new faces. The new organizers bring a slightly new politic to the conference; a subtle difference perhaps, but still real. This partly reflects the different interests of the individuals in this group compared to those who comprised the committees of the past, but it also reflects the changing politics of the movement as a whole. This reality is neither right nor wrong; times simply are changing. What was once a conference devoted to examining "systems of oppression" from a feminist point of view is now increasingly social. What once seemed to hold more political urgency and an opportunity to vent one's anger is now more focused on music and dancing. I don't want to overstate the difference, for both elements have always been present. It is more a subtle shift in emphasis. The workshops haven't really changed much: Defining Bisexuality, Bisexual Advocacy, Living in One's Personal Culture, Safer Sex Is Hot Sex, Bound for Pleasure, and Personal Photography; there is something for everyone. Perhaps the change reflects what one national bi community leader suggested to me: The time for anger is passing, and now it's time to celebrate. We'll see.

Friday evening at past conferences was reserved for a keynote speech and reception, but in keeping with this year's conference theme, "The Art of Being Bi," an art show and reception was held instead. It was a low-key affair, as many of the weekend's attendees apparently chose to wait until Saturday to arrive. Therefore, not many people were around the BECAUSE check-in desk when I arrived. Located near a large conference room where much of the weekend's activities were to be held, the check-in desk buzzed with volunteer activity and featured a banner, T-shirts for sale, and program folders. Working the desk was Becky, a twenty-something woman who was both volunteering at and attending BECAUSE for the first time. A professional woman who lost her job due to the terrible economy, Becky was somewhat emotional about being here. She told me being involved with the bisexual community "used to make me upset. It's so much to deal with. But I'm getting better. I think I dove in too fast at first." Coming to terms with being bisexual can be a trauma for many people, and Becky was young in her struggle.

Also new this year was Allen. Allen differed from Becky in that he seemed quite comfortable there. Allen is in his early thirties, works in computers, and is more than a little interested in science fiction. He is becoming something of a rising star on the planning committee and is "so excited to be here. It's been great."

Brent was everywhere. It is his second time at BECAUSE, the first being last year when it was in Milwaukee, also at a hotel. Brent is a new leader in the community—a fast rise considering he first drifted into the community like a lost puppy just a couple of years ago. Since then he has settled into the community and made friends. He had done quite a bit of the heavy lifting that weekend and promised to "crash, man. As soon as this is over I'm out. I'm gone. You won't hear from me for weeks." No one, of course, held him to that, and everyone expected he would be hard at work wrapping up BECAUSE the day after the conference.

The conference's coordinator, Kathy, was a bundle of nerves. Understandably so, she has worked hard for the past year to ensure these next three days go well. Of all the planners, she has the most BECAUSE experience to bring to the table, as this was the third conference she worked, and the second at which she was at least co-coordinator. Kathy is in her thirties with one child at home whom her partner, Mark, is taking care of this weekend. She, similar to Becky, is unemployed, having been a contract employee working in HIV/AIDS prevention, a job with very little security.

These four people, plus five or six more, were responsible for putting on the oldest regularly held conference on bisexuality in the United States, the second oldest in the world. They are all volunteers and achieve this event on a shoestring budget made up of one small grant and conference fees. If they are lucky, they might break even.

The big question is, Why have a conference on bisexuality? About ninety people attended, from various economic classes, mostly college educated, nearly all white, and nearly all liberal to left-wing. Most came looking for the same things. Not sex, although there may be opportunities for that if one is looking. Not for politics in a traditional sense; not even one workshop addressed the topic. The only political booth set up in the informational area was the Green Party, and they didn't look busy. No, these attendees came to find community, something woefully lacking for bisexuals. They came to vent, to blow off steam from the seemingly endless stream of slights, insults, and erasures they must put up with during the rest of the year. They came to understand, to learn what it means to be bisexual, if not in the workshops, then by spending time in a room full of people who are, at least in this important way, just like them.

THE WORKSHOP

I was at BECAUSE that weekend to give a workshop. As time goes on, one stops attending workshops and instead begins leading them; as this was my ninth BECAUSE, I'd long since reached that point. My workshop du jour was the "Top Ten Myths About Bisexuals." I'm more interested in workshops that are about fundamentals and about the whole community rather than a segment of it, such as a leather workshop. Not that either is wrong; I'm just more of a big-picture man.

When it comes to presenting workshops, I could spend all day prattling on about bisexuality from a sociological point of view. Instead, I was there to listen. I think it is much more interesting to hear what is on other people's minds. Besides, in most instances the combined wisdom from any room full of people is far greater than anything I could say. My goal for the workshop was to generate a list of the most tiresome, irritating, angering, irksome stereotypes, myths, and other falsehoods heaped on bisexuals. I was going for visceral, not intellectual. I was looking for people leaping to their feet saying, "Yeah! That drives me crazy!"

I wasn't disappointed. Although I don't recall anyone leaping to their feet, the topic was certainly a hit, with about twenty-five people participating enthusiastically. We had a rambunctious time, made all the more entertaining by the Christian revival meeting* taking place next door. We had no problem generating a list we all could agree on.

---

*This strange bed-fellow arrangement seems to be the norm. In 2002 BECAUSE shared meeting space with a women's bowling group, and in 2001, while the conference was at the University of Wisconsin, the hotel for out-of-towners hosted a Mary Kay Cosmetic Conference. Isn't America great?

Indeed, the problem came in paring it down to only ten, so I'll go with thirteen:

1. Bisexuals are easy; they are indiscriminate about whom they have sex with.
2. All bisexuals are swingers.
3. Bisexuals have the best of both worlds and are twice as likely to get a date.
4. Bisexuals are unable to commit to either gender.
5. Bisexual women are all wives just trying to please their husbands, and bisexual men are all married guys cheating on their wives.
6. Bisexuality is just a phase on the way to being lesbian or gay.
7. Bisexuals are unable to be happy, have low self-esteem, or are mentally ill.
8. Bisexuals are disease carriers.
9. Bisexuals are a very small part of the population.
10. Bisexuals are just trying to maintain heterosexual privilege.
11. Bisexuals can't be feminist.
12. People call themselves bisexual to be trendy.
13. Bisexuality is a choice.

Myths must come from somewhere, so where did these ideas come from? How much truth is there to them? Perhaps most interesting, what brought twenty-five people out to a hotel in the middle of nowhere on a beautiful April afternoon to make a list of the myths about them that anger them the most? Perhaps now would be a good time to look at the relationships between bisexuals and bisexuality in both the straight and the lesbian and gay communities. What does it mean to be bi in America?

Chapter 2

Relating Bisexuality to the World

Being bisexual in this culture is a gift and a curse. It gives you—it gives me—a certain flexibility of thinking, and I don't know that it does that same thing for everyone, but I think it's forced me to live outside the box in many ways. And that, of course, that makes things a little more difficult sometimes. I've been married and divorced and had many different relationships both with men and women. I'm in one right now, and I think it's been harder to get kind of overall community support for relationships that include and recognize bisexuality. (Scott B.)

"BRING OUT THE BISEXUALS": THE JERRY SPRINGER SHOW

I had heard of the *Jerry Springer Show*. One would have to live in a cultural vacuum to not have, but I can honestly say I had never sat down and actually watched it. Not to be a snob, but I can't imagine myself ever saying, "Turn on the TV. Jerry's almost on." That said, a few months ago, while happily channel surfing, I was stopped by that evening's show, titled "Bring Out the Bisexuals."

Indeed. Let's bring them out. First we met a female stripper who left "her man" for the arms of another female stripper. Second was a transsexual who left a wife for the arms of his gay male lover. Third was a woman who left her man and now was in the arms of her *sister.* Add in yelling and screaming, men in black restraining the guests, loud beeps, censored squares, and a chanting audience, and you have the idea—cheap, trashy fun for the whole family.

It strikes me that this, and places similar to this, is where most people get their information about bisexuality. Of course, most Americans have little or no information at all, but when they do see the word *bisexual,* it is when surfing past shows such as Jenny Jones, Montel Williams, and Jerry Springer, or when reading (or at least looking at) *Penthouse Forum, Hustler,* and *Playboy.*

This is a great contrast to what I see. At the BECAUSE conference, I found an interesting, intelligent, articulate, compassionate community bearing no likeness to the one on TV that night. I see a community of gentle people, hardly willing or able to tussle on a stage with several bouncers in black. What I see are people demonized and discriminated against by many in straight society through the structures of homophobia. What I see is a gay community, faced with discrimination and hatred from many in the straight community, struggling with the concept of bisexuality and a bi community. I see people linked by their shared experience of having attractions to people of more than one gender who rarely enjoy the cover or the support of a functioning community. Isolated by the larger American culture that denies their very existence, bisexuality is dismissed and bisexuals are ignored. Bisexuals are nearly forgotten in society, largely invisible in the media, and inconsistent with many people's beliefs about sexuality.

THE INVISIBLE BISEXUAL

To the degree that people continue to operate with an implicit theory of sexual orientation as dichotomous, bisexuality is invisible.

Joseph P. Stokes and Robin L. Miller
in the *Canadian Journal of Human Sexuality*[1]

A lack of public exposure is perhaps the biggest challenge for the bisexual community. Invisibility simply removes bisexuality from the discussion—any discussion. It has often been said that if everyone who is lesbian or gay would come out, because of their sheer numbers there could be no more discrimination. The idea also applies to bisexuals; however, even if they did all come out, they would still be invisible.

The reason for this invisibility is obvious. Consider my neighbors two doors down. They are two gay men who own their house together—nice guys. They walk their dog together, keep a nice yard, and go to all the block parties. We have a friendly, neighborly relationship: say "hi" when we cross paths, make small talk, and complain together when it snows too much. Please note that I called them my *gay* neighbors. I have never asked about their orientation; all I know is that they are in a relationship. One or both could be bi. Short of knowing them better, there is no way for me to know, unless of course they flew a big flag saying, "We're Bi." On the other hand, my partner (a woman) and I live two doors down from them. I can attend all the bi events I want, write books, and so forth, but I bet when they walk by with their border collie (if they think about it) they say, "There's that straight couple." Maybe there are twenty bi people living on my block; how would I know?

Most people make assumptions about sexual orientation according to the gender of one's partner. It is both easy and practical, since it is often or even usually right. Sometimes, however, it is inaccurate; that assumption makes bisexuals invisible.

Dan is a forty-one-year-old blond-haired man who lives in a mobile home in the suburbs of Minneapolis. In several older suburbs of the Twin Cities, mobile-home parks have been grandfathered in and now co-exist with newer, more expensive developments. These few parks are the only place left for working-class people to live in these much wealthier communities. Dan is a good example; he works hard to get by, replacing auto glass for a living during the day. With no significant relationships at this time and no real interests unless one includes television, the evenings generally find him home in his recliner. All in all, it is a quiet life, punctuated with the occasional night out at a local bar with his work friends, or the irregular visit to the Gay Nineties, a gay nightclub downtown.

"I never thought about that," Dan replied when asked if he was ever curious to get to know other bi people, just to know them. "Not really. I'm not very comfortable talking about it. I'm really more interested in getting a girlfriend." This is a possibility he feels is looking up now that a new neighbor moved in next door. "I just every once in a while like to have sex with a man," he told me. I asked him what he considered himself, and he said, "Bisexual, definitely."

In America, a man his age with a job and in good shape has a good chance of finding a woman to settle down with. One could theorize that Dan suffers internalized homophobia, which occurs when people turn their fear and hatred of homosexuality inward against themselves. In other words, although people may be bisexual or homosexual, they do not always like their orientation or themselves. If it were not for that, Dan might consider having a more intimate and longer-lasting relationship with a man. Maybe someday he will, but at this time that is not what he is looking for. Quite possibly he will meet a woman, get married, or otherwise make a partnership and then in regard to his same-sex attractions either be monogamous or not. He would continue to be considered straight by nearly all who know him. Perhaps, however, he will find a man who meets his needs. In that case, regardless of what he calls himself, his bar friends will likely discuss how Dan is now gay. It is unlikely (but certainly not impossible) that he will become an out and loud member of the bisexual community. Dan is just like many, many others, trying to achieve their goals and find some peace, if not fully reconcile their attraction to more than one gender. He is like the vast majority of bi people: invisible.

Bisexuality in the Public Eye—Or Not

The media has built on this inherent invisibility, sometimes to the point of absurdity. Take for example the wedding of Robyn Ochs and Peg Premble. Ochs, who is introduced more fully in Chapter 9, is one of the most visible and active leaders of the bi community in the past twenty years. Ochs and Premble wed, after seven years as a couple, on May 17, 2004, the first day of legal same-sex marriage in Massachusetts. In addition to a packed courtroom of other same-sex couples waiting to be married, attending the ceremony were their friends and a reporter from the *Washington Post*. The reporter had chosen the couple for a story in the following day's paper to present the human side of the marriage debate. And there it was, May 18, 2004, on the front page of the *Post:* "A Carefully Considered Rush to the Altar: Lesbian Pair Wed after 7 Years Together."[2] *Lesbian pair?* A lifetime of bi activism, erased in the swipe of the pen.

Film is another good example; a spate of films have been released in the past few years about people who are attracted to both women and men: *Chasing Amy* (1997), *Bedrooms and Hallways* (1998), *High Art* (1998), and *Kissing Jessica Stein* (2001), to name only a few. Yet all these films have in common one very unexpected trait: almost never is the word *bisexual* uttered at any time. The "almost" is because in *Kissing Jessica Stein* and *Bedrooms and Hallways* bisexual is used as a disparaging remark; in these films about people having sex and/or a relationship with both men and women, the word bisexual is a pejorative.

These films are a rare exception in that they deal with the subject at all. It is unusual for anyone but straight people to appear as central film characters. This must be especially difficult when the film is a biography of a bisexual person, but this is usually handled by merely ignoring the uncomfortable facts. For example, the subject of the film *A Beautiful Mind* (2001), John Nash, married to a woman, was well known to have had male lovers.[3]

I have personal experience in how this works. In 2002, I wrote a play, "Manfinders.com," about two men hooking up while cruising for sex on the Internet. One of the characters was gay and one was bisexual. That the character was bisexual was incidental to the story, and it came up only briefly. At a production meeting with the director and cast, the director (a gay man) questioned why the character was bisexual. He needed a reason for the character to be bisexual rather than gay (besides the fact that some men who cruise the Internet are bisexual). He saw no need to go there. The actor playing the bisexual character resolved it in his own mind by deciding that the character was confused and had not yet come to terms with his homosexuality. This confusion was most certainly not part of the script, but the actor played the character as confused about his sexuality anyway. Even in this scale of theater where one would think freedom to experiment and challenge an audience would be the rule, the choices available were to write bisexuality out or play the character as a stereotype.

Although most films ignore bisexuality, a few public figures have, if not proclaimed their sexual orientation, lived their lives of multiple-gendered loves in a public way. Mick Jagger, David Bowie, Sandra Bernhardt, Madonna, Courtney Love, Michael Stipe, Anne Heche, Sophie B. Hawkins, and model Rachel Williams, to name a few, are all to varying degrees out, if not loud, about their attractions. Indeed, in a more political vein, the National Organization for Women's (NOW) Patricia Ireland has been public about her dual relationships with her husband and a female companion.[4]

Even this little bit of visibility matters. Scott, who was quoted at the beginning of this chapter, is a fifty-something therapist and a long-time leader in the Twin Cities bi community. He has been out publicly since the 1960s. He attributes his willingness to come out then, and stay out now, to having been

[l]ucky enough to have seen, and been presented with, role models of people who were bisexual who were admirable in many ways . . . Eleanor Roosevelt, Errol Flynn (who I was so smitten with as a kid). . . . So I guess I had plenty of reasons to think that it was positive. As I say, people like Patricia Ireland, Elton John, many others saying publicly, "Yup, I'm bisexual," probably helped. Having role models. I think there are a lot of people who don't have those as role models for whatever reason. They didn't hear it. They didn't see it. It didn't mean anything to them. So all they have are negative role models, and that makes it hard to claim that identity.

Scott's story highlights why invisibility is a real problem and why the Jerry Springer episode, "Bring Out the Bisexuals" is so egregious.

Removing Bisexuality from the World

As one man said to me at a national twelve-step conference a number of years ago, "I don't really believe there's anything like bisexuality anyway." You know, like he should know me. I mean, that's what's so amazing is that we assume that we know, that someone would assume that he or she knows me better than myself. I mean that's just bizarre to me. (Anita)

Anita has encountered the most obvious form of oppression experienced by bi people: the denial of their very existence.[5] It is a view created in part from, and certainly facilitated by, the problem of bisexual invisibility. As long as people can believe they do not know anyone who is bisexual, as long as bisexuals do not show up at the table and claim their identity, it will be possible to deny they exist.

Such lack of recognition is born of a desire to understand the world by simplifying it. Wouldn't it be easy if there were only two kinds of people? If there were only two answers to every question, yes or no, right or wrong, or only good or evil? No grays, only black and white? No ambidextrous people, and everyone fitting neatly into census racial categories? And everyone is exclusively heterosexual or absolutely homosexual? Although that world may be easy to understand (if incredibly boring), it is also not *this* world. This world is full of grays, not to mention pinks, greens, and yellows. There are very few absolutes, especially when talking about humans. We are, to our benefit and our detriment, complex, multifaceted, unpredictable, and unique. We do not fit into little boxes well. As convenient as it would seem to be, we are not simply heterosexual or homosexual.

Homophobia and Either/Or Thinking

Many people subscribe to the dualistic view of human sexuality. They believe in the one-drop rule: a person who is attracted to someone of the same gender, regardless of how he or she feels about other genders, is homosexual. This viewpoint is very popular with homophobes, neatly dividing the population into "we normal folks" and "those sick fags." In this view there are no grays, no need or reason for nuance. Homophobes spend no time differentiating their hatred; they just hate those who are different from (or in some cases the same as) what they are.

And people in the GLBT communities *are* victims of hatred. Verbal assaults, physical violence, hate crimes against personal property, job discrimination, and more are the inheritance for people who are not straight. The effects of homophobia are well documented: "Students with a history of same-sex sexual experience appear more likely to have felt threatened and to have experienced personal injury or damage to their property as a result of physical violence."[6] Or "15% to 20% of same-sex [attracted] students . . . reported behaviors at the extreme end of the suicide risk scale, as compared with only 2% to 6% of their other-sex [attracted] peers."[7] When it comes to the bisexual community, no "gay basher" stops to ask exactly where someone falls on the Kinsey scale. No one is only *half*-bashed because he or she is bi.[8]

THE RELATIONSHIP BETWEEN THE BI AND THE LESBIAN AND GAY COMMUNITIES

Interestingly, and what might seem counterintuitive, bisexuals do not fare much better in the gay and lesbian communities. Bisexuals are routinely accused of being "tourists" or "half gay"; they "can't make a choice" and "only want the best of both worlds." Indeed, many lesbian and gay people deny bisexuality's very existence. A survey for the *Advocate,* a magazine targeting the gay and lesbian population, found one-third of respondents did not believe in bisexuality.[9] Bisexuals are pressured into accepting the label of gay or lesbian and joining that community, pressured into choosing between their relationships and being authentic. The result for many bisexuals is either disassociation from or marginalization within the gay and lesbian communities.[10] For example, from the online support group:

> I don't feel welcome in the overall gay community. . . . In general I feel that most of the gay and lesbian people I've met think I'm using "heterosexual privilege" or that I just haven't fully come out as homosexual. Now, I'm not gay bashing. I go to pride parades [and] I'm president of my campus gay-straight alliance, etc. But I have been asked to leave groups and mailing lists because they were for "homosexuals only." Or because, as one woman told me, "Having a bisexual here would bring down the quality of the group." (Kimberly)

This problem is especially difficult for bi women. When I asked about their experiences with the gay, lesbian, straight, bisexual, and transgender communities, 59 percent of bi women I surveyed online found the straight world welcoming, but only 25 percent found the lesbian community welcoming. Men had a better experience with the gay community: 60 percent found it welcoming, while 52 percent said the same about the straight world.

How can this be? Being lesbian, gay, or bisexual does not automatically confer immunity to homophobia. A gay man may say to himself, "I am gay. I am gay, and I can't help it. There is no choice to be made; there is no gray area. I am one hundred percent gay. I have been told all my life I'm one of 'them,' and so are you." Homophobia appears in other ways too. For example, a lesbian might believe, "It's wrong to have sex with someone of the same gender. I'm sick, but I can't help it. But if you are bisexual that means you can."

> Our society is not very tolerant of the homosexual orientation. All of us are raised in an environment that says being gay is not normal (thank God this is beginning to change for some). Many, many gays grow up trying to be "normal" just like everyone else. They go through years sometimes trying to fit into the mold. As they begin to realize their own orientation, they move into accepting they are bisexual, still trying to fit into the boy-dates-girl mode of society. Finally, they come to the realization that they're who they are and accept that it's okay to be gay. This is/was their reality. They have never experienced the bisexual feeling of maintaining their attraction to both sexes, so they don't feel that bisexual is anything other than THEIR reality which was a transition to being open and accepting their gayness. . . . If you've never experienced something, it's often hard to see that perspective (at least for many). (Trista)

Our society is very tough on gay and lesbian people. It is often a challenge for someone who has gone through so much to heal all the scars homophobia has left behind.

In Search of a Gay Gene and What That Means to Bi's

Many people believe sexual orientation is a biological imperative. Much of this view hangs on the search for the gay Holy Grail: the "gay gene," the genetic marker making one destined to be gay or lesbian. It is comforting to many to be able to say, "Hey, look, I can't help it. I was born with it!" It sure seems right, doesn't it? Something so much a part of who a person is, feelings so fundamentally undeniable, something that seems so immutable as sexual orientation would seem to be a good candidate for biological basis. What does this biological basis for homosexuality say about bisexuality, and just what does a "gay gene" mean to a bisexual person?

Once again, bisexuals are removed from consideration. For example, a lesbian suffers the usual challenges nonstraight people face: shame, family disapproval, harassment, and so forth. She finds peace in the view that she "can't help" her same-sex attractions. She may also assume other lesbians similarly can't help it. However, if she meets a bi woman—a bi woman who gets to choose relationships with a woman or a man—it could challenge her beliefs about the nature of sexual orientation and may even cause her to requestion her own orientation.

A gay gene or genes may exist. Indeed, a biological component for sexual orientation seems likely. I am not a researcher in genetics, and I cannot offer anything new about the subject. But two facts are certain: First, many other factors shape people's sexuality—and sexual identity—besides biology, including culture and psychology. Second, and more important, we as a society must ask ourselves, What does it matter? In other words, what if a person could "help it"? Would it then be wrong to be lesbian, or gay, or bisexual? Certainly not. It is a fundamental human right to love whomever or however we choose with other consenting adults. It is not a sickness in need of a cure.

I would suggest there is no need to call into question the imperative nature of sexual orientation but instead to broaden it. Like lesbians and gays, bisexuals also cannot help how they feel—they just feel.

Just like many straight people who cannot imagine ever having sex with someone of the same gender, and many gay and lesbian people who cannot imagine having sex with someone of a different gender, many bi people cannot imagine being attracted to only one gender. A gay gene may or may not define one's orientation, but it would be right to say bisexuals cannot help it either. Sexual attraction is complex, mysterious, wonderful, and pretty darn tough to generalize. Isn't it great?

Kevin, a quiet, bearded man in his thirties, explains his growing awareness of the imperative nature of his bisexuality:

I was born bisexual. And I think I knew it, and I think that awareness became more front-brained as I got older, probably in my twenties.

When asked if identifying as bisexual is now a more accepted option, he appeared indignant:

More of an option? No, I think we're born who we are. It's more of an option to be out. I feel like [sexually], and I will say for me because I'm not going to define sexuality for other people, for me it's a natural alignment. It's part of myself.

Are Bisexuals Really Homosexuals on the Way to Coming Out?

It is often the case that on the journey from the societal default of heterosexual to the eventual self-identification as lesbian or gay one considers the possibility of being, or even identifying as, bisexual for a time. Indeed, one estimate indicates that 40 percent of lesbian and gay people have identified as bisexual at some time in the past.[11] It seems human nature that people would look at all possibilities when exploring their orientation. Unfortunately, it is also a common human trait to generalize or project our experiences onto other people. Therefore, "I thought for a time I was bi before coming out as gay" becomes "All bisexuals are lesbians or gays who are in the process of coming out." Again, we are human; we are all different. No one experience fits all of us. Although a lot of people identify as bisexual for a time before coming out as gay or lesbian, many other bisexuals will always identify as bisexual. Indeed, participants in the online survey have identified as bisexual for an average of 10.3 years, which is a very long transition indeed.

Several years ago I was visiting Chicago, and I found myself at a nice little bar in "Boy's Town," the city's gay bar district. I was chatting with an older man at the bar; I would guess he was in his late sixties or seventies. At one point, I mentioned I was bisexual. He said, "Oh, bisexual. I used to think I was bisexual. You'll come out someday." He meant, of course, to come out as gay. I took a chance, considering his age, and asked, "How long have you identified as gay?" He replied, "Eight years." At the time I had identified as bisexual for twenty years.

Bisexuals in GLBT History—Or Not

Denial of the existence of bisexuality means bisexuals have often been written out of the history of the GLBT movement. The invisibility of bisexuals in Hollywood and in popular media has already been discussed, but it isn't only the mainstream media that makes bisexuality disappear. Rob, a long-time bi activist and HIV/AIDS educator, is well versed in the popular press of the GLBT communities:

> The *Advocate* recently did a story on queer youth who were starting groups in high schools . . . against much opposition. [There's] very important activism going on in our community right now, especially among the youth. In an eight-page article the word "bisexual" appeared twice; once was by the right wing or citizens alliance, so the right wingers remembered us, and once was by a young lesbian who recognized that the gay-straight alliances that are being started in schools need to be inclusive in welcoming bisexual teens because so many teens are using the term now and not wanting to pin down to one or the other. So we need to get the community, especially our community's media, in line with recognizing that we exist, looking for the bisexual aspects of stories, stop lumping Ani Difranco in with gay and lesbian artists. . . . There are so many bi-identified artists now that just get lumped in with gay/lesbian artists, and there needs to be more respect for people's self-identification.

More Reasons for Lesbians and Gays to Dislike Bisexuals

Many more stereotypes and myths about bisexuals are winding their way through the gay and lesbian communities. Perhaps the opposite of "all bisexuals are merely gay or lesbian people in the process of coming out" is the belief that bisexuals are all straight people who are experimenting or merely recreating with same-gender sex. I applaud sexual experimentation, but it is a long way from experimentation to the adoption of a sexual identity. Have we reached a point where, at least in some circles, a straight person must consider bisexuality before coming out finally as straight? Perhaps, but this does nothing to change the feelings of all those who consider bisexuality on their way to identifying as bisexual.

Bi women also face two burdens that bi men do not. First, bi women are accused of bringing sexually transmitted infections (STIs) to the lesbian community. Second, bi women have been accused of being "traitors to feminism." Both of these points will be discussed at length in Chapters 5 and 8; here it is sufficient to say that both accusations are unfair and untrue.

A problem bi women and men both face is that they are accused of holding onto "heterosexual privilege," the special advantages straight people have in American society. In truth, anyone in a different-gender relationship is the beneficiary of heterosexual privilege. In the previous story about my "gay" neighbors, if someone were to discriminate against one of us for being sexually suspect, the victim would most likely be my neighbor, not me. I am the beneficiary of heterosexual privilege by virtue of my invisibility as a bisexual. That said, those bisexuals in same-gender relationships enjoy no more privilege than a lesbian or gay person in a same-gender relationship. For that matter, many closeted gays and lesbians also seem to enjoy heterosexual advantages. Last, I would be remiss if I didn't point out the privilege of being part of an extensive lesbian and gay community—complete with institutions, culture, and history—something bisexuals do not currently enjoy.

Related to seeking the safety of heterosexual privilege, others believe that bi people will always ultimately "go back" to the safety and social acceptance of a different-gender relationship. In other words, "Bisexuals will always break your heart." I find it interesting that the dissolution of a relationship involving a bisexual person cannot simply be about the usual reasons such as incompatibility or snoring. Several years ago, my circle of friends included a particular female couple; one identified as lesbian, and one identified as bi (even though when she said her orientation aloud, her lesbian partner would correct her with, "You are not! You are not!"). They fought like cats and dogs. In hindsight, I don't think there could be two less compatible people. After they broke up, a mutual friend mentioned that the lesbian partner had gone out on a date, but he was very concerned, since the date was with a bisexual woman. He said "Just look how it turned out last time!" even though the issue was compatibility, not bisexuality.

What Bisexuals Say About Relating to Gays and Lesbians

People's experiences are always unique to them, but when enough people are asked, common themes develop. Also, it must be kept in mind that some bisexuals travel extensively in the GLBT world, while others have little or no exposure to the culture. Dan, introduced earlier, has no experience to speak of with gay male culture, nor does he want any. On the other hand, Brent, an attendee at BECAUSE in Chapter 1, is in many ways similar to Dan. He's a forty-ish white male who spent many years in much more conservative communities than St. Paul, his home for the past two years, yet he feels tension because of his orientation:

> Over the course of my life generally I have associated strongly with the gay community, . . . with measurable acceptance and "success." When I went to a predominantly gay situation with my female partner recently (a social function mind you), these people acted completely different than they ever had before with her not around.

Even as a consummate insider, Brent finds his orientation to be an issue:

> I work for arguably the largest GLBT publication (or one of) in the upper Midwest. . . . As a writer and photographer, my beat is the bi and trans communities. When I am around "the gang" they almost always bring up my sexual identity—I never do. I am now dating one of those people, and in an effort to endear himself to me recently after an intimate experience, he wrote me an e-mail that said, "You're pretty good for a bi guy." Did he mean I was only half as good as a gay guy or what[?] . . . Why couldn't he just say that he had a nice time[?]

On the other hand, Shannon, a man in his mid-thirties who has been out since he was twenty-one, reported generally good experiences in the gay community:

> I'm a single bi male living in Minneapolis, which is a pretty great place to be openly gay/lesbian. As far as being openly bisexual, I have not experi-

enced any extreme hostility. I have experienced some "friendly ribbing" from friends, most of which has come from my gay friends. . . . I have heard some bi folks express feelings of not being comfortable either in the gay or the straight communities/bars. I feel fortunate in that I move in both with relative comfort and ease.

He also understands the questions his gay friends have for him:

My straight friends tend to "question" my bisexuality less often than my gay friends. That may be simply because they are used to taking their orientation for granted, which my gay friends perhaps are not. I think that any flack I do get is mostly based on people's inability to understand what it would be like to be open to physical intimacy with someone regardless of their gender. (Emotional intimacy seems to be less of an issue for them.) This used to bother me, until I realized that I do not understand what it would be like to NOT be open to such intimacy.

Other people have had cause to be angrier. For example, Daniel said:

I have encountered a great deal of opposition from my friends who are gay. None of them believe I'm bi. They think I'm in denial and/or trying to hold on to some semblance of normalcy and approval. My issue with this thinking is this: how can one condemn me for finding myself . . . especially when that person was probably condemned when he/she was trying to find him/herself? It seems a little hypocritical and insensitive to me.

Daniel's solution, for now at least, is to be in the "gay closet":

This is why I tend to just say I'm gay. . . . that way I don't have to deal with comments and looks and opinions.

Several women in the support group expressed feeling hurt specifically by a lack of acceptance from the lesbian community. According to Kimberly:

My ex-girlfriends (both lesbians) were BOTH very anti-bi, toward me and my bisexual friends. . . . I get the feeling that I was their girlfriend to make them feel superior somehow (part of the reason I'm no longer with them). My first ex would always say, "You're not bad for a bi chick!" like that was a great compliment.

Cool has a similar story:

I had a blast all summer hanging out with my cool 23-year-old female roommate (and former best friend) while she came out, and came more out, and more and more out until she not only works in a gay club now, but ONLY hangs out in the gay club-scene-world. She did her best to try to hook me up into her new world, but I feel exactly the same level of comfort/alienation in gay bars as straight bars. So, her gay friends have let it be known they don't like me because I'm too "straight" for them and she has (understandably) chosen them over me and the uncomfortable straight past I represent.

Cool finds herself in limbo between two unwelcoming communities, unable to feel part of either:

To me the two worlds are exactly the same; equally limited, judgmental, and bourgeois . . . just mirror images of each other. I truly like and overlap [with] some of the gay world, but my roots just refuse to take hold there and grow. Unfortunately, my well-established roots in the straight world are simultaneously shriveling and dying too, leaving me feeling extremely unstable.

I asked the support group about how they felt about Pride celebrations. "Gay Pride," or "Gay and Lesbian Pride," or "LGBT Pride" are *the* community events for nonstraight people, but how welcoming are they for bisexuals? For Eric:

For the past four years, I have made sure Pridefest (Nashville) is an event for me and other bisexual men and women. I've hosted a table alongside the Rainbow Community Center (Nashville's GLBT center)—of which we are now an official program group. I have literature out for people to take with them that tells about bisexuality, our group (Bi the Way—Nashville), book lists (with some of the listed books on display), and this year the info and registration forms for the upcoming North American Conference on Bisexuality. Reactions to us being there vary from (A) a few who are totally knocked out and excited to find us there, (B) most who are genuinely friendly, but "just looking," and (C) a few who treat us like their illegitimate cousin. I had one lesbian tell me this year the she "used to identify as bi, but then decided to come out"—oh, really? I assured her that I had decided to come out, too, but as a bisexual man. . . . Overall, I find the event to be a LOT of fun and enjoy being there.

Unfortunately, bisexuals where Julie lives are not enjoying this kind of success:

I think the local pride here [in Michigan] is LBGT pride, so at least the title is inclusive. . . . However, last year when I went, which was my first year going as an out bisexual, I had an experience which made me feel pretty excluded. There was a comedian performing who was asking "who all here is a lesbian" and all the lesbians cheered, "who's a gay man?" and all the gay men cheered, "who all is straight" and the handful of straight folks cheered . . . then she asked who all was bisexual, and only two of us cheered, and then the comedian got all this attitude and made fun of us and told us "pick a team already why don't ya?" My experiences at Pride and other pride-like events are that bisexuals are just invisible. We're assumed to be gays and lesbians, unless of course we're holding a big bi-pride sign or something—so we're usually under the radar. But when we do come out and distinguish ourselves, it opens up all the "fence-sitter" type comments.

In my experience, this feeling that bisexuals are not welcome in the gay and lesbian world causes the greatest pain for bi people. Perhaps it is naive, but many bi people hold the common belief that a great big happy LGBT community will be waiting with open arms for them when they come out. Logically, the shared experience of homophobia unites us in our oppression, right? This hope makes the disappointment that much more painful.

If it seems as if I have spent a lot of time discussing the relationship between the gay/lesbian communities and the bisexual community, this is quite true, and for good reason: It is this relationship that gives rise to bisexuality as an identity.

Chapter 3

Bisexuality Defined

"SOMETHING MEN JUST DO"

The last time I was in San Diego was 1978. A friend and I were driving around the country in a beat-up, borrowed Peugeot, and we slept on the beach for a few days. Now, twenty-four years later, this visit was very different from my first. This time I had a rented Dodge Stratus in much better shape than that old Peugeot (working door locks!) and a room all to myself in a good hotel. My motives for being there on a beautiful California weekend in October 2002 were very different from those sleeping-on-the-beach days. I came to San Diego to attend the Bisexual Men's Conference, put on by the local bi group, the Bi Forum. Okay, I admit it—I'm a conference junkie. I don't know why. Maybe it is the allure of a hotel lobby, or the plastic name-tag holders which never seem to work right, or perhaps the opportunity to go around for introductions with a whole new set of fellow audience members every hour and fifteen minutes that makes me crave the conference life. Or maybe it is the snacks.

Coming from faraway Minneapolis, I expected to meet only Californians at the conference, but any hope of winning the "traveled the farthest award" (if there were such a thing) was quickly dashed. Indeed, men had come from all over the United States, plus Canada, but the winner of the nonexistent "traveled the farthest award" was a man who came from Germany. His name was George, and he was a handsome, stocky, middle-aged Web site designer who spoke perfect English.

George's workshop was about a poll he had conducted at Yahoo group sites catering mostly to bi males looking for sex. Although his findings were interesting, more interesting for me was an offhand comment George made about the nature of sexual orientation as an identity. Being from Germany, his experience with other cultures was of course different from our American perspective. He referred at one point to "the Turks and the Spanish," who, he said, viewed having sex with men as "something men just do."

Something men just do. It strikes me that believing sex between men is "something men just do" is probably a minority view both in his country and in the United States. Yet it has been the model for sexuality for nearly all of human history and continues to be the model for most of the world. "Something men just do" implies two things: First, men having sex with each other is common. Second, men having sex with each other is just not a big deal. What do we know about the validity of this view, and can we generalize it to women's behavior?

SEX, HISTORY, AND CULTURE

Although the details are often obscured, it is clear that throughout history and throughout the world, people have had and are having sex with other people of the same gender. We know this from documented history; we know this from art; and we know this from anthropology.

Anthropologically, one need only look at our closest relatives in the animal world, the bonobos. Often called pygmy chimps, bonobos are very different from their cousins, the chimpanzees, in that they have an unusually peaceful and egalitarian society. They also have a lot of sex. They have sex to bond, to acquire food, and seemingly just for the fun of it. Not only do they have sex, they have sex in every possible combination and in many ways and positions. They have sex in twos, threes, and fours. They have sex face to face. They have oral sex as well as intercourse. They have sex with other bonobos of the same sex—often.

In human history, it is hard to gauge the full scope and meaning of same-sex sexual practices. The major reason for this is that same-sex behavior is removed from history, either by those who would have us believe it never happened or by those who are merely too shy to mention it. Even in the example of the bonobos, a quick check of *Encarta Encyclopedia* finds a listing for bonobos and their use of sex in the social order but no mention that they engage in same-sex behavior.[1] Similarly, I attended architecture school at the University of Minnesota in the late 1970s and early 1980s and learned only recently it was not unusual for friezes in Rome to depict sex acts and men with large erections. Also, Christians in the past did a remarkably thorough job removing the genitalia from ancient Greek and Roman nude sculptures, both physically and allegorically helping to rewrite the history of sexuality.

However, evidence of same-sex behavior in many places and times does still exist. Perhaps the society most well known to Westerners is Greece. Ancient Greece is famous for open and accepted male same-sex relationships, especially between boys and older men and to a lesser extent between older and younger women. These relationships were an accepted part of their culture and were governed by a formalized code of honor. This code was centered on the idea of *areté*, or male strength, symbolized by the athlete and warrior.[2] Indeed, Alexander the Great was well known for his sexual interest in men (a factor to consider next time the issue of gays in the military comes up). Less well known are the lives of women in ancient Greece, but what we do know helps shape our vision of women who love women. Indeed, the term *lesbian* derives from the Island of Lesbos, where the poet Sappho lived. To listen to Sappho, at least on the island of Lesbos if not throughout Greece in the sixth century B.C.E, women were able to express their same-sex attractions with a great deal of freedom.[3]

In Middle Ages Europe, the Christian Church's rule resulted in prohibitions against sodomy. Sodomy was rather loosely defined as not only anal intercourse and oral sex, but also coitus interruptus, intercourse with the male in any other position than on top, or sex between Christians and Jews. Christian philosophers, from early on, believed any sexual activity not for procreation was sinful, as was sexual pleasure in general. Yet evidence of homosexual behavior is described within letters and poems of the time, especially those written by the men charged with controlling sin. There appears to have been a subculture of male-on-male sex within the monastic communities, especially in the tenth and eleventh centuries. In fact, while the European Christian Church was quite clear about its prohibitions against any sex not for procreation, this rule was not enforced uniformly over time or in all areas. For example, the German code of law enacted in the thirteenth century was very comprehensive yet unusually silent about sexuality, probably because ruler Frederick II was accused by the pope of being a sodomite. Frederick II was not the only European ruler known for same-sex lovers. For example, Richard the Lionheart and Edward II both had relationships with men, and Queen Anne had a relationship with a young woman.[4]

Meanwhile, in Asia, same-sex behavior enjoyed a heyday during certain periods of Chinese history, especially the Zhou dynasty (1122-256 B.C.E.), and continued well into the twentieth century. In Japan, similar to many areas of the world, marriage was a social arrangement. For companionship (often including sexual activity) men turned to prostitutes and their male friends and boys. The samurai had sex as a matter of course with younger males in training.[5]

On the other side of the world, in parts of sub-Saharan Africa woman-to-woman marriage was and still is a common practice.[6] In many African cultures, women married each other for economic reasons, family support, and procreation (the "husband" arranges male lovers for the "wife" in order to have children). Interestingly, the woman who assumes the role of "husband" obtains the status of a man in the community (a topic discussed more in Chapter 5 in considering the construction of gender). But do the women have sex with each other? According to R. Jean Cadigan in the *Journal of Comparative Family Studies,* this is a matter of debate.[7] Doesn't it seem strange a practice described as "common" has this fundamental detail left unclear? Not if we consider this: if same-sex behavior between men is obscured, sex between women is doubly so. In patriarchal societies (which is pretty much all of them) men write the history. Not only is same-sex behavior written out of history, but female sexuality usually is not written about at all.

Another group of interest are the Sambia, a tribe in the eastern highlands of New Guinea. Similar to many other cultures, they use male initiation rights to mark the passage into adulthood. Unlike other cultures, their initiation rights involve the younger boys orally servicing the older boys in order to gain their semen. The semen serves as a substitute for mother's milk and is thought to help them grow. Also, it is thought that semen is not produced in a body but must be acquired from older men. Eventually, the older boys move into arranged marriages and usually no longer practice the initiation with the younger boys, especially after fathering a child.[8]

Today both the ubiquity and, in some cases, oppression of same-sex behavior continue. For example, Maura Reynolds, in the *Los Angeles Times,* wrote about the common practice of Pashtun men keeping male lovers.[9] How common? She reports a mullah, speaking out against the practice, said 90 percent of men have the desire to commit this sin, but only 20 to 50 percent do. *Only* 20 to 50 percent? Apparently, Kandahar has especially beautiful *halekon,* or attractive, effeminate young men. Sex between men is an open secret, even though, according to Reynolds, the stated penalty for such acts is burning at the stake, being pushed off a cliff, or being crushed by a wall. Perhaps this is a good example of how sexuality is erased. In a hundred or a thousand years, will Afghan history include this detail of their culture, or will it be removed from their history in the same way the Christians removed the genitalia from statues?

The Pashtun are examples of a common, perhaps the most common, model of sexuality. Much of the world, for example Latin America and Arab regions, views male sex in the context of a feminine and masculine model depending on who is the insertee and who is the inserter. In this model a feminine man carries a stigma, yet if a man receives oral sex from another man the recipient's masculinity is not questioned.[10] Here, as in historical Europe and many cultures all over the globe, people are *not something,* an identity; they *do something,* an action. They may break taboos, but that does not mean they redefine who they are. Therefore, a man receiving oral sex from another man or a man performing anal sex on another man is not considered gay or bisexual, or in any way different or suspect. The man performing oral sex or receiving anal sex is suspect and is considered less of a man. In this model, sexual identity is entwined in gender identity.

North America

North America is a tapestry of various cultures, sometimes separated geographically and sometimes coexisting in the same cities, workplaces, and schools. Within this exists considerable variation on what it means to have sex with someone of the same gender.

Even before Europeans moved in en masse, North America had great cultural diversity with about 500 Indian nations. Within this diversity, most American Indian cultures had some variation of what is now called "two-spirit" people. Also known as *berdache* by the French missionaries, being two spirited is about both gender and sexuality. Those who are two spirit often have the role of shaman in the tribe. Instead of being oppressed, they are held in high esteem.[11] Although one might think of two-spirit people as only people who were born men, people who were born women were also included in many Indian cultures.

In Northern European cultures, prior to the last half of the nineteenth century, same-gender sex was viewed as unnatural but certainly not unknown or even unusual. It was a sin, but so were many other things people did, such as swearing and adultery. For example, in eighteenth- and nineteenth-century Europe, a history of romantic friendships between women is apparent in their lives and explicit in their writings. Also in the late nineteenth century in New England, "Boston marriages," or long-term relationships between women, were quite open and common. One reason why this could be done so openly in an otherwise sexually repressive time was because men did not take women's sexuality seriously. For example, in 1811 a Scottish judge acquitted two women accused of lesbianism because he thought sex between women was too fantastic to consider.[12]

Perhaps Boston marriages reflect a more important and, for some, a more surprising fact: Institutional discrimination against same-sex sexual behavior is relatively new. Discrimination against GLBT people seems so ubiquitous it is hard to imagine it was ever any other way; however, while there have been occasional examples of persecution, it had never really been enfranchised into the culture until relatively recently. In the now-famous 2003 Supreme Court sodomy case *John Geddes Lawrence and Tyron Garner v. the State of Texas* ten professors of history filed an amicus brief in support of the petitioners.[13] In it they assert:

> The government policy of classifying and discriminating against certain citizens on the basis of their homosexual status is an unprecedented project of the twentieth century. . . . Sodomy laws that exclusively targeted same sex couples, such as the statute enacted in 1973 in Texas . . . were a development of the last third of the twentieth century and reflect this historically unprecedented concern to classify and penalize homosexuals as a subordinate class of citizens. . . . Widespread discrimination against a class of people on the basis of their homosexual status developed only in the twentieth century . . . and peaked from the

1930s to the 1960s. Gay men and women were labeled "deviants," "degenerates," and "sex criminals" by the medical profession, government officials, and the mass media.

What happened?

The Medicalization of Sexuality

One clue is that the term *homosexuality* was first coined in 1869. The timing was no accident; the end of the nineteenth century was the Victorian Era, a time of sexual repression for people of all orientations. At the same time, science was on the rise. Not only were traditional sciences leading the way into a brave new future of cameras and telegraphs, but the new sciences of sociology and psychology were also created. People now believed everything could be explained through science, including human behavior. Indeed, psychology sought to explain human sexuality as a medical issue, with homosexuality as an illness.[14] For example, perhaps the most influential psychiatrist to date was Sigmund Freud. Freud believed homosexuality resulted from problems in a person's development,* with homosexuality as the result of an "Oedipal complex," "penis envy," or "anal fixation."[15] Homosexuality began to be seen as pathological, with the client needing to be cured, or stopped, at all costs. Same-gender sexual behavior became an illness for the first time.

This medical model became the dominant view of sexuality in America. Indeed, one could argue the terms *homosexual, heterosexual,* and *bisexual* were developed by Europeans to be used like phyla to divide and classify humans. Far from benign, this model has been used to divide and discriminate against certain people ever since.

---

*Freud's views on homosexuality were complex and evolved over time. For example, late in his life, in a 1935 letter, he displays a positive attitude to homosexuality, "Homosexuality is assuredly no advantage, but it is nothing to be classified as an illness; we consider it to be a variation of sexual development." Some would say his inconsistency and evolution relates to his own same-sex attraction. According to Colin Spencer in *Homosexuality in History,* in the 1890s Freud had a relationship with a Wilhelm Fleiss and again later with a psychoanalyst named Sandor Ferenczi.

Culture and Sexual Orientation

This Northern European medical model of sexual orientation is now so dominant that it is hard for some whose roots are from Northern Europe to imagine any other. However, it isn't the only model of sexuality in the United States. Indeed, Latino culture has its roots in the Mediterranean and has followed the masculine/feminine model. Although with the increasing influence of Northern European culture in parts of the Latino community, this tradition is facing pressure. For example, when U.S. Latino men who have sex with men interact with sexual health programs, they may be labeled with a gay or bi identity that is not their own. In other words, how can an HIV-prevention program reach Latinos with programming for gay men? If a Latino needs such services, he may be forced into accepting this different cultural model of who he is.

Similarly, to a degree African-American culture also uses the masculine/feminine model. Here again, culture and sexuality are made complicated by the omnipresent Northern European culture and by racism. Victor Raymond, a long-time activist who has facilitated workshops about bisexuals of color many times at BECAUSE, explains:

> In the African-American community you hear about people on the "down low," the DL. They may be gay, they may be bi, but it's not talked about. It's very coded language. . . . Those are men who have sex with men. It's also the reason why if you were to say to an African-American man, or even a Native American man, "We're trying to get a message out about safer sex because it's really important to gay men," they would be with you up until you say "gay." Then they'd [think], "Oh, you must not be talking about me.". . . You're not going to see these terms get used. You are going to see them have their own terms in their own communities.

The "on the down low" that Raymond describes means not accepting a gay identity. Although "gay" as an identity is, of course, all around African Americans in the larger American culture, for many it is not seen as a possibility within their own culture. According to Paul Rust, "[To] identify as bisexual, lesbian, or gay would be tantamount to rejecting not only one's gender role but also one's family and one's ethnicity."[16] Indeed, for many gay men an important part of the coming-out process has been to move to the "gay ghetto," a part of town where they can feel safe and at home. For African Americans, that may mean exposing themselves to racism and leaving behind the support of their extended family and community.[17]

Despite the clear existence of other models of sexuality, some still argue that the only true way to think about sexuality is in the Northern European, homosexual/bisexual-heterosexual paradigm, in which those people who have sex with others of the same gender, regardless of culture, are homosexual. In most of my examples, the behavior might more accurately be described as bisexual. So are these individuals homosexual or bisexual? The answer is that they are neither.

Our European medical model of sexuality is just as culturally based as two spiritness or the *halekon* of Kandahar, and it is wrong to demand this is the only possible view of sexuality. We must not impose or generalize this model to the rest of the world. Two-spirit people are not gay, they are not bisexual, and they are not transgender, even though they may share some qualities with all three groups. They are two spirit; any other answer risks being ethnocentric. The one factor that is different about Europe's model of sexual orientation, and the reason it seems so ubiquitous, is that it is rapidly spreading throughout the world alongside McDonalds, Hollywood, and aircraft carriers.

It is important to note that thinking about orientation in a cultural context does *not* mean we can choose our orientation in the same way we choose our music. Certainly not, although I would be remiss if I didn't point out that we don't choose our culture either. As I discussed in Chapter 2, I believe the popular wisdom that there is a biological determinism behind sexual orientation. Whether it is genes, prenatal environment, or something else, we are brought to our sexual desires and do not choose them. However, biologically based or not, the point is that the sexual *identity* of bisexual, heterosexual, or homosexual is cultural; *feelings* of attraction are organic. People are hammered into molds, albeit their own culture's mold, the world over.

While exploring sexuality and models of orientation using terms such as bisexual and homosexual, we must keep in mind just what it is we are talking about: Northern Europe's cultural model of sexuality.

MODELS OF SEXUAL ORIENTATION

The Kinsey Scale

With that in mind, probably the most important moment in bisexual history occurred in 1948 when Alfred Kinsey published *Sexual Behavior in the Human Male* and then in 1953 *Sexual Behavior in the Human Female*.[18] These books changed everything for two reasons. First, Kinsey found that homosexuality was much more common than previously thought. Second, he created an entirely new paradigm of sexual orientation when he proposed the Kinsey scale. This scale is a number line from 0 through 6; 0 represented exclusively heterosexual and 6 exclusively homosexual. People can fall anywhere along this continuum, being a "Kinsey 2" or "4" or "1 ½." Kinsey had created the present model of bisexuality without ever once using the word bisexual.

The Kinsey scale clarified two issues. First, there is a great variety of sexual orientations. He said:

> The world is not divided into sheep and goats. Not all things are black, nor all things white. It is fundamental of taxonomy that nature rarely deals with discrete categories. Only the human mind invents such categories and tries to force facts into separate pigeonholes. The living world is a continuum in each and every one of its aspects.[19]

As with any number line, there are infinite points along the Kinsey scale to choose from. Kinsey thought sexuality was not an either/or proposition, or even a three-part system, but distinguished by infinite variety.

Second is an implication that perhaps all of us on this continuum are in the same boat. Heterosexuality isn't primary or held above all "deviant" behaviors? Straight people are ranked in just the same way as homosexuals? Perhaps a Kinsey 4.5 is no better or worse than a 1.5. Revolutionary! The world has never been the same since.

Fritz Klein and Even More Variety

As helpful as the Kinsey scale is, it is only a crude model of what constitutes a person's sexual orientation. Kinsey was interested in behavior and attraction, but what if behavior doesn't match well with attraction? What if people usually enjoy sex with one gender but only fall in love with the other? What if a person's past doesn't reflect his or her present feelings? Sexuality is much more complex than 0 through 6.

Enter Fritz Klein and the Klein Sexual Orientation Grid.[20] As a psychiatrist, researcher, and founder of one of the first bisexual support groups in the country, Klein has unique insights into the complexity of sexuality. Klein adapted the continuum model of Kinsey, in this case with 1 being exclusively heterosexual and 7 being exclusively homosexual. Klein then asked seven different questions:

1. Sexual attraction: Whom are you visually attracted to?
2. Sexual behavior: Whom do you have sex with?
3. Sexual fantasies: Whom do you think about?
4. Emotional preference: Whom do you fall in love with?
5. Social preference: Whom do you spend your time with?
6. Lifestyle: What community do you feel part of?
7. Self-identification: What do you call yourself?

The Klein grid then asks for answers to these questions when thinking about only the past year. Next one answers by reporting on the past (an average of past feelings and actions before this year). Finally, it asks what is seen as the person's ideal, his or her future. Completing this assessment by ranking each answer ala Kinsey on a 1 through 7 scale gives a total of twenty-one different numbers. This model certainly has considerable room for variation and nuance in what constitutes sexual orientation.

The online support group demonstrates the flavor of how this works. Surveying only self-identified bisexuals created a bell curve of responses centered on 4 (the middle) for nearly all the questions asked, and many had significant numbers in the 2 and 6 categories.* In other words, there was a great amount of variation in what it means to be bisexual in this group. Indeed, it raises an important point about

---

*Interesting is where the largest deviation from a rank of 4 takes place. Both the bi men and the bi women surveyed leaned toward being more visually attracted to women. Also, the bi men in the survey tended to be more romantically inclined toward women. For the complete results, see Appendix A.

sexuality in general and bisexuals in particular. For example, people who call themselves bisexual would choose 4 on the self-identity scale. But perhaps a person is more sexually attracted to men but more emotionally attracted to women. All of his sexual experience is with women, but men still occupy his dreams. Another bisexual may also be a 4 on the self-identity scale but be more sexually and emotionally attracted to women while his sexual behavior and fantasy life has revolved around men. How much do these two men have in common? Even though both identify as bisexual, it means very different things to each of them. The result is that *bisexual* is a catchall term for everyone who is not overwhelmingly a 7 (gay or lesbian) or a 1 (straight). In reality, bisexuals may or may not have much in common in regard to their individual sexuality. One reason this is important is in building community; imagine trying to organize such a group. It can be like having a club for people from Slabodia but no two people agree on where Slabodia is or who the people are who come from there. I will delve more deeply into the implications of this issue for the bi community in the next chapter.

A Multiple-Variable Model

M. D. Storms provides another important model,[21] one I find compelling. Storms suggests we look at sexual attraction to different genders independently of each other. Imagine a scale with one end representing no attraction to men and the other end high attraction to men. Likewise, there is a scale for attraction to women with one end low attraction and the other high. In this model a straight male, for example, would be at the high end of the attracted to women (ATW) scale and at the low end of the attracted to men (ATM) line. A lesbian might have high ATW and low ATM. One can imagine a great variation within this model. A lesbian may also be a medium ATM and a high ATW, or a straight male a high ATW and medium ATM. A bisexual might have both high ATM and ATW, or perhaps medium ATM and ATW, or some other combination still not in conflict with their behavior or self-identity.[22] A person with low ATM and low ATW may best be described as asexual. Although transgender people were left out of the discussion, a scale could be created for trans folks too. For that matter, one could be done for feminine males and masculine females.

Having known people who have identified as such, this is one reason why I like this model: it includes people who are more asexual. Another reason I like it is because it describes attraction to women and men as two separate variables, as two different aspects of me, if you will. This feels right; it seems to capture how I approach my own sexuality. That said, there are many more bi people who would disagree completely with this sentiment. Many bisexuals describe their feelings as falling in love with the person, not the gender, and that a person's gender doesn't matter. Conversely, gender does matter for others (including myself).

Regardless of orientation, many factors go into our choice of sexual identity. Klein uses seven variables, but we could imagine others, such as politics. (Especially for women. A large political component in the lesbian identity is not part of the gay identity. I discuss this in Chapter 5.) Not only could we have a larger group of variables, but wouldn't some matter more to certain people than others? Models are useful in many ways, but all are doomed to be approximations, problematic, and likely not very useful on a person-to-person basis. We all have very personal reasons why we identify as we do, and if we disconnect behavior from orientation (as I will discuss soon) we are left with no easy measure of someone's sexuality.

PERSPECTIVES ON BISEXUALITY

So we have various models to help us understand the nature of sexuality, but we still haven't answered the question, What does it mean when people identify as bisexual? That they rank themselves as a 3 on the Kinsey scale? What about people who are a 4 or 2? A 1 or 5? Does it mean some particular combination of Klein numbers? Models aside, what are people trying to tell us when they say they are bisexual, and conversely, what are we saying when we categorize someone as bisexual?

Although this problem may sound rather esoteric, in fact it has huge implications. When researchers look at sexual orientation, they need to have a definition of the word. How can you study bisexuals if you haven't decided exactly what *bisexual* means? It is not as clear-cut as it sounds.

The Academic Literature

> Bisexuality is difficult to define. Must one engage in sexual activity with both sexes to assume a bisexual identity? What if a person has sexual or affectional desires for both sexes but does not act on them? What if a person is involved in a monogamous, long-term same-sex relationship but has had previous satisfactory heterosexual relationships?
>
> From *Bisexuality, Not Homosexuality:*
> *Counseling Issues and Treatment Approaches*[23]

Which definition of bisexual have researchers and writers used in the past? When we look at academic literature, we find several definitions that are not in agreement. For example, Beth Firestein offers the following definition:

> "Bisexual" means of or pertaining to one's experience of erotic, emotional, and sexual attraction to persons of more than one gender. Such individuals may identify as bisexual, homosexual, lesbian, gay, heterosexual, transgendered, or transsexual or may choose not to label at all. . . . Bisexuality here is defined as the capacity, regardless of the sexual identity label one chooses, to love and sexually desire both same and other-gendered individuals.[24]

Firestein argues bisexuality is independent of self-identification and raises the possibility of a person being a lesbian/bisexual or a gay/bisexual. However, Dr. Gail Elizabeth Wyatt, a UCLA professor of psychiatry, argues the complete opposite in a 1992 *Essence* story: "The individual must define for herself what her sexual preference is and under what context she has reached that conclusion." She adds, "Someone cannot identify her sexual orientation for her based solely on behavior."[25]

Another definition comes from William Wedin, director of Bisexual Information and Counseling Services. He believes bisexuality is "the capacity to be aroused by either gender through fantasy or physical contact."[26] Elizabeth Smiley's definition in the *Journal of Mental Health Counseling* appears to be the most complex yet:

Bisexuality is a sexual orientation where an individual: experiences a combination of sexual and affectional attractions to members of both sexes; engages to varying degrees in sexual activities with both sexes; and self-identifies as bisexual in a way that is consistent with personal, social, political, and lifestyle preferences.[27]

Finally, Kenji Yoshino, in the *Stanford Law Review,* argues there are three factors we might use to define a person's sexual orientation: conduct, desire, and self-identification.[28] Yoshino argues that considering only a person's behavior is flawed, for reasons I shall discuss shortly. Yoshino also suggests that considering only self-identity is also a mistake in that it removes too many who would identify as bisexual if it were not "a stigmatized identity." Yoshino finally concludes, "Which axis or combination of axes is best suited for our purposes? I believe the answer is a pure desire-based definition."

A definition is necessary. Looking again to the Oxford English Dictionary (OED)[29] for guidance, the second definition* for bisexual agrees with Yoshino, defining *bisexual* as being "sexually attracted to individuals of both sexes." That's good, but in order to include the transgender community, I'd tweak this a little by defining *bisexual* as being sexually attracted to individuals of more than one gender. I believe defining bisexuality based on desire is both simple and intuitive, as when someone says they are bisexual, this is usually what they mean.

BISEXUALITY AS AN ORIENTATION

Like homosexuality or heterosexuality, bisexuality is a sexual orientation. Being an orientation implies two things: (1) being bisexual is much more than behavior and (2) bisexuality isn't a lifestyle choice. Bisexuality means a person is attracted to more than one gender; it doesn't mean all bisexuals are having sex with more than one

---

*Interestingly, the first definition is "having both sexes in the same individual," a usage predating not only the second definition of bisexual but also homosexual by half a century. Now in colloquial language we would say "intersex" or "transgender," not bisexual, as discussed in Chapter 6.

gender. Bisexuality is not is a mere description of behavior. Ask the online support group:

> To me, bisexuality is about while you might be in a relationship, that relationship does not define whether you are attracted to men or women. That sort of thing does not go away, just because you have a relationship. . . . You might be committed to your partner, who may be same-sex or opposite or in between, it does not mean that you are able to stop finding people of either gender attractive. (Dominique)

Bisexuality cannot be determined by the gender of the sexual partners. This applies to all sexual orientations: just because a person identifies as straight doesn't mean he or she hasn't had or doesn't still have sex with people of the same gender. Conversely, many gay men have had or do have sex with women, and many lesbians have had or do have sex with men. Indeed, as reported in Family Planning Perspectives, a survey conducted by the *Advocate* found 75 percent of lesbian respondents reported having had sex in the past at least once with a man, and 6 percent said they have had sex with a man in the past year.[30] It must also be kept in mind there could be as many reasons why someone would choose to have sex with people of both sexes as there are people doing it. Situational same-sex behavior (as in prison), curiosity, opportunity, and sex work are among the many reasons. Sexual orientation is about feelings and attractions, not just actions. Note the following from an essay in the *Boston Bi Women's Newsletter:* "A person can be bisexual whether they are celibate, or date one gender while having fantasies about the other, or have partners of both genders at different times (or at the same time), or anywhere in between."[31]

Indeed, we see bisexuals with all varieties of partner choices. Kayley Vernallis reports in the *Journal of Philosophy,* "Some people identify as bisexuals although they have only experienced sex with one gender, perhaps because they have sexual desires for and fantasies about both genders."[32] They may or may not have had lovers of different genders. They may or may not be monogamous. They may or may not ever have had sex in their entire lives. Take for example a Catholic priest who has been celibate his entire life. We can all agree this person has a sexual orientation, and he may identify as straight or bi or gay. This is a very important point for bisexuals, because many people believe bi's need both a man and a woman as sexual partners. For example, if a self-identified bisexual woman is in a monogamous relationship with another woman, she is now assumed to be lesbian. As mentioned in the previous chapter, such thinking makes bisexuals invisible.

Acknowledging bisexuality as an orientation helps us assert being bisexual is not a choice, just as being gay or straight isn't a choice. There is support for this point of view in the literature. An article in the *Journal of Humanistic Counseling, Education and Development* says, "The assumption that bisexual individuals 'choose' their orientation, a common societal myth, may be unfounded."[33]

As touched on earlier, this is a hot issue for lesbians and gays. Do they choose to be gay? Can they change their mind? It is absurd. There may or may not be a "gay gene," but it is clear people are not in control of their sexual attractions. They are in control of their actions, but I argue no one is in control of their feelings. I can't stub my toe and decide not to let it hurt: it's a feelings thing. Look at it another way: if it were a choice, there would be very, very few nonstraight people. After all, why would anyone put up with the abuse this culture doles out for being attracted to the "wrong" gender if they had a choice? Several ministries promising to make people straight, or at least act straight, have been wildly unsuccessful. Can anyone really believe people who sign up for this program fail because they really don't want to change? All of them? As a friend who attended such a program told me, "If it were possible to pray hard enough to become straight, I would be straight now. No one can pray harder or want to be straight more than I did."

In addition to this argument that never seems to quite go away, bisexuals add yet another wrinkle understandably confusing to some people. A straight person dates people of the opposite sex, right? And a gay person dates people of the same sex, okay? But bisexuals can choose either sex to date; they have a choice! They can choose to be straight, or at least have a straight relationship, right? Again, just because someone is in a relationship with a person of a different gender doesn't mean they are heterosexual. Bisexuals can choose their partners, but they cannot choose their orientation. If a bisexual woman marries a man, she hasn't chosen to be straight. She can choose to be out or not, to be monogamous or not, but she can't choose who she is attracted to any more than a person who is straight or lesbian. She is still bisexual.

Part of the problem is that language is confusing. Quick: What is a straight relationship? What is a gay relationship? Now what is a bisexual relationship? Similarly, we get what is meant by "lesbian sex" and "straight sex," but what are we talking about when we say "bisexual sex"? The answer is we are being imprecise with language when we refer to relationships this way. When someone says "straight sex" or "straight relationship," what they really mean is different-gender sex and different-gender relationship. Similarly, "gay sex" would be more accurately described as same-gender sex. Perhaps the people participating in "gay sex" may both be bisexual. In this case, how would that be gay? Yet once more, bisexuality becomes invisible.

How Permanent Is Bisexuality?

As discussed in the previous chapter, it is a commonly held belief that bisexuals are only future homosexuals. Bisexuality is a stop on the way to identifying as gay. Yet when we go to the literature again, we find in the *Journal of Sex Research:*

> Bisexual activity appeared to be relatively stable over time: the recruitment criterion was any sex with a man and a woman in the previous three years, yet 60% were bisexually active during the past six months, and 56% began their bisexual activity at least five years prior to the study.[34]

This, too, is in keeping with what I have seen. I mentioned in the previous chapter that on average the online support group identified as bisexual for 10.3 years. Indeed, when I asked how comfortable they were with their orientation, 82 percent reported being very or mostly comfortable with identifying as bisexual.

Does orientation change over time? Yes, I think it can. Heresy you say? Maybe, but hear me out. I suggest this from my experience with support groups. Many times I have watched people try to create a new world for themselves when they come out, a new world that denies their old one. For example, take a fifty-year-old man who has raised children to adulthood and has been married for thirty years. Now he identifies as gay. He may decide he was mistaken those fifty years he thought he was straight; after all, he's told there is a gay gene so either he has it or he doesn't. Besides, he really can't remember how it felt to be attracted to a woman in that way. Could the past fifty years really have been a mistake? Could he have been fooling himself all these years? Possibly. However, I do think considering a life of fifty years to be suddenly now invalid is far too dismissive of what it means to be human and far too simplistic regarding sexuality. While there certainly are people who knew all along their words and actions didn't match their feelings, there are many more whose orientation evolves and reveals itself over time. As for why he can't remember how it felt to be attracted to a woman, I would think that's natural. Have you ever broken up with someone and can't remember why you were ever attracted to that person in the first place? You remember you were there, but the feelings may seem completely foreign. Hey, at one time in my life I had a huge crush on Donny Osmond. I remember it, but I can't feel it. You change; you grow. The same is true with orientation. Just because a person can't recall feeling a certain way doesn't mean it wasn't real at the time. So rather than say everyone whose sexual identity changes over their life was previously in denial, perhaps it is simply more accurate to say some people, for whatever reason, experience change in their sexual attractions, and thus their sexual orientation.

While orientation can change over time, there is one important thing to keep in mind: *you* can't change your orientation. In other words, it may change but you don't get to choose how it changes. As my friend found out, no amount of praying will make a person straight, even though he or she may have been straight at one time.

Aren't humans interesting?

How Many Bi Folks Are There?

As we've seen, there is little agreement in academia as to just what bisexuality is. With this question unresolved, we have little hope in finding the answer to how many bisexuals there are; after all, we have to know whom to count. As reported in the *Journal of Sex Research,* "Estimates of prevalence are confounded by the lack of a single widely accepted definition of bisexuality."[35]

A further check of the literature about bisexuality reveals a scarcity of useful research. Indeed, this isn't only a challenge for bisexuals, but affects all sexual minorities. Too often studies seeking to quantify different orientations are either flawed or of limited use. In the *Gay and Lesbian Review,* Christopher Bagley and Pierre Tremblay state when counting homosexuals, "Arriving at a reliable estimate has proven difficult . . . fueling the controversy over numbers."[36] They suggest the difficulty lay in methodology. One example they cite was the use of a randomly selected sample to be representative of the entire population. The problem is cities are easier to sample, and lesbian and gay people are concentrated in cities. Another potential methodological problem is how the data are obtained. Using the same sample group, there would be very different results depending on if the study was done with an anonymous survey or face-to-face interviews. An example of this cited by Bagley and Tremblay was a 1993 study, "The Sexual Behavior of Men in the United States,"[37] which used face-to-face interviews to find only 1.3 to 2.3 percent of eighteen- to twenty-nine-year-old men were exclusively homosexually active, a figure I think is obviously too low. Yet another statistical mistake would be to use a self-selecting sample or a "sample of convenience," such as polling those around you, in a class you teach, or at your place of work, and assuming they are typical of all members of the population. Alfred Kinsey's research in his famous studies, *Sexual Behavior in the Human Male*[38] and *Sexual Behavior in the Human Female,*[39] was flawed because the group studied came from such a sample of convenience (they were volunteers, students, and prisoners) and was anything but a representative sample of the general population. These are all common problems in research no matter what the field of study, and all of them have been applied to the study of sexual minorities at one time or another.

What information do we have about how many bi's there are, given the difficulties in gaining definitive answers? Let's look at two groups: (1) those who behave bisexually and (2) the population identifying itself as bisexual.

How Many People "Behave Bisexually"?

People who behave bisexually, defined here for our convenience as people having sex with people of more than one gender, obviously make up a larger group than those who identify as bisexual. ("Behave bisexually" could mean a lot of things—perhaps going to conferences counts!) Given this, how common is bisexual behavior?

First, let's look at Kinsey's studies done in the 1940s and 1950s. He found 37 percent of men had had at least one sexual experience with another man at one time in his life (including adolescence) and 10 percent had only so-called "homosexual sex" for a three-year period as an adult (which is where the famous 10 percent figure comes from). He found 4 percent of men have had sex only with men from adolescence on.[40]

Second, published in 1994, the National Health and Social Life Survey (NHSLS) found very different results. It utilized face-to-face interviews of 3,432 people to find approximately 9 percent of men and 4 percent of women having ever had any same-gender sex partners. In addition, 2 percent of men and just under 2 percent of women reported same-gender sex in the past year, and 6 percent of men reported they were sexually attracted to men, while 5.5 percent of women reported they were attracted to other women.[41]

What are we to learn from all this? Not much, other than how difficult it is to count bisexuals. And as I've already discussed, behavior and identity are often not the same thing.

How Many People Say, "I'm Bisexual"?

The next big question is, How many people identify as bisexual? First, we'll turn to the National Health and Social Life Survey again for some numbers. This study didn't differentiate between bisexuals and homosexuals, but what it did report was 2.8 percent of men and 1.4 percent of women in the survey identified as homosexual or bisexual. A very small number, which it defends by pointing out the national gay population seems larger because of its concentration in major cities. Indeed, the study found in the twelve largest cities 9 percent of men identified as bisexual or homosexual.[42] However, I think the small numbers in this survey have more to do with their methodology. Again, not only was the survey done using face-to-face interviews (and thus some participants were reluctant to reveal intimate details to a stranger), but in about 20 percent of the interviews another person was present, usually the interviewee's children or, in 6 percent of the cases, spouse. While questions about sexual orientation were asked in a written questionnaire, the presence of an interviewer and many times family members is bound to result in an underestimate of homosexual and bisexual prevalence.[43]

Another study, *The Janus Report* by Cynthia and Samuel Janus, found significantly higher numbers of homosexuals and bisexuals.

Their results from a study, done at nearly the same time as the NHSLS study, showed 4 percent of men and 2 percent of women are homosexual, while 5 percent of men and 3 percent of women are bisexual.[44]

So which is study is true? Who knows? It really doesn't matter. When it comes to the core issue of human rights, it's immaterial if 50 percent of the population identified as or behave bisexually or if it were just one person. I believe it is a fundamental human right to love whomever or however you chose to love (except when lacking consent due to factors such as age and coercion). If you were the only person in the world who was attracted to both sexes, you wouldn't be wrong to feel or act that way. It's that simple.

Unfortunately, an old expression fits here: it shouldn't matter, but until it doesn't matter, it matters. We live in the real world, and the voting booth often determines our rights. There is strength in numbers and there is support in numbers for sexual minorities in a hostile world. This is why the lesbian and gay communities and their supporters have held on tenaciously to the erroneous number of 10 percent from Kinsey's studies.[45] This is why the government stopped funding for the NHSLS study,[46] which was forced to scale down their project and obtain private money. The political right didn't want to find out how many lesbian and gay voters there actually were for fear of the political consequences (how ironic it would turn out numbers so small.)

Still, despite the confusion of numbers, one fact seems clear: there are a lot of bisexuals in the United States. Even if a low estimate of 2 percent is used, that means there are 5.5 million bisexuals. That is a lot of bi folks.

Why Don't More People Identify As Bisexual?

One reason there are more people behaving bisexually than call themselves bisexual is there are cultural barriers to adopting it as an identity. Of course there are great societal barriers to bisexual behavior, but there are these same barriers to identifying as one and more. It's safe to assume that among individuals who have or have had sex with men and women and don't identify as bisexual, some number of them would identify as bisexual if it were easier to do so. I won't venture to guess what proportion of the population this is, but it is surely a significant number since it is no easy decision to call oneself bisexual.

What are these barriers? First, we live in a society where there are many homophobic people. Some people are deterred by the threats of violence and discrimination from identifying as bisexual, or behaving bisexually, or both. Considering the legal sanctions and physical and psychological abuse that many must endure, it is a testimonial to the power of people's basic needs that anyone behaves or identifies as bisexual at all.

Another barrier to identifying as bisexual could be that the person can't find a bi community. It is more difficult to identify with a group you have never seen or perhaps assume doesn't even exist. The bi community, or lack thereof, will be examined in the next chapter.

Take for example Rob, whom we first heard from in the previous chapter. Rob is an attractive man in his early forties with short dark hair and a goatee. He has been very active in bi politics for the past ten years and is an HIV/AIDS prevention worker. He is a free thinker, someone who knows his own mind and isn't easily swayed by peer pressure. Yet:

When I was about twenty, I was at a college that had a very gay-supportive atmosphere, and literally, on my twentieth birthday I woke up and realized, "Gee, I'm not just open-minded, I like this sex with guys thing; I must be gay." So I identified as gay for ten years—sometimes I identified as gay with a footnote, "I'm gay, ah, some women I like." I did that for a good decade. I identified as gay until I was interviewed by a young Minneapolis activist named Joe Duca, and he was doing a "needs assessment" of bisexuals in the Twin Cities probably nine or ten years ago. And we made an appointment—he said the interview would take a half of an hour, maybe forty-five minutes if we were gabby; he came over at seven thirty in the evening and left at one thirty in the morning. I had never talked to anyone who identified as bi before and had been through so many of the same things as I had, and literally that night, that's when I started identifying as bisexual and realized that was the appropriate word for me.

Nancy from the online support group says:

Throughout my teen years, I had crushes on girls, but I placed my feelings on a back burner because I was confused about my feelings and thought they were abnormal. I had never heard of the terms "bisexual" or "bi." I did know what "gay" was. Throughout my teen years and most of my adult years I lived the "straight" lifestyle and dated only men. I learned I was bisexual in 1997 when I read about bisexuality on the Internet. I finally knew my feelings were not abnormal and I certainly was not crazy. I felt a great weight had been lifted from my shoulders!

You can see what a challenge it is to adopt a bisexual identity when you have no models with which to work!

Another barrier may be a person's relationship. For example, imagine people who are bisexual and happily married and are content not to explore their same-sex feelings. Nothing has changed—they are still monogamous, and they are still committed to their partner and their relationship. How many people would tell their partner they are bisexual or even tell themselves? Certainly some people do, but to be sure, many do not.

One's faith may be a barrier. Most religions in the United States do not accept bisexuality. How difficult is it to follow a religion that teaches bisexuality is wrong and to still identify or behave bisexually? Although many still do, it is problematic.

Education can be a barrier. For example, one bisexual man in his fifties who grew up in rural Minnesota started having sex with men in his early teens and with women a few years later. He maintained this pattern all his life until discovering the word "bisexuality." That's right, rural Minnesota schools (not to mention just about anywhere else) did not and do not teach about bisexuality. An example of the flip side of this is a middle-aged woman who told me that as a teen she heard Elton John was bisexual and found out what this meant. With that knowledge she decided there must be others, because they wouldn't have invented a word just for her and Elton John!

As discussed in the previous chapter, culture is a barrier. If you don't have a word for bisexual, or for the concept of bisexuality, how can you identify as one?

There are probably many other barriers, including workplace, family, and on and on. They all add up to fewer people identifying as bisexual than there could be, whether they behave bisexually or not. According to Ronald of the online support group:

In my experience, from those bisexuals whom I've met, the bisexual community is all over the map in terms of how we "deal" with our bisexuality and the level of comfort we have with being bi. My personal guess is the bisexual community is big. . . . However, only a very small segment of the bisexual community has become comfortable with themselves to a level where they identify themselves as "bi." To some degree, that comes with age/maturity . . . and as a result of social pressures.

However, attitudes are changing. If greater numbers are a good thing, good things are coming our way. Barriers are diminishing. Continued education, continued changes in our culture, continued aging and dwindling of the age groups suffering the most homophobia, and continued success for gays and lesbians in mainstream media all mean more and more people who might identify as other than straight will find their barriers to doing so reduced. In other words, success of the gay liberation movement is bound to have a positive effect on the numbers of people who call themselves gay, lesbian, and even bisexual and transgender.

BISEXUALITY AS AN IDENTITY

I've discussed how bisexuality is poorly defined, and that there is confusion whether it is an orientation or a behavior. Even among those who do call themselves bisexual there is tremendous variation. We know there is discrimination. It is the case that you don't have to identify as bisexual to have sex with people of all genders, and most who do don't identify as bi. Given all this, why would anyone identify as bisexual at all? I offer two answers: one personal and the other sociological.

I have often wondered: if most people who have sex with more than one gender don't identify as bisexual, what is it about me that I do? How I *feel* is not a choice, but how I *identify* is, and I identify as bisexual. Again, the world is full of people who make different choices. As I've discussed, barriers and culture play a decisive role, but I now want to leave a little room for personal agency. Fact is, a major reason I identify as bisexual is because I'm stubborn. After a lifetime of people saying "you don't exist," "you are fooling yourself," "you'll come around someday," and "you have to decide one way or the other," many people understandably accept what they are told. Me, I said horse hockey. I am attracted to men and women thus I am bisexual, and if that doesn't fit into someone else's view of the world, that's about them, not me. Sometimes stubborn is a very good trait.

I asked my online support group about this, and they mostly agreed.

My mom always used to say, "Girl you are so contrary. If everyone is going up you go down just to be different, and I would say "no Mom I am always headed in my own direction not going with the norm or going the opposite way just to be different from them." It's just in my nature to follow my own path despite the outside world. (Tezza)

Yeah, some people have called me stubborn too. I've always refused to call myself a lesbian because, like a bad shoe, it just didn't seem to fit. (Ravenmajel)

Another issue to consider when understanding the bisexual identity is the relationship between identity and oppression. Let's go back to the bi men's conference in San Diego and George's workshop. George said, "It's something men just do." What changed to bring us from "just something men do" to a bisexual identity?

If we look at the lesbian and gay communities' history, again, they didn't exist as an identity until the Victorian era, when sexual oppression and medicalization of sexual behavior began. I argue homosexuality as an identity is a direct result of discrimination. Homophobia created the homosexual identity. Ostracism from the larger society pushed people out from the mainstream and brought them together as their own community, creating the very thing society wanted to stomp out. How ironic. Men have been having sex with each other for all of history, but it took Oscar Wilde being arrested to define what it meant to be gay.

Bisexuals were not differentiated from the greater transgender, lesbian, and gay world. Defined by discrimination and traveling together for safety, it was truly one community. Then this greater gay community started having success. In some cities, what was once a good way to be arrested is now a good way onto the city council. Not that success is total, not at all; there still is a long way to go. But the formerly united community has come far enough to be able to splinter into its constituent groups. First lesbians started speaking out about their own issues and demanding to be full partners. Then trans people and bisexuals spoke out about no longer wanting to be second-class members of the community. Indeed, many bisexuals, especially bisexual women, found themselves unwelcome in a community they previously were part of or felt to be their birth-right. Beth Firestein makes the case in the *Journal of Sex Research:*

In a very real sense, the lesbian/gay movement created bisexuals as an oppressed group by creating a discourse in which lesbians/gays and heterosexuals, but not bisexuals, were defined into political existence. Thus, the lesbian/gay movement not only altered the political arena by creating a new political tradition; it also created the need for a bisexual movement.[47]

Just as the lesbian and gay communities are the offspring of exclusion and discrimination, the bisexual community is the offspring of exclusion and discrimination from the lesbian and gay communities. Not that all or even most bisexuals feel discriminated against by these communities, but there are enough who do, enough to create a separate and distinct bisexual identity. Indeed, for many bisexuals, their relationship with the lesbian and gay communities is defined by one simple conflict: what does it mean to be attracted to people of the same gender while in a relationship with someone of another? How can you be queer and in a relationship with someone of the opposite sex?

Which brings us to the next question: Is there a separate and distinct bisexual community, complete with its own culture and institutions? If not, why not?

Chapter 4

In Search of a Bisexual Community

THE PICNIC

The day of the picnic was an uncomfortable 97 degrees and sunny. Let's just say I wasn't very enthusiastic. As a life-long Minnesotan, I am more accustomed to the biting cold of winter than the blistering sunburn of summer, but since I was in charge of the charcoal I had little choice but to go. No charcoal, no barbeque. No barbeque, no end to the abuse I would have to endure over the next year because of it.

Held in a lesser-used area of Como Park, a large and popular park in St. Paul, the picnic site featured parking nearby and a wonderful old cottonwood shade tree. Both features would turn out to be key: the shade was an absolute necessity and there was no way people would be walking a great distance from their cars to a picnic site carrying grills, coolers, and chairs. It was a good place for the picnic, especially considering the organizers didn't want to pay to reserve a spot (which would have allowed for setting up a canopy for more shade and greater visibility). Beggars can't be choosers.

The event began, theoretically at least, at 1 p.m. A few people arrived about then, but most drifted in over the next few hours. Grills were started, chairs set up, lawn toys deployed. Threats of a game of volleyball were quickly squelched in favor of a far more heat-appropriate plan of lounging under the cottonwood tree. Inactivity was the rule, except for three children who seemed content to exhaust themselves. At its peak twenty people were playing, eating, chatting, and trying to keep cool. Anyone driving by on the road next to our picnic wouldn't have paid us any notice. Other than the bisexual community's tri-color flag hanging from the cottonwood, there wasn't a clue that this was the "Annual Bi Community Picnic."

The picnickers that day were a fairly homogenous group. All the picnickers were white and all were dressed casually: shorts, sandals, hats, and the occasional Hawaiian shirt. No one wore a bathing suit, despite the heat. They fell within a narrow age range, the youngest an attractive young woman in her mid twenties (who was new to Bisexual Organizing Project [BOP] events) to several people in their mid to late forties. Some of them came as couples (but none with more than one partner) and most as singles. Most knew each other well—in some cases too well—but on the whole, they were generally friends. The event was a success, considering the hot weather. By and large, everyone appeared to have a good time.

I had a good time as well. I've known most of these people from their years of activism with bisexuality issues, and I enjoy their company. I especially enjoy the feeling of being with my tribe; it is comfortable being with a group of people who are bisexual like me. That is why I went to the picnic on that hot Sunday: to find my community.

I spent a good deal of time sipping lemonade and catching up with Lou while sitting under the cottonwood tree. Now in her forties, Lou is seen as the grande dame of bi activism in the Twin Cities. I am a big fan of Lou's; she exudes balance and wisdom built on years of hard work and activism. She attended the picnic with her husband Martin and their two sons; Lou and Martin have been together for seventeen years, married for twelve:

Even though I am legally married, I'd just as soon get rid of the institution all together. . . . We got married on April first. It was kind of a commentary on what we think of the institution of marriage: that it is a joke. But we take our relationship seriously. . . . We wrote our own vows [because] we wanted what we said . . . to be an accurate depiction of what we actually wanted our relationship to [stand] for.

Lou has been active in bi politics since the late 1980s when she and Martin joined the Bi Connection, a local bisexual organization that had its heyday in the late 1980s and early 1990s. Lou is one reason why the Twin Cities was an early adopter of the term *GLBT* to describe the larger nonstraight community and abandoning the use of "gay" as a catchall term. She says:

Having been around when the first wave of name changes went through, I can say it did make a difference. The first group we picked was the Twin Cities Pride Committee. We didn't just go in there; we did several years of volunteer work. I have tremendous respect for these people.

Also at the picnic is Brian. He is a slight man with long hair and glasses and is soft spoken and intellectual. He is far more interested in intellectual conversations than lawn sports. Brian is there without his wife, Connie, who wasn't interested in putting up with the heat. They are pursuing a polyamorous relationship. "We've had a couple of short relationships. We are in the process of nurturing another relationship now. I don't know where that's going to go."

Kathy, who we met at BECAUSE in Chapter 1, brought her two-year-old son Meridian. Kathy is more than busy keeping him out of trouble. She is clearly a loving mother and is always present for "Mer." Her husband, Mark, decided to stay home, probably again because of the heat. Kathy is in her thirties and wears her hair cropped very short with two thin braids, one on each side of her face. She is on the board of directors at the BOP, the local bi organization sponsoring the picnic, and was one of the planners for the past two BECAUSE Conferences held in the Twin Cities.

Tina, in her mid-twenties, the youngest member of the BOP board (and perhaps the most socially active), is a one-woman welcoming committee for the picnic. Tina planned the picnic as she planned many social events in the past. She has a way about her everyone likes; her sincerity is apparent and appreciated.

Jen and Steve were also involved in planning the picnic. They are now officially an "item," having met while working on the board of directors of BOP. This is an anomaly: the board is all about hard work and is as far from a singles club as you can get. Steve is a middle-aged man who, like me, has a thing for Hawaiian shirts. Jen, a younger health care worker and co-chair of BOP, came to bi activism through church work and is a former seminarian. They take opposite approaches to the day: Jen stays put on a blanket as Steve keeps trying to start the volleyball game.

We welcomed a few newcomers, friends of Jen's, including her ex-husband. We also welcomed back Bridget and Arthur, Lou's old friends and activists from way back, who both worked in the early days of BECAUSE.

These people, plus a few more, made up the bi community picnic. One could not argue they are typical of anything, including bisexuals, for they are too small a group and reflect only people motivated enough to come to a park in the heat. They are, however, typical of the attendees for many local bi community events. Multiply by five, add in about fifty people new to the conference, plus a few people of color, and there you have BECAUSE.

This example of a "bi community event" raises major questions in my search for a bi community. What is it these twenty people have in common, besides being bisexual, that brought them together? Why only twenty people? Where were all the bisexuals that hot Sunday afternoon? Indeed, the larger question is, Is there a bisexual community at all?

WHO ARE THEY?

We know there are a lot of bi folks, but what do we know about them? What kind of generalizations can we make about the population?

First, let's think about how useful generalizations are. It must be remembered, as with all generalizations, they are describing characteristics of a group and say nothing about an individual. For example, if I were to suggest bi people tend to like the color red, it is not safe to assume your friend who is bisexual must like the color red, or if you are bi and don't like the color red you must not be bi or you should start liking the color red. Important too is that generalizations, at least the ones I'll be making, are not value judgments. In other words, saying bi's tend to like red isn't to say that they are defective for not liking blue more or that red is clearly a superior color.

Another problem with generalizations applied to bisexuals is found in the very nature of their group. Bisexuals in our culture are a very diverse group, reflecting many different cultures and beliefs. But even more, "bisexual," as discussed in the previous chapter, tends to be a catchall term for people who are neither homosexual nor heterosexual. In other words, many bisexuals have nothing in common, not even agreement on what the word *bisexual* means. While it is very problematic to make generalizations about any group, it goes doubly for bisexuals.

Indeed, this is the first generalization about bisexuals I would suggest: they do not have a well-defined culture. When someone says they are bisexual, it does not give much of a clue about the individual's life. Some bisexuals are monogamous; some are not. Some are interested in love relationships with both sexes at the same time; some are interested only in serial monogamy; and some are in long-term relationships with a partner. Some are interested only in casual sex; some seek only emotional connections. Some are swingers, and some have severe judgment for swingers. Some are highly educated and informed on issues surrounding bisexuality, and some never think about it save when they cruise for sex. Some seek out the queer or gay culture; some have no interest in it whatsoever. Some attend or volunteer for Pride celebrations every year, and some have never and will never attend such an event. Some are liberal, both personally and politically, and some are conservative. And on and on.

To understand the bi community better, one thing we can do is look at bisexuals according to their *community of origin.* Which community, the straight, gay, or lesbian, did people come from before identifying as bisexual? In our society, the default is clearly heterosexual: people are straight until they declare otherwise. Given that, a significant number of bisexuals identified as lesbian or gay before identifying as bi. It has been suggested that one-third of bisexuals previously identified as gay or lesbian. One reason bisexuals might call themselves gay or lesbian is obvious; there is a supportive community waiting for gay and lesbian people, and there really isn't one for bisexuals. Another reason, as discussed in Chapter 2, is the "one-drop rule": if you are the least bit attracted to someone of the same sex, you are homosexual. Case closed. For some people it is only later when that label doesn't seem to fit very well with what they are feeling that they choose to continue their journey through introspection and education until a bisexual identity emerges.

Possibly related to the community of origin is *community of affinity.* Of interest here is the idea of "gay bisexuals" and "straight bisexuals," as bi's in the lesbian or gay community may not have very much in common with bi's in the straight world. As with the community of origin, which community a bisexual is part of may be reflected in their politics and culture. A potential factor in picking a community affinity may be a person's level of attraction to different genders, because as discussed in the previous chapter, a bisexual person may be more attracted to one or the other. This distinction between gay bisexuals and straight bisexuals may also be very important regarding sexual behavior and HIV/AIDS risk. (We can all look forward to more research in this area.)

A bi person's communities of origin and of affinity are important because they tend to color their view of bisexuality. For example, bisexuals who have no previous relationship with the lesbian or gay communities may not see a role for alliances between a bisexual community and gays and lesbians or share a common political and social mission with the Gay Liberation Movement. Instead, many bisexuals coming from the straight community may emphasize a mission of "sexual freedom." Bisexuals in the swinger community usually come from the straight community's point of view. Bi's who come from the straight culture may have little knowledge of lesbian or gay culture and may not identify with the label *queer.* Alternatively, a person who has strong ties to the lesbian and gay communities may see GLBT as the model and believe in the shared mission of "gay liberation." They tend to see the bi community as a necessary ally to the gay and lesbian communities and share to some extent its culture. They may also identify with the moniker *queer.* In contrast, a person who comes directly from the straight community may not have considered these political issues at all.

So here we have a brief thumbnail sketch of bisexuals. We know there are a lot of bisexuals, and we know there is little we can generalize about them. We are left with the million-dollar question: Is there then a bisexual community?

IS THERE A BI COMMUNITY?

Let's go back to our little picnic that hot, sunny afternoon. If we agree for now to go with the *Janus Report* numbers of 3 percent of women and 5 percent of men identifying as bisexual, and assuming there isn't anything different or unique about the Twin Cities attracting or repelling bi's, we are looking at a potential pool of picnic participants of about 120,000. We are left to ask, Where were the other 119,980 bisexuals that Sunday?

The answer is obvious. They were doing what everyone does on a summer afternoon: working, gardening, spending time with their families, watching television, but not going to a bi community picnic either because of lack of interest in, knowledge of, or access to (for example work commitments or physical barriers such as the heat) such an event. Why are so many bisexuals apparently uninformed about or uninterested in community events?

What Is a "Community"?

The fact is, few bisexuals are part of a bi community. Part of the reason is definition. I chose not to use *community* in the loosest sense of the term of merely having something in common, but more in terms of being a functional group brought together by commonalities and sharing a culture of some kind to some degree. For example, a few years ago I was looking at a bicycling magazine. In it they referred to a "bicycling community." A bicycling community. Hmmm. I guess there must be at least 200 million bicycles in America. I wonder how many bicyclists identify as part of a bicycling community? I would bet very few, only those invested enough in bicycling to include it in their list of community affiliations. Indeed, when leading workshops, I often ask participants to give their name and what communities they are a member of as an icebreaker, and never once has anyone identified as part of the bicycling community. (Just about everything else you can imagine, but never bicycling.)

I would suggest this is one criterion for being part of a community: that you *feel* part of it. Other people may assign a person to a community, which could have the effect of reinforcing or even creating a person's allegiance to it, but ultimately a person has to *feel* part of a community to truly *be* part of it. Conversely, for a community to exist there needs to be people who are part of it, participate in it, and help define a culture particular to it. You need individuals to feel part of the community to have the community. Therefore, I suggest merely being bisexual doesn't mean you are part of the bi community, and just because there are bisexual people doesn't mean there is a bisexual community.

How can we know if a community exists? The primary outward manifestation of a community is its institutions. The bicycling community has stores, magazines, clubs, and Web sites. The lesbian and gay communities have bars, stores, newspapers, clubs, Web sites, and on and on. What about the bisexual community? Does it pass the institution test? It looks pretty grim. In most cities there are no bi institutions whatsoever. There isn't one self-declared bisexual bar, nor one store, nor one general distribution newspaper at this time anywhere in the country. As David said to the Bisexual History Project:

I wish it were bigger; I wish it were more of a community . . . I wish . . . I could go into a café and know that there can be a lot of bisexual people there who can relate to the life that I live. I can find that in gay space, but it's not the same somehow. . . . I want to have that bi space.

This issue is a concern for those seeking to counsel bisexual clients. As Sharon Deacon, Laura Reinke, and Dawn Viers suggest in *The American Journal of Family Therapy,* "While homosexuals have been able to identify with a community that receives social and emotional support, bisexuals do not have a community in which they can belong."[1] Janet Lever and Sally Carson report in the *Journal of Sex Research:*

> Without social recognition, there can be no bisexual community comparable to the gay community with its networks and institutions. And without community, there are no reference groups, supportive norms, or available symbols to counter the pull toward the two extremes of the continuum.[2]

Why Does It Matter?

The lack of a community can have major consequences for people who are bisexual. What if someone who would otherwise identify as bisexual doesn't believe there to be a bi community? They may believe their only choice is identifying as gay or straight.[3] Sometimes this can be a conscious choice: "I may be bi, but I am the only one. I want to be part of a bi community, but that's not an option." For others it could seem there is no choice: "There are no bisexuals, and bisexuality doesn't exist. Therefore, I can't be bisexual." This happens often; indeed, it may even be the rule. If all people who behaved bisexually were to identify as bisexual, there would be no question as to whether there is a community.

This problem of a lack of community would be bad enough if it took place in a neutral environment, but we know the world is anything but neutral about bisexuality. As discussed in Chapter 2, many in our culture reject bisexuals. Indeed, according to a report in *The American Journal of Family Therapy,* "Before the 1970s, professional psychiatric and psychological literature described bisexuals as neurotic, mentally unstable, masochistic, repressed, and egocentric, among other things."[4] In this environment of homophobia, bi phobia and sex phobia, bisexuals need a community to turn to for support.

MEET THE BI COMMUNITY

Fortunately, there is some hope. While much of the country has no sign of bi institutions and thus bi communities, in some cities there are. As we will visit in Chapter 9, Boston has the Bisexual Resource Center. Until recently there was a national magazine, *Anything That Moves*. There is BiNet USA. There are regional conferences, in the Northeast, in Texas, in the Midwest. There is the men's conference in San Diego described in the previous chapter. There are many Web sites offering community. In the Twin Cities there is the Bisexual Organizing Project and the Bi Community Picnic.

So in some areas of the country the bi community passes the institution test. For example, Ronald says:

A community? Isn't that where we support one another? Help each other? Be a sounding board for each other? Join together when "attacked" verbally by homosexuals? If this makes a community, then we have one in Las Cruces. Our meetings are more than just going places. It is the above.

What about the first question: Do bisexuals feel part of a community? Clearly some do. At least twenty people that weekend in St. Paul did, and probably more. When BOP hosts other events, they usually count on a core group of fifty to a hundred people to attend. Attendance at BECAUSE runs from a low of seventy to a high of two hundred. Here, you will hear many individuals say they are part of a bisexual community.

So we find in some areas of the country, there is a bi community, however small. Eric in Nashville has a community but also wonders why so few participate:

We all know there are huge numbers of people who have had bisexual experiences, but finding/reaching out to them is challenging because many (most?) don't make the "bisexual identity" leap. Either their experiences aren't that meaningful to them, or they're too fearful of that label. . . . In conservative cities like Nashville, outward sexual conformity is alive and well.

I've seen a lot of people come and go through our bi group. Some were obviously just looking for a hook-up. Others were either scared off . . . or must have decided that it wasn't important enough to invest in building a "community" with common insights. And, to be fair, some don't have the time to invest for a host of reasons.

We continue to have a small core of people (5 or 6) who are almost always at group meetings and dinners, another 7 or 8 who make irregular appearances, plus the occasional new person. Sometimes I can't help but be a little envious of cities that have larger groups, but then, even when it's just the small core, we have some of the best discussions at the meetings and always have a great time socializing at dinners and other activities. We do advertise, but in a fairly conservative area, it takes a lot of courage to step away from conformity.

If so many people pursue sex partners of both sexes, and so many people identify as bisexual, why are so few people participating in a bisexual community? Eric offers some good insights. There are others. First and foremost, bisexuals are invisible. As discussed previously, this problem of invisibility is key to understanding the bi community. How can a community form when its potential members can't find one another? Making it even harder is that many bisexuals don't want to be found, as most bisexuals live happily in either the straight or gay/lesbian communities. For example, one participant of the online support group says:

I've never found a worthwhile book on bisexuality. I don't belong to a bisexual group, and I don't feel part of a bisexual community. Most of my friends are straight. I think that being bisexual is a personal experience and nobody else's business. I am happy to be bisexual and it works. (Happy)

Many bisexual people go to work in the morning, walk their dogs, take care of their children, love their partners be they of the same or different sex, and otherwise live a happy life. Why would they seek out a bisexual community? Why, if they weren't after something, would anyone want to stir up trouble for themselves? Why would anyone put out a flag saying, "Bisexual lives here"? For example, Brian told the Bi History Project:

I'm aware there's a community out there. I don't really feel I'm very connected to it. This is my fourth year at the BECAUSE conference, and it's like I run into people here and there, but I'm pretty much overwhelmed just dealing with my day-to-day life and I don't have enough time to participate.

Yet some do. Some have a reason to hang a flag. Some people need to feel part of a group of people who are like them. We are tribal; we seek the support of people like us to help feel right with the world. We want to believe we are not the only one of our kind. Everyone needs support, and many people need a community to get it.

Others seek a bi community for social reasons beyond support. Just as straight people generally look for straight partners, gay people for gay partners, and lesbian people for lesbian partners, some bisexuals come seeking love. Sometimes in the most traditional ways, meeting at a picnic for example. Other times in more unusual ways, such as on the Internet. And sometimes they come to meet people in more specific ways, such as at a sex party or swingers group. None of these are unique to bi people, just a little more challenging for them due to a lack of community resources.

Another reason a person may be part of the bi community is because they are politically motivated. There are those bisexuals who are motivated to fight for their civil liberties, and they need a community of allies to fight with and fight for. Also, let's not forget invisibility is the main barrier to community for bi's. For any cause, political action is all about becoming visible.

Last, there are those who, whether they choose to be or not, are visibly part of the bi community. By the very nature of their lives they are hanging a flag. For example, a person who goes to a family reunion every year bringing both their male and female partners with them. Or perhaps you are a member of a community, such as the polyamorous community or the pagan community, or whatever reason putting you out there to be seen. Whatever the particulars, for a small number of bisexual people invisibility isn't a reality.

This then makes up the bi community: the politically active, those seeking support or partners, and those who have no choice. Not only does each of these groups come to the community for different reasons, they each have different needs, goals, and perhaps even ideas of how to go about achieving them.

One important point is this: the motives bringing people to the bi community set them apart from the majority of bi's who don't share those motives; therefore, members of the bi community are probably not representative of bisexuals in general. Issues of concern to the vastly smaller bi community may or may not be of concern to the much larger group of all bisexuals or to those behaving bisexually. Unfortunately, this makes it a challenge for the activists to advocate for all bisexuals. Not that it can't be done with sensitivity and fairness, but it must always be kept in mind the bi community is a unique subset of all bisexuals with their own issues and concerns.

What Does the Community Look Like?

What else can we say about the bi community, from the Bisexual History Project and the online support group, and from the Bi Community Picnic? Marcia Deihl, who we will meet again in Chapter 5, says:

> One of the smartest things I've ever heard was from a man named Norm Davis; I met him at a bi conference in 1983. . . . I can think of exceptions, but he said, "If someone really enjoys being a bohemian or an antiestablishment person and they've had bisexual experiences, chances are they call themselves bisexual. If someone is very traditional minded and doesn't like to make waves, chances are they call themselves straight or gay." This is only for someone who is bisexual, I'm not talking about people who really are straight or gay and are sure of it.

In other words, Deihl isn't saying all bohemians are bisexual, only that most self-identified bisexuals are bohemian. If we narrow it to bisexuals who are members of the community, I would certainly agree. For Deihl:

> I couldn't stand the white bread lifestyle, . . . I'd go nuts. . . . Not that you're doing it on purpose, but it comes from within. And you enjoy having a bit of a fringe, rebel fringe, a bohemian thing.

To describe members of the bisexual community, one would have to first note that in general they are above average in education. Indeed, the online survey shows half the participants having a bachelor's degree or higher. However, it's not just about formal education, but more about being very well self-educated. Many of them can speak with authority on many topics—especially in matters surrounding sexual orientation. Here is a group of people that has devoted a lot of time questioning issues and developed their own answers. As Brian says:

> With different groups I have to keep different things undercover, and it really just seems like the bisexuals are the only ones that are willing to accept everything and willing to accept the polyamory and the pagan in one place.

Community Norms

The bi community, as is true of all communities, has norms. A clear set of beliefs, politics, language, and standards of conduct form the bi community's culture and community norms. For example, Brian finds an accepting bi community to be polyamorous and pagan, and indeed I would suggest this is a bisexual community norm.

One thing that is not a norm for the bi community is to be accepting of all beliefs and lifestyles (although many in the community might believe this to be true). For example, political conservatives wouldn't feel welcome. Several years ago at a workshop at the BECAUSE Conference I (a lifelong liberal) caused something of a rhubarb (a Minnesota term for a dustup, fracas, row, run-in, etc.) when I posed the question, "Would a Republican feel welcome here?" Believe me, there were no conservatives in the room. If this group had been appointed to elect the president in 2000, Ralph Nader would have won in a landslide. There is as much uniformity in political beliefs as at an NRA convention. Brian fit right in; Charlton Heston would not. Being left-leaning politically is a community norm.

Fundamentalist Christians also wouldn't feel at home. At my first BECAUSE conference, I went to a large room where the workshop "Bi 101" was to be held. There was a large group, about thirty people, and we were told to get into a circle on the floor before the start of the workshop. Candles were lit, and the lights went out. A man in a brown robe with a large hood, much like I imagine a druid would be dressed, entered and began a long, low chant. After several minutes even newbee me figured out something was not right. Then someone got up and left. One by one, others followed. Finally, I left. In the hall outside the room, the people who left before me were gathered in conversation. Apparently the workshop rooms were switched: Bi 101 was down the hall, and we had been sitting in on the beginning of a workshop on spirituality. I must admit, while I wished I stayed to see more I had to ask, Is this spirituality to bisexual people? In support groups, I've seen many people fight mightily with issues around their own spirituality, usually about how Christianity fits in with their same-sex attractions. In the bisexual community's culture, Brian's pagan beliefs are supported. Christians may feel less so, especially if they went to that workshop.

Another norm in the bi community is that the culture is clearly feminist. Indeed, as I discuss in Chapter 9, this is key to the history of development of the bi movement. For now, suffice it to say Phyllis Schaffley wouldn't feel any more welcome than Heston.

One community norm is the acceptance, if not adoption, of the identity "queer." "Queer" is very popular in the bi community. Not that everyone in the bi community calls themselves queer, but there is a widespread acceptance of its use. In the online survey, about half the participants identify as queer. Most people who call themselves queer use it as something of a secondary identity—identifying as, for example, gay first and queer second—however, a significant number of people refuse to accept any other label. Calling someone queer was a popular insult in the past (and to some degree, the present), but many in the LGBT communities have reclaimed the word. However, it remains controversial. I take a look at "queer" in Chapter 10 when considering possibilities for the future.

On the other end the spectrum of self-identity from *queer* is another label: *bi curious*. The term has a special place in the bi community, namely as the recipient of overwhelming scorn. It's seen most often in personal ads: "MWF, bi curious, seeking another WF to join my husband and me." On one level "bi curious" implies that the person is exploring their sexuality. You would think there would be a lot of support for this, wouldn't you? In fact, you'd have to look long and hard to find people who embrace "bi curious" in the bi community. Ask the online support group:

The term "bi curious" makes me very angry. I feel it is the biggest oxymoron in the bi world. As one of the first bi women I talked to told me, "Either you like girls, or you don't. There is no maybe." You don't have to "try it out" to see if you are bi! I mean, you should know if you like members of the same sex! (Nancy)

I hate it too. It can also mean "I'm a straight girl who wants to sound hip" or "My boyfriend gets a hard-on from thinking about me with another woman" Grrrrrr. . . . I don't wanna be anyone's science experiment—even if she is cute. (Julz)

I hate the "bi-curious" term because it gives the impression one can change one's mind and orientation at will, instead of coming to terms with the fact you're attracted to members of the same sex. (Cool)

Bi curious strikes many bi's the wrong way because it reinforces stereotypes of bi's not being committed to working in the LGBT communities (never mind most bisexuals stay in the straight world and aren't committed to this, either) or being firm in their own identity. Bi curious also gets attacked by many because of its association with couples looking for a third person, usually a woman, to share their bed, a stereotype many bi women are very, very tired of. To many, bi curious seems to be less about exploring one's feelings and more about being a tourist and never really coming out as bisexual.

For me, if the label bi curious works for an individual, I say, good for them. That may be difficult for many in the bi community, but it seems a little strange to me to become judgmental about other people's sexuality. It is difficult to figure out how to navigate this world as a bi person, and I think people have to travel the road they are on.

What Does the Bi Community Say?

Nearly everyone participating in the Bi History Project discussed their relationship to the bi community. Some talked of the support they get from being a part of it, and some talked about their lack of connection to it, but none doubted its existence. Anita, a middle-aged woman with a beautiful voice (everyone who meets her comments on her voice), said:

I feel that I have claimed a place in the community that I've always felt akin to. I have supported the GLBT community, but I feel now that I claim a place, that I really belong in that community whereas before I sort of viewed myself as a straight person who was attracted to women. . . . I feel a real sense of belonging . . . having met people more and more [that] are bisexual (because at first I was the only person I knew who was bisexual).

We will get to know Anita more in following chapters, but for now we need to know that BECAUSE has been a key part of her vision and connection to the bi community.

You know, at first (this is the third BECAUSE Conference I've attended). . . . I don't know what I thought, that there were going to be people who looked just like me or something; it was very weird. But now—and however much is just my own day-to-day living with myself and seeing more people that I've met at the conferences—I do feel connected through this conference and through some of the people that I've met, and I want to know people who are bisexual. And what I'm finding out is that we're just as diverse a community as is any community—each community of diversity, each community of religion, each community of nationality—in all the ways that people differ, so do we. And we just happen to have an interest or the same values in common.

Carey, a woman in her late twenties, is a former organizer for BECAUSE. She's wearing bib overalls and has short hair. She has an intensity to her that is common to some of the participants of the History Project, perhaps born of innate intelligence coupled with years of personal work and clarity of mission. Carey has long been an outspoken advocate on several fronts, including the transgender community and on feminist issues.

I do, in a sense, feel connected to a bisexual community. I feel connected to people here. I haven't been as active in the bisexual community recently; I used to be very involved. I helped organize BECAUSE for several years. I've been very involved in the Bi Women and Friends group. Even though that hasn't been my focus lately, it's still home to me. It's kind of like I've gone off into other things, [but] to me this is still the place I come back to, and it's not quite as much about bisexuality per se but it's about people who are really open to different things and have a different view of the world than mainstream culture, people who tend to be active and present and caring.

We met Scott at the beginning of Chapter 2. He's a bi activist of long standing, having first come out as bisexual in the 1960s, and he has been key to the development of several local organizations, including BECAUSE. Scott is a middle-aged man with a round face, curly hair and a ready smile. When asked what BECAUSE meant to him, he said:

I know a lot more people who are bi than I did before. That's been one of the greatest things. I mean, what BECAUSE is now is wonderful, and it's due to many, many other people who [if it wasn't for BECAUSE] I wouldn't have known.

Alix is a short, solid young man with glasses who also exhibits a quality of several History Project participants; he has at least the appearance of working in academia. One could imagine Alix at home in Cambridge, Massachusetts, preparing to teach an English Lit class at Harvard. Alix, a first-time attendee of BECAUSE, presents the kind of wonder I remember well from my first conference.

It's offered me a whole new community to network with because I was not even aware of the bisexual community, so that's been pretty exciting. . . . This is my first year. I just thought it would be another support system for me and I was really interested in the topics and the willingness to really go out there and think about things that are out of line for a lot of people.

Bi's in Other Communities

While of course people who are part of the bi community are also members of other communities, there are significant overlaps between the bi community and some other specific communities. Some communities have been especially welcoming of bisexuals, and as a result many bisexuals call them home. Indeed, we will need to look at whether some may constitute a bi community of their own.

The Polyamorous Community

One important community to many bisexuals is the polyamory community. According to the polyamorysociety.org:

> Polyamory is the non-possessive, honest, responsible and ethical philosophy and practice of loving multiple people simultaneously. Polyamory emphasizes consciously choosing how many partners one wishes to be involved with rather than accepting social norms which dictate loving only one person at a time.[5]

The bi community has a complex relationship with nonmonogamy, with many people feeling stereotyped as being necessarily not monogamous because they are bisexual, yet there are undeniable links between the "poly" and bi communities. I discuss this at length in Chapter 6.

The Science Fiction Community

Also common in the group is interest in science fiction. I have to admit, I rarely read science fiction myself and for years wondered what the connection was all about. Brian cleared it up for me at the picnic:

> [Being bi] has a lot to do with science fiction. The authors have been free to explore relationships that our society won't accept in any other framework, so people who grew up reading a lot of science fiction have been exposed to all different models of relationship.

Science fiction commonly explores topics taboo for most literature, such as gender, polyamory, and, yes, bisexuality. Because of this, there is a lot of overlap between the two groups, with some science fiction stores almost serving as bi hangouts. Indeed, I know at least two of the picnickers have helped to put on a local annual science fiction convention. This is not unusual of the bi community throughout the country.

The Pagan Community

Another thing setting the established, visible bi community apart is there are a number of people who identify as pagan. Not all, or even most, but certainly far more than average in the greater society. That is why the spirituality workshop I described earlier was in fact about paganism. Brian said:

I don't have a separate identity as a bisexual and as a pagan. I identify who I am, and who I am is always going to mix together. There's really no way to separate them out.

He describes his beliefs this way:

Bisexual, polyamorous, solitary, eclectic figure—that all fits together. I mean pagan is a broad general heading. If you ask ten different pagans how to define it, you'll get twelve different definitions. . . . [For me], I don't follow any one written tradition. I have kind of assembled my own religion over the years through my own experience and things I've found that communicate to me.

Magenta is a middle-aged woman with very long reddish hair. She wears lots of jewelry, and one would guess it is all jewelry with a purpose: a medicine pouch, a crystal, and various symbols. She says:

I had long hair—I've always had long hair. I'm a witch. And one of my teachers said witches don't cut their hair.

She describes the connection for her between her pagan beliefs and bisexuality this way:

I've been very, very active in the pagan and Wiccan community in Minneapolis. I'm actually one of the leaders, one of the people who founded a lot of things, and my primary identity has always been as a witch; my sexuality has always been in the context of my sacred spirituality.

The Transgender Community

For many there is a close link between the transgender and the bisexual community. Indeed, some of the Bi History Project participants identify themselves as transgender. When I first found the bisexual community I wondered what drew these communities together. The connection didn't seem obvious. Was it only a marriage of convenience due to exclusion from the lesbian and gay communities? Or were there other levels to the connection?

Turning to Alix again, he offers good insight into the inseparability of his bisexual and transgender identities.

I identify as a transgendered man, F to M and bisexual. I was actually married in my twenties, had a son, came out as a lesbian for twenty years, came out as a transgender a couple years ago, am in transition right now, just had chest surgery last year, hormones for a month, so I'm brand new. I realized I was bisexual last year when I started meeting the trans community, some of the transgendered men, and realized I had an attraction for both, M to F and F to M. So it's been probably less than a year that I've had that.

Scott also offers a personal view of the relationship between different aspects of his identity and bisexuality:

Within the . . . GLBT community I also identify as transgender. I think that does tie in, very much, for me. I'm also a polyamorous pagan and those tie in and seem to be part of the community spectrum right now, for which I'm glad.

Carey offers her perspective:

I really enjoy how I see the bi and transgender movement together. . . . One of the things I'm really proud of, actually, is here in the Twin Cities and Minnesota that the bi-trans movement has really been pretty cohesive . . . and that, you know, we'll come out sisters and brothers, and our gender flows through in a lot of ways.

The transgender community is discussed more fully in Chapter 6.

Are There Other Bi Communities?

Are there other bisexual communities than those we have been talking about? It would be good to say yes. The polyamorous community, the science fiction community, the transgender community, and, one described in Chapter 7, the swinger community, are some of the other communities having a large number of bisexuals. But are they then bisexual communities? I would think not. Just because bisexuals may feel comfortable or at home in these different communities doesn't make them a bisexual community, and it would be a disservice to claim them as such since there are also many people in these communities who are not bisexual.

What about geographical differences in bi communities? Given that there is at best a loose connection between bi communities around the country there are still remarkable similarities. Perhaps what variation that would exist between communities has been diminished with more books on the subject, helping create a more unified culture. Perhaps it's the Internet and the early adoption of it by many bisexuals that helps define a more uniform community. More likely it's the common root to bi activism that has made for similar results. The differences that do exist between regions of the country seem to center on how closely the local bi community is affiliated with the lesbian and gay communities. For example, BiNet Atlanta (the area bi group offering social activities and support groups) had, when I visited a few years ago, no relationship with the Gay and Lesbian Center of Atlanta. When I contacted them after my visit, BiNet Atlanta expressed only animosity toward the center. In Minneapolis, on the other hand, the bi community is closely allied with many lesbian and gay organizations, especially major statewide agencies such as Outfront Minnesota, the state's equivalent to a gay resource center. Still, this difference has little effect on the bi culture of the cities. If I attended one of BiNet Atlanta's support groups, I would expect to hear a very similar discussion about relationships, family, and coming out as I would attending the Twin Cities' Bi Forum discussion group.

BACK TO THE PICNIC

Here on that hot afternoon in Como Park is the bi community, albeit a tiny subset of those who identify as bisexual. Perhaps at first glance this recognizable, acknowledged community is pretty unremarkable, certainly not flamboyant or outrageous. It is hard to guess what an outsider would imagine the participants of a bi community picnic to look like, but if they were looking for a bunch of weirdos, they would be sadly disappointed.

I would maintain, however, this community stands out for being free thinkers who are truly accepting of others in a way few communities can claim. Perhaps it's the difficult journey of identifying as bisexual and of trying to accept themselves in a near absence of community support that helps them see and support the struggles of other people. Perhaps it's something inherent in those who choose to call themselves bisexual, as opposed to calling themselves straight or gay and behaving bisexually. Perhaps it's a quality of those who are willing to create a community where none existed. Lou, Kathy, Brian, Bridget, Tina, and all the rest would find a home in this sketch of the bi community.

Now that we've taken a look at what constitutes a bisexual community, lets step back and look at the experiences of bi people that inform both the community and bisexuals in general. I'll start with the very different experiences women and men face in their struggle to discover what it means to be bisexual in America.

Chapter 5

Women's and Men's Experiences: *Penthouse* Bisexuals and Support Group Men

KISS THE GIRLS

On February 6, 2003, I crawled out of bed just like any other day, bleary, bedraggled, and befuddled. As had been my habit, I'd stayed up way too late and got way too little sleep because, as you might have surmised, I was writing this book. As has been my habit for the past twenty-five years, I threw myself in a chair with my coffee and Raisin Bran and opened up my local paper, the Minneapolis *Star Tribune*. When I got to the entertainment section what did my eyes behold but "Kiss the Girls,"[1] a story about women television characters kissing each other. Neal Justin, an entertainment writer for the paper, tells about the appeal two women kissing seems to have for television viewers, or to be more precise, male television viewers. As Justin says, "A kiss is just a kiss—except when it's two gorgeous women puckering up on TV." By my count, he cites nineteen cases in which women kissed on prime-time television. And not just any women, we are talking about Pamela Anderson, Carmen Electra, Heather Locklear, Denise Richards, Michelle Williams, Kylie Minogue, and many other "gorgeous women" of prime time. According to Justin, Scott Seomin from the Gay and Lesbian Alliance Against Defamation calls these television characters "Penthouse lesbians" after the men's magazine, *Penthouse*. I'll call them *Penthouse* bisexuals.

I'm usually pretty slow in the morning, but two facts about this story caught my eye. First, the word *bisexual* appears nowhere in this story, even though throughout he is talking about female television show characters who are otherwise straight but are now kissing women. One would think "bisexual" would at least be used as an adjective. "Jennifer

Aniston's character's bisexual behavior . . ." Something! This is another excellent example of, as I discussed in Chapter 2, how invisible bisexuality is in the media.

What I think is more interesting about this story, however, is how it informs us about the different struggles women and men face when it comes to same-sex attraction: in our male-dominated culture bi women are eroticized and bi men are ostracized. The phenomenon is, I think, fascinating. It calls into question exactly what is the problem our culture has with bisexuality. After all, if it were truly about abhorring what some might call unnatural sexual behavior, what's up with the Miller Lite commercial with two women wrestling in the mud? Granted, there is a great diversity of opinion in our culture and there are sure to be people who find that commercial and the other examples of women-on-women sex in the media appalling. But the marketplace has voted, and women kissing women has won by a landslide.

I think opposition to same-gender relationships and public displays of affection has more to do with people's gross out factor than puritan morality. As Wayne Bryant, the author of *Bisexual Characters in Film,* says:

> I think there are a lot of differences for bi men and bi women. Bi women tend to be looked on as sex objects by society, and bi men more as outcasts. In some ways, it's cool to be a bisexual woman and it's disgusting to be a bisexual man.

Perhaps the typically male producers and other potentates in the media are judging the desirability of a same-sex kiss based on whether it excites them or threatens their masculinity. It has been said (by a straight guy), "What's better than one naked woman? Answer: two naked women." For many straight guys, any number of naked men are too many.

BISEXUAL WOMEN

Straight Men and Bisexual Women

HOT SWM
5'11", 180 lbs., healthy, seeking hot and sexy bi
female couple, 18-35, for hanging out and having fun. No drugs or psychos.

SEEKING BI FEMALE

Attractive, fit SWM, 43, 6'1", seeking bi female or bi female couple for intimate encounters. Must be fit and healthy, pretty legs and feet a plus.

BI FEMALE WANTED

By this attractive, 5'8", blond, 20-something, MbiWF. Come over and fulfill my fantasies! My husband is 43, 6'0", 240 lbs. and wants to satisfy us both. Serious replies only.

Anyone who has perused the back pages of any city's alternative weekly has seen ads similar to these. Hey, in my opinion they are the best part of the personals! Page after page of people looking for their soul mates isn't as interesting as "submissive bi sought for water sports." But hey, that's just me.

One might think in this climate bi women have it made, that they can have their pick of all these men and couples who pay good money to advertise to find them. Perhaps some bi women do feel that way. More often than not, however, bi women aren't answering any of these ads. Indeed, to what might seem to be an advantage, many bi women are saying thanks, but no thanks:

> I really am not interested in threesomes, though I hear a lot of assumptions that I should be. Finding other women who want to be with a woman one-on-one but can deal with the bi thing seems really hard for me and many other bi women I know. Why can't we find each other and hook up without men in the middle? (Julz)

I argue that Julz is more typical of bisexual women than the women of the girl-on-girl pictorials gracing the insides of many *Penthouse* magazines. Many men may hold having a threesome with two "bisexual chicks" as their ultimate fantasy, but I have yet to find among bi women any desire to be treated as a piece of meat. Not many women enjoy being objectified. Monogamous or not, bisexual or not, most people, both women and men, are more interested in finding a good relationship and a compatible partner than in fulfilling someone else's fantasies.

The pressure to please a man, as I discussed in Chapter 4, is sometimes at the root of women calling themselves "bi curious." Sometimes bi or otherwise straight women are willing to give their men their ultimate fantasy. I won't criticize it; that's their choice. But I will point out that the bi community generally has little patience for it. A great deal of judgment is expressed in the community for these "part-time" bisexuals. For example:

In my personal experience, I have corresponded with, or known personally . . . quite a few women who are not really bi but are just being with women because their male partner wants them to . . . and they are too afraid of losing their male partner to say no to the threesomes. (Valia)

Who is and who isn't really bi isn't for me to say, but it does seem that we might have here an example of situational same-sex behavior (for example prisoners, sailors, college roommates, etc.). Instead of actual sexual attraction, the situation—a woman's partner encouraging her to have sex with another woman—leads to sex with more than one gender.

Trendy Bisexuals

Also on the edges of the bi community and bi women's culture is the adoption of the label of "bisexual" in a more temporary way. How can I be delicate about this? Some young women in America today call themselves bi to be trendy. There, I said it. Lori, from the online support group, says it too:

Being a bi female is trendy. [They do] not consider themselves bi but say they are to be cool . . . being trendy has everything to do with everything. (Lori)

What does it mean that calling oneself bi could be trendy? I think it is only good news for the bi community. Even if a young woman calls herself bi only while at Smith College, that is one more person out there using the word bisexual; and it is one more person knowing something about the issue throughout her life; and it is one more person to speak out against homophobia. Besides, as I talked about before, I'm all for malleability in sexual orientation.

Interestingly, there is support for this phenomenon in the academic journals. As reported in the *Journal of Social Issues,* "Scholars from many disciplines have noted that women's sexuality tends to be fluid, malleable, and capable of change over time, . . . in comparison to men, whose sexuality and sexual orientation are viewed as less flexible and more automatic."[2] It is difficult to say if this is a true picture of women and men's sexuality or if nature or nurture create this dynamic. Perhaps being free of the huge cultural weight that is masculinity and enjoying encouragement from straight men (albeit often unwanted) give women more license to explore their sexuality. Regardless, again, I think it is only good news. Perhaps the question shouldn't be why young women are exploring bisexuality, but what keeps young men from doing the same?

Homophobia

This is not to say bi women get a pass from homophobes. Certainly not. First, regardless of one's stated orientation, anyone in a same-gender relationship suffers at the hands of institutional homophobia. At the time I am writing this, other than in Massachusetts, two women in the United States cannot marry and thus face barriers in many services such as spousal rights in medical situations, retirement, housing, contracts, and so on. In many areas of the country, bi women, like bi men and gay, lesbian, and transgender people, enjoy no protection from active discrimination at the workplace, in housing, and other places that put them in contact with people who may hate them. When two women are murdered in Oregon, or stalked and killed when hiking along the Appalachian Trail, we are reminded women are not exempt from being victims of so-called gay bashing. When two women who are friends of mine have obscenities yelled at them from a car window, or a man in a truck chases another friend with her woman partner—in both cases for committing the atrocity of holding hands—we know *Penthouse Magazine* doesn't protect them from those who hate.

Like the situation in which bi and gay men find themselves, women who love women threaten gender roles. Like bi and gay men who pose a threat to masculinity (which I will discuss soon), bi and lesbian women don't so much threaten femininity as they challenge masculinity. Historically, women become threatening to the patriarchy (a social and political system in which men are in charge of or have a disproportionate amount of power) when they cross over to do

"men's" jobs, drive cars, defy cultural norms in dress or sexual behavior, or be become assertive. Carolyn Dean, in her book *Sexuality
and Modern Western Culture,* says:

> Women's sexuality garnered little attention until it crossed the
> line to defy gender roles. Women's sexuality of the late nine-
> teenth century was defined by passivity; lesbianism threatened,
> and excited, men of the time. . . . In the late nineteenth-century
> Europe, it was not lesbian desire as gender inversion that domi-
> nated medical and literary discourses but lesbian desire con-
> ceived as the destabilization of gender boundaries.[3]

Bi women who know their place, in the pages of *Penthouse* and
putting on a show for their man, aren't a threat to the patriarchy. Bi
women who are in charge of their own sexuality—a sexuality that
might not include a man—are. And bisexual women in the bi community are overwhelmingly the latter.

Feminism

Feminism and political activism play a key role in the culture of the
bisexual community. Many bi activists cut their teeth in feminist
work before working on bi issues. Indeed, as I will discuss in Chapter
9, most leaders in the bi community are women, and the bi movement
is clearly feminist. Speaking from the point of view of a man, Bryant
is very clear about the role of women and feminism in the bi community:

A lot of bisexual activist women came from a feminist background, and so
I think that's had a lot of effect on how the movement grew. And back in the
early days of the movement, most of the organizations were led by women,
and probably the majority are now. I'm glad of that. (Wayne Bryant)

Marcia Deihl, one of those early bi activists from Boston, says:

I came out of feminism, going to lesbian feminism, to a search for integrity
in every area of my life. . . . But there was this other bunch of people [the bi
community] who understood me, regardless of my partner. . . . My friends
who knew me from coming out as bi, they really honestly support me, regardless if my [partner] is a woman or a man. . . . That's all I ever wanted.

Deihl works at Harvard University and was a member of several musical groups in the 1970s and 1980s, such as the New Harmony Sisterhood Band and The Oxymorons, a four-person a cappella group (three of whom were bisexual). She says of the relationship between women and men in the bi community:

[Bi women in the movement] seem to be much more politically oriented than they are cruising oriented. . . . [Cruising is] something I know the least about. I'm a hopeless romantic and monogamous. . . . I think there's a huge sexual social component that might be larger in the male community than the women's. Not that some women aren't interested, but there's this whole "what books are you reading, Ya Ya Sisterhood" in the women's movement.

Why are leaders in the bi community so linked to feminism? One reason is that feminist politics have served as a training ground for generations of activist women, whether we are talking about unionism or civil rights. Wayne says it better:

Bisexual women . . . at least the ones who formed the movement in the early eighties, were grounded in feminism and support groups and knew a lot about organizing. Bisexual men didn't have those skills.

Another possible reason women have assumed more of the leadership roles in bi organizations is because bi women seem to see bi activism as more political while men see it as more personal. This is a sweeping generalization but one I think is generally valid when considering the whole activist community. I think in America, a woman having any sexuality of her own is a political act. As I discussed previously, crossing gender lines is a threat to the order of our patriarchal culture, and women asserting their sexuality, any sexuality, crosses those lines. To be in charge of one's own sexuality, any sexuality but doubly so for bisexual or lesbian sexualities, is inherently feminist.

Lesbians, Feminists, and Lesbian Feminists

"Feminism is the theory, lesbianism is the practice."

Ti-Grace Atkinson[4]

Another reason activist bi women have tended toward feminism is that bi women have been put on the defensive about their credentials as feminists. One might think lesbians and bi women are the most natural of allies, but sadly this is not the case. Bi women, by virtue of their relationships with men, are often attacked as traitors to the feminist cause. Some more radical feminists view lesbianism as the natural extension of feminism: rejecting men and building a better world of their own. Bi women are thus less "pure."

I argue what is more feminist than bisexuality? The bold assertion of a woman's right to her desires, even though scorned and discriminated against by the greater society and rejecting dogma in favor or authenticity, makes bi women, for me, the champions of feminism and sexual politics. As Corrinne Bedecarre says in *Hypatia*, "A common feminist challenge to bi identity is: what is political about being a bi woman or man? The short answer is that anything people resist as much as they resist bisexuality must be political."[5]

Alas, many do not share this belief. As discussed in Chapter 2, in general the past rejection of bisexuals at the hands of the lesbian and gay communities is key to understanding bisexuality as an identity now. Indeed, much of what we know as the present bi community has been defined by this tension between the lesbian feminist community and bi women. It is this casting out of bi women that gave the bi community its leaders, its organizations, and its flavor.

This lesbian/bi women split affects more than community organizing; it deeply affects individuals. Again, Bedecarre says of lesbian attitudes toward bi women, "Cynical, skeptical or dismissive are the attitudes that I have mainly found," and "Bisexuality is more often resignedly tolerated than it is pro-actively supported."[6] Many bi women feel abandoned by their former friends and allies. Deihl felt the pressure to conform: "No one would support loving a woman in 1965, but no one would support, in my crowd, loving a man in 1975."

Indeed, it is revealing that in the survey 59 percent of women feel welcome in the straight community, but only 25 percent feel welcome in the lesbian. This issue was a favorite with the online support group. For example, Maria says:

Many people have told me that I have very low chances of meeting a woman for a long-term relationship (and that's exactly what I'm seeking) if I don't stop calling myself bisexual, and told me that since I'm only interested in pursuing a relationship with women, I should call myself a lesbian. However, I stubbornly disagree with this point of view. I have no desire to lie or to deny part of who I am. I did love my ex-boyfriend, and I see no reason to hide it or pretend that seven years of my life was a mistake (or whatever). What upsets me the most is the lack of trust toward people like me on the part of lesbian community.

What Bi Women Say

When the women of the Bi History Project tell their stories of struggle and redemption, of love and hate, it becomes harder to generalize about what it means to be a bi woman. All the generalizations about the community I've been making mean little on an individual scale. There is no surprise here; everyone's story is unique.

Kathleen is an attractive thirty-nine-year-old woman who looks likes she would be more at home at a book club than a bi conference. She speaks confidently and frankly about her personal journey:

I came out to myself twenty years ago when I was nineteen. I went to a Halloween party and realized afterward that a woman was interested in me, and I was oblivious. My roommate was telling me, "Oh, this woman, she was really attracted to you, and didn't you get any of these hints?" And I was like, "No, I didn't." I hadn't ever thought about a woman being interested in me, and when I realized that, I thought that was kind of interesting that a woman might be interested in me. . . . It just sort of entered my head as something that was a possibility. It was really scary at first. It was like, this isn't something I've ever thought of as a possibility for me. So it was scary, but once I finally met somebody that I wanted to date, then it was fun, then it was exciting. It was still like not something that I ever thought of as a possibility for me though. . . . I guess I just thought I would get married and have kids and have a house and never tell my family any of this. I was brought up Catholic, so there was all of this repression and not okay to be sexual at all, much less date women. It was always the monogamy and marriage rule, you know, and be a virgin till you're married.

Kathleen is now in the process of divorcing her husband of thirteen years.

He knew that I was bisexual when shortly after we met, I told him. We dated for five years before we got married, so I was with him for most of my adult life. . . . I never intended to get married and get divorced. I thought if I would get married, I would just stay married. I think that there's just more to me than just being the stay at home, be the good wife, be a mom, keep the house kind of person. Now I'm becoming more involved in being more of an activist. I'm one of the leaders of the BGL group at my college. I went back to school to be a teacher. I feel like I'm more vocal now, and I'm stronger than I was before.

Elizabeth is a forty-four-year-old woman. Her curly dark hair and black clothes gives her a decidedly uptown look. Yet, like Kathleen, any stereotypes about what a bi woman looks like are lost, as she fits the image of neither a *Penthouse* girl nor a lesbian separatist. Breaking stereotypes and defying roles is old hat to Elizabeth.

I come from a family—my mom's a teacher, my dad's a preacher, and I was the only girl, and I was supposed to be frou-frou—they had very predetermined ideas about who I was supposed to be, and I just never fit them. I'd try, and I'd be so uncomfortable and unhappy, and I'd sort of slide back, and that's been most of my life. I've tried to meet other people's expectations, but really, I always knew it wasn't quite me, and I'd give up for awhile and be myself, and then I'd go back to trying to please people. I also went to a church school. It was pretty clear about gender roles and people's behaviors. However, it was in that school that I met my first three girlfriends and we were lovers on and off for many years, and I felt . . . great about it, but I couldn't talk about it.

Like many people Elizabeth had an "aha!" moment when she discovered there was a name for what she was feeling:

When I was in my early twenties, one of my roommates came out as a lesbian, and she was very open about her experience and we talked a lot, and I told her, "Well, I've always had boyfriends and girlfriends. What does that make me?" And she said, "Oh, there's a name for that, it's "bisexual!" And I just will never forget that. It was like, "Oh, I have a name. Wow!"

Jodi, a graduate student in social work, grew up in Minnesota farm country. Her journey brought her to New York City, where politics played a large role in her development as an activist and bisexual:

I'm not one of those people who is like, "Well, when I was nine, I knew I was different and it really freaked me out." I was, like, really a girl, really heterosexual, you know. . . . What changed was I moved to Manhattan and all sorts of things opened up for me. I [was a nanny] for this family who were labor lawyer activists and [it] exploded a lot of things that I believed about the world. And [I] also met some lesbian and bi women and began to think, "Oh, wow, just like I can challenge everything else, I'll challenge my sexual orientation!" . . . Shortly thereafter I met my male partner that I was with for so long, and so it all happened kind of at once. And looking back I think I should have put the brakes on that relationship until I figured out what was happening in my head, because it was hard, it was very hard, to leave, but there was such a huge part of me that was so unhappy staying that I just couldn't.

Jodi's sexual orientation exemplifies the fluidity discussed previously. When asked if she identifies as bisexual, she answers:

Yes, I do, though now I'm kind of questioning that because right now sleeping or dating with men just isn't very appealing. . . . I was involved with a man for a very long time and ended that relationship because I just really wanted to explore dating with a woman. [I] have found out that it's a lot better, and I'm really happy, and I really like that. I'm very attached to the bi label because the bi community helped me feel very safe. . . . I think to do with that fluidity of [orientation] . . . right now I'm not attracted to men but I can't guarantee when I'm fifty I might not be—I kind of doubt it, but who knows? So there's that part. But also I found the bi community and I actually met bisexual people . . . it's just been a very accepting, very warm place to be, so I think it's out of sheer loyalty that I always will [call myself bisexual]. Because calling myself a lesbian just doesn't fit. It just doesn't fit at all.

It's been said bi women have more trouble with the lesbian community than the straight, while bi men have more trouble with the straight community than the gay. Another sweeping generalization to be sure, but as seen here, there is some truth to it with bi women. What about bi men?

BISEXUAL MEN

The Twin Cities Men's Center is in the basement of a building so nondescript that it is nearly invisible. The center has been there for about twenty of its twenty-eight years, and its twenty-year-old furniture (already used when they got it) is showing its age. The center is a compact group of meeting rooms featuring literature from organizations throughout the country, books of special interest to men, posters about domestic violence, and safer-sex supplies. When I arrived one evening I found the previous evening's coffee cups undisposed of on end tables and bullet-points from last night's anger-management class on the blackboard. If this is the center of the patriarchy, the patriarchy has fallen on hard times indeed.

However, despite the furniture, the Men's Center is a very comfortable place to be. Something about its earnestness makes it work, or maybe it's just the windowless, low light, quiet rooms that can relax a person. This is a good quality to have in a space like this, one that sees so many men, so many groups, so many different topics all to help men grow spiritually and emotionally. Most evenings the center hosts two or even three activities. "Divorce and Uncoupling," "Gay Issues," "Twenty-Something," "Men's and Women's Issues," and "Survivors of Abuse" are all support groups meeting here. Add anger-management classes and weekly presentations, and you have a very busy little nonprofit organization.

On Friday evenings only one group meets here. Since it's the start of the weekend, Friday nights are not generally thought of anywhere as a good night to have a support group. Regardless, this is the night of the bi men's support group.

I've come on a particularly cold and dreary evening. I haven't been here for quite a while; the Men's Center is just as I left it. At one time I was quite involved, working on the board of directors, facilitating support groups, and generally getting a taste of social service work, something that would eventually refocus my career aspirations. The Men's Center also gave me my first taste of organizing—six years ago a friend and I started this very same bi men's support group.

On this particular Friday, however, I am one more attendee. Ten other men came to the group this evening. I've been gone too long and, to my mixed emotions, know no one there. Although part of me wishes to see an old friend or two, that's not why I came. I've come to touch base, to come home to a place that was crucial in my own growth through some hard times. I've come not seeking a reunion, nor have I come as a voyeur, but as a man seeking the comfort of a supportive place.*

We meet in the library. I feel good about that, because that's where we always used to meet. It is the more relaxing room, with couches and easy chairs, as opposed to the larger room where the seating options are more uncomfortable. Besides, the wall of books in the room gives it a warm feeling. The men filter in, most alone, some in pairs. Were these pairs friends before they went to this group? Some of the men obviously know one another; they have the aura of being regulars. Some of the men say nothing and sit quietly. It can be an awkward moment, with some guys talking with each other as if the other men weren't there at all.

---

*In general, all of this book's anecdotes are true stories, although I sometimes change names or details so as not to expose someone. However, due to confidentiality issues, this story about attending a support group is a synthesis of people I've met over the years of facilitating the group. In other words, although the people here are typical of this support group, they are not actual people.

The facilitator for the evening is Dan, who is a handsome man with long white hair and a full white beard. His eyes crinkle when he smiles, which is often, and his accent identifies him as a life-long Minnesotan. It turns out Dan is married and has a boyfriend. Dan's wife knows he is bisexual and knows his boyfriend, too. They've reached not so much an accord as a stasis. Their relationship has found its own level of comfort and continues to work for them.

To my left is Ryan. He is an older, distinguished-looking man nearing retirement even as he navigates a career change. Ryan has either been a Lutheran minister or planned to be one for his entire life. As a bi man he doesn't feel comfortable keeping secrets from the church, but he doesn't see any possibility of successfully being out, not in his synod. He is recently divorced and now lives with his male partner in a distant suburb.

Mark sits on the other side of me. He is a quiet man; even though he is a regular, he doesn't say much. Mark is in his late forties, suffers the middle-age spread and is just starting to lose his hair. He tells me he is a mail carrier and has been for over twenty years.

Tim is a young man, probably under twenty-five, with a full head of blond hair. He is very vocal; it screams of the insecurity of being a young man in a room of older men. He works at a coffeehouse, not a trendy independent but a chain shop downtown. He is obviously a regular at the group.

More men come. Jackson and Sam come in together but sit apart. They, too, seem to be regulars. They are both in their thirties and seem to be well liked. Taylor is a quiet man whom MGM central casting would call if they needed a banker. There is Robert, another quiet man, Allen, and Ben, all three of whom are in their forties.

The check-in gives a glimpse of each man's life. Not having been in the support group with these men before, their check-ins are like stories I am joining in the middle. Ryan updates the group as to his job hunt; Tim tells everyone about a sad visit with his drunken father; Jackson is struggling through a divorce; Taylor and Robert are at the group for the first time, with Taylor married and trying to sort out just what he feels, and Robert single and living alone his entire adult life.

After check-in, the group turns to "taking time," which involves each individual telling what's on his mind and getting feedback. As had been the pattern before, the regulars want to talk about issues in their lives other than bisexuality, while the new and newer people want to talk about sexuality issues. The regulars were once new and urgently wanted to talk all about their bisexuality, but now they have moved on to new subjects. Still, they come seeking the support of being with their community.

This is the bi men's support group at the Men's Center: a good spread in ages, some professional, some blue collar, some socially skilled and some more awkward. All are white. Some of the men are out about their bisexuality and some are not. Some are married, but only Dan is out to his wife. A couple of men appear to have led lonely lives. Some see themselves as about to throw away a perfectly successful and basically happy life in favor of an unknown. Some are out and proud and are enjoying life in a way they never imagined possible. Some are in transition; others are not but find this at least one place to feel part of a community. As we've seen throughout this book, there is nothing obviously unusual about these men. Indeed, if you walked in not knowing what the group was, you would be given few clues as to its purpose. Also, like other groups of bisexuals we've met in this book, there is little you could generalize about these men. In this room of only eleven men, you could find someone to either reinforce or bust just about every stereotype there is.

Some things do stand out, especially within the context of the issues I've been discussing in this book. These men are clearly not hooked up to the bi community as defined in Chapter 4. They may have developed their own small community of men from the support group, but they are unattached to the community of men and women who attend BECAUSE or community picnics. None of these men seem to be invested in the GLBT communities at all. That has not always been true of this group. While coming from a straight point of view is most common, usually a couple of guys have traveled some in the gay community. None of these guys have crossed paths with bisexual women enough to know anything about their experience or the role feminism has played in the bisexual community. Nor are they likely to care. In general, they do not seek a bisexual community as such—what they do seek is more authenticity in their lives.

What Can Be Said About Bi Men?

Bisexual men are in a very different position in the greater culture than bi women. Rather than being objectified by straight culture, they are scorned. Rather than being ostracized by the gay male community as bi women are from the lesbian community, they are trivialized and dismissed. If their role in feminism is the defining struggle for bi women, the meaning of masculinity is the defining struggle for bi men.

Bi and gay men share much in common. Both share a complex relationship to what it means to be masculine, and as a result both suffer at the hands (both allegorically and literally) of the greater culture. Men who have sex with men bring into question just what a man is. Is it defined by genitalia or by something more? As I've discussed previously, in many cultures gender is in part determined by one's sexual activity. A person who inserts is masculine; a person who is receptive is feminine. In Northern European and American culture, an identity politic has developed around the choice of one's partners. Despite that, the old masculine versus feminine relationship continues also. Men who have sex with men are considered feminine and their masculinity called into question.

Why should this matter? Why do people care so much if they are feminine or masculine? The problem is that we live in a patriarchy, as can be evidenced by simply looking at the gender breakdown of government and corporate boardrooms. Women are seen as less than men. Therefore, a man who is feminine is less than a man. For that matter, as previously discussed, a woman who is masculine is a threat, since the system can't have people born women choosing to take on the mantle of a member of the patriarchy. When a man calls another man a "bitch" or a "woman" or uses phrases such as "cry like a girl," he is calling another man's masculinity into question by equating him with a woman and thus less than a man. It seems the worst insult one man can heap on another is to compare him to a woman.

Bi Men and Gay Men

While bi women feel more at home and more accepted in the straight community, bi men find a warmer welcome in gay male society. Enjoying the absence of the feminist political infighting, the online survey indicated 60 percent of bi men feel welcome in the gay male community, while 52 percent feel the straight world is welcoming and accepting.

Bisexual and gay men have much in common. In this culture, bi and gay men both suffer at the hands of homophobia. Both are often presumed to be child molesters, sex addicts, or mentally ill. Both are condemned by many major religions. Neither can openly serve in the military, nor can they marry partners of the same gender in forty-nine out of fifty states. As discussed in Chapter 2, homophobia makes no distinctions between bi and gay men. Jesse Helms does not hate bisexuals only half as much as gay men. Gay bashers do not stop to ask where one ranks on the Kinsey scale. A man does not lose only half of his job.

Bi men and gay men do part company on some other issues. Gay men have a well-defined community, with institutions such as bars, newspapers, and stores. Gay men also have a well-defined culture. There are standards of behavior, community norms, and, to a degree, standards of dress and appearance. There is a gay history, complete with gay heroes and heroines. These are things bi men and bi women do not have.

While bi women face anger and ostracism from many in the lesbian community, bi men face condescension and dismissal of their identity at the hands of many gay males. Certainly bi men are generally welcome in gay male spaces and are not so much a threat to community paradigms as bi women are in the lesbian community. However, bi men are seen as lesser members of the club. Given the scale of the gay culture and lack thereof for bisexuals, it is easy to see bi men as not full partners with gay men. Then, add in all the stereotypes and misunderstandings about bi people previously discussed—bisexuals are merely gay people who haven't yet come out, bi people are sex addicts, bisexuality doesn't really exist, yadda yadda—and the result is bisexual men have a role of almost junior members of the gay male fraternity.

Bi Men and Bi Women

Bi men and bi women have much in common. Both suffer from the myths and stereotypes defining bisexuality in the greater culture. Both struggle with homophobia, and both suffer in the lesbian and gay communities, albeit to different degrees and in different ways.

There are other subtle and not so subtle ways that they have very different experiences. For one, there is not the political component to sexual expression for men as there is with women. Men are expected to claim their sexuality and to engage in sexual behavior regardless of their orientation. That some men visit parks to engage in anonymous sex with other men is usually explained by pointing out, quite correctly, that if a similar park were filled with women looking to find male sexual partners, straight men would fill the park. Men are assumed to be sexually out of control, and women are seen as needing to always be in control. As I pointed out before, women being in control of their own sexuality, and choosing to assert it, is a very political act. There is little political about men being in charge of their own sexuality.

This brings up another difference between the experiences of bi men and bi women. While some bi women in different-gender relationships are allowed or even encouraged to explore their same-sex desires (as long as it is for the enjoyment and under the supervision of her male partner), bi men do not have the same deal. Instead, bi men have access to various institutions to express their sexual desire for men if they so choose. Who knows how many bi men have or do cruise for sex? There are certainly some, and even if they don't take advantage, the option is out there. So for some men, instead of an activity for the couple, it can be a solitary, lonely act. In the survey, when people were asked to pick all the ways they meet potential relationship or sex partners, 23 percent of bi men meet partners by cruising, 27 percent at sex or swinger parties, and 33 percent meet men on the Internet. When looking for sex, 52 percent of men met or meet partners through friends, work, relatives, or church. For women, 86 percent meet partners this last, more traditional, way, and 44 percent meet their partners at bi or polyamorous community events, such as picnics or conferences.

Yet another difference for bi men and women is how often they have sex and how many partners they have had. To be sure, bi men do have more same-gender sex than bi women. In my survey, the average bi man has had sex with twenty-eight men, while the average bi woman has had sex with five women.

Finally, bi men, like bi women, in same-gender relationships are simply invisible. However, because bi men can travel more successfully in the gay male community than women can in the lesbian community, there is less need to separate from the greater community of men who have sex with men. Therefore, I would suggest there is less need for organizing around an identity politic, as bi women have been forced to do.

Bi Politics

The effect of all this is that women are the leaders of the bi community and of bisexual political thought. Informed by feminist activism, bi women have defined bisexual organizations' structures as more consensus run (a more female or feminist model) and less hierarchical (a more male and patriarchal model). Bi political thought often includes ideas such as "systems of oppression," or seeing the linkage between power and homophobia, racism, sexism, and other isms. It is a feminist political theory. Wayne likes it:

I'm happy to be part of a movement where the men aren't running everything and dictating how everything should be. Because, God, that's boring. But I think also having a strong feminist presence has had a really good effect on bisexual men. A lot of the bisexual male activists identify as feminist men. When the Boston Bisexual Men's Network was still in existence, it identified itself as a feminist men's organization and had that as part of its mission statement and printed it in every one of its newsletters.

I like it, too. It is refreshing to be part of a group largely both feminist and woman run. If only there were more such spaces! That said, I do have to wonder if it is a barrier to more people feeling part of the bisexual community. Previously, I told the story of asking, What if a person was Republican; would they be welcome? Now I'll ask, What if a man disagreed with feminism, would he be welcome? The answer is no—not in the bi community out there going to conferences, attending picnics, etc. Thinking in terms of systems of oppression and working to end racism, sexism, etc., is good work, and I'm right there. However, many people, perhaps especially a lot of men, have no desire to work to end racism, sexism, etc., and they won't be coming to the party. It is something of a conundrum if the bi community desires to grow and accept everyone. How does a community avoid excluding people while staying true to itself?

What Bi Men Say

Kevin is a man in his mid-thirties and showing signs of premature graying. He is a quiet man, but when he does speak he shows himself to be an intelligent and thoughtful person:

I'm Kevin, [a] happily married bisexual man. . . . We were lucky, my wife and I were lucky, in that we both knew that each of us was bisexual before we got married. I see a lot of couples kind of struggling with that later as they realize, you know, "Well, maybe I'm not what I thought I was," and so it hasn't been too much of a struggle for us.

Kevin adores his wife of twelve years:

We're ecstatically happy. I don't know about other bisexual marriages. I do see other bisexual couples discover that later and struggle. . . . We're floating on a cloud.

Even though he's married, Kevin feels most at home in the gay male community. He explains:

I have to say I feel a little more connected to the gay community because I am very interested in gay activism. I feel fine about the bi community being, maybe not a part of, but being very closely connected to the gay community. I know that . . . there are [bisexual] separatists. . . . That's fine, whatever.

Kevin sees why bi men and gay men may unite politically:

I think the bisexual community and the gay community resist a very unjust system, and I think that's part of why we have a community; in that, we're resisting the ridiculous system of one gender oppressing another or straight sexism oppressing bisexual or gay sexuality. We're holding out.

Kevin and his wife have agreed to practice nonmonogamy:

I think that it's good for people to see a married couple as one example of a bisexual couple. In our case we happen to be a man and a woman who are married, madly in love, very, very, very close, and we're so close we're practically the same person, and adventure outside the marriage doesn't hurt anything. In fact we can get together over details and giggle.

Kevin was asked how out he and his wife were:

We have a rainbow flag on our house, but as people get to know us, obviously very soon after they get to know us, they realize that we are bisexual. In conversation it becomes pretty obvious. And they see a very, very close couple who have trouble sometimes even realizing that we're separate people, really, because we're very, very close.

The online bisexual support group had many stories about men's lives. Some of the men had been successful at navigating the waters of their bisexuality and others had not. Eric's life with his wife is one that many men at the Men's Center Friday night bi group would envy:

I live just outside of Nashville, Tennessee—a fairly conservative part of the country, but not hopeless. I identify as bisexual, have been aware of it all my life, have experienced both same and opposite sex, but have only become really comfortable with myself in the last five to ten years. I'm in a monogamous marriage and out to my wife. Though Nashville has a modest gay/lesbian community, there was nothing in place for the social/support needs for bisexual people. So, I started a social/support group for bisexual men and women. Our group, Bi The Way–Nashville, will be three years old this November and was one of the best things I could have ever done for myself—and it has apparently been good for others as well.

Like Kevin, Eric fights the invisibility common to bisexuals:

I knew everyone perceived me as a straight, married guy—which was totally inaccurate—and the "straight" label was really starting to suffocate me. That's when I started the social/support group.

Eric has little patience for men who deceive their wives and themselves. Their relationship is monogamous, at least for now:

Let me first say that I've experienced conversations where some men will say they consider themselves "monogamous" when, in fact, what they're really saying is that they don't see other women, but they do have sex with other men—most without the knowledge of their wives—and still consider themselves monogamous. It's their way of rationalizing the situation. Some don't appear to be comfortable with the "bisexual" label and usually don't come back to the group meetings. With the exception of an invited third person (male) about thirteen years ago, my wife and I have been in an exclusive relationship for fifteen years. This has become more important to her in recent years than to me, but I value her needs and respect them. As I became more and more comfortable with myself, my needs (social, emotional, physical) as a bisexual person demanded more and more expression.

That said, it hasn't always been easy for Eric:

Being a married, monogamous, bisexual male, though definitely rewarding in my particular relationship, can be extremely difficult. And, as liberal as my wife is (truly, she enjoys group dinners and socializing with people from the group), I don't think she realizes just how difficult it can be sometimes. Ideally, I would like a secondary relationship with a male partner who is in a healthy . . . relationship with his wife, all above board and ethical, the definition of polyamory. Given my wife's needs for monogamy, though, I don't see this happening in the foreseeable future and I have no interest in separating from her. Therefore, the friendships that I've made (of various depths and intimacies—all non-sexual) from having started the group have become extremely important to me and go a long way in making me feel fulfilled as the bisexual person I know myself to be, even though I'm not having sex with someone of the same sex.

Most of the time, monogamy is absolutely no problem for me as there are no women that I have strong enough feelings for to compete with the feelings I have for my wife. As for men, beyond the "eye-candy" factor, there aren't many that I find really attractive to me.

Every once in a while, though, I'll connect with one guy at a very deep level of both physical and emotional attraction and suddenly monogamy becomes incredibly difficult, almost to the point of depression. It's not (at all) that I'm suddenly not attracted to my wife—just that I'm acutely aware of potential, quality relationships that I'm not free (by agreement) to fully explore.

Eric has a great understanding of the complex relationship between bisexuality and nonmonogamy:

Though I don't think bisexuality and non-monogamy are necessarily synonymous, embracing bisexuality does, in fact, cause you to at least consider the different types of relationships that are possible—more so than the average straight or gay person would tend to do.

Aaron is someone many bi men can relate to, including some of the Men's Center support group. He's seventy-four years old and still struggles to find definition for himself:

When I was a kid, I really wasn't aware of sexuality. . . . I did have some fun experiences with some of my friends. I remember the first time—probably— was in a culvert by my friend's house, a big culvert. We found this very novel because we sucked each other a little bit. We had no idea what it was. We thought it was kind of cool to do that. [That was] grade school, fourth or fifth grade. It was like what boys do, no big deal.

When I was thirteen I became sexual with a friend of my dad's. Later I understood that it was sexual abuse, because I was thirteen and he was in his thirties. He had all these right phrases to tell me, how wonderful I was. This went on for quite a while. He also did it with a friend of mine. I don't know how long that went on, but I realized then that I really enjoyed that, although I still didn't know anything about being gay or bi, or what orientation was all about. I didn't know much about that until I got to college . . . in the early forties. You heard the word "queer," but you never heard the word "gay" or "homosexual."

Then I went away to college, and I met a guy. We were active on the weekends. . . . He told me later that I was his first lover. Lover! I had no idea about that! Even then I was denying that whole thing.

Then I came to Cleveland, I thought I probably should get married. I found my wife. People gave you the idea that . . . if you got married it would be okay . . . that the feelings would go away.

Aaron has been married for over forty years. He chooses to act on his same-sex feelings outside of his marriage:

So I got married but realized I was still attracted to men. But I was married, so nothing happened. It wasn't until I had been married for 18-20 years . . . [I met a man] and we met about four or five times when he came to town. . . . He also got married and has a family. I haven't seen him in a long time. After that first time I felt, oh yeah, this is kind of nice.

But then it's hard to find a person and a place. But then, as I get more to today, there was [a] bi group [I was part of], those kinds of groups [are] sort of like a band-aid, soothing a little bit. It helps to me keep from being too compulsive. . . . That compulsivity has really been hard for me. I've been contacted by guys who'd like to get active. Fortunately, most of them don't have a place either. I say fortunately because it keeps me from being more active. But there's always that awareness of it, that passion. I love to hug men; I think I get a lot from that. . . . Hugging has helped me . . . to continue being married. Having a circle of male friends has helped me, being in a group like that.

Guys going through divorce have said, "Get a divorce. You're gay; get a divorce. Your wife will know; it'll be all better then." I think, jeez, I can't do that. I try to be a person of integrity, but that little bit of me is not too congruent with integrity. And I think, you know, I'm really being so dishonest with my wife. And yet, if she does know is that better than if she doesn't know? Maybe she knows, but doesn't want to say anything. She knows I have men as friends, I don't know if she understands I like them sexually or not. But she knows how important it is to me to have male friends. So all that has helped a lot. I think, as I get older, I don't need that as much as I did, but still a big thing about it is beyond the sex part of it; it's a feeling of being incomplete. . . . There's a loneliness. I don't know if that would ever go away if I were more active with men or if it's just there because you don't get that kind of support from your wife that you get from other men. It's kind of a lonesome feeling in there.

I've facilitated many bi support groups, and it is a lot easier to judge someone like Aaron before you hear how much pain they are in, and how much they've given up to do what they believe to be the right thing, to keep their family together at great personal cost. As Aaron says:

Some people say, if you're bi, you have the best of both worlds, and I don't believe it. For me, I don't have the best of either of them.

Ron's story starts out very much like Aaron's, but it has a happier ending:

I came out at forty-four to myself and a few people (gay men I was having sex with!). I was never going to come out to family, friends, work, etc. [Then] at forty-five, I could no longer be not out. . . . My wife accepted me. I told my children, my family, and work. My mom did not talk to me for the next five years. She recently (a couple of weeks ago) started talking to me again. One of my four sons stopped talking to me. He, just a couple months ago, began talking to me again. [In] 1998, I married Bobby with my wife standing at my side. The three of us have been living together since then.

Happy has a somewhat less resolved situation with his wife:

I'm married to a straight woman and we have three kids. My wife accepts my bisexuality. She doesn't want to hear about it and we have an agreement to keep [my] life and our family separate. I can mess around, but not with anyone within our circle of friends. I can have a "boyfriend" as long as it doesn't interfere. She makes me promise that I'll never fall in love or embarrass her. I think that my wife generally knows if I am dating, but we don't talk about it. I know that it hurts my wife sometimes, but we usually talk through the issues and I think that she genuinely understands me. We tried a three-way once, but it was not a good experience.

But now he has a new relationship, and it's working for him:

I've been in a relationship with a gay man for the last two years and I don't think that my wife knows. I see him when traveling for work. I am monogamous with this man and I do love him. It is good. He is good about helping me and making sure that my wife and family come first. My relationship with my wife has never been better, both in bed and out. My male partner makes me appreciate my wife and love her more.

This chapter has some of the experiences of bi women and bi men, how they are similar and how they are different. Both bisexual women and men struggle to find their home while not quite fitting in straight society or the lesbian or gay communities. Meanwhile, bi men and women face very different challenges from very different groups, creating challenges for community formation and political activism. However, one important group has not been discussed yet, as I've talked about men and women: the transgender community. What is the relationship, and the connection, between the bisexual and the transgender community?

Chapter 6

The Transgender Community

BI CITIES!

The television studio is not what most would imagine a studio to look like. Sure, there are three cameras forming something of an arc around a set; fresnel lights hang from the ceiling, and there is a booth in the back of the room. But the room is small and the ceiling low; the equipment is obviously quite used, and the set is filled with run-down furniture. If you were to look a little harder, you would find the booth equipped with state of the art in video recording gear; state of the art, that is, if this were 1985, not 2005. The set of the *CBS Nightly News* it is not.

But that's cable-access TV. It's a free service begat from a contract signed long ago between a cable television provider and the city with which it wished to do business, and, being free, beggars can't be choosers. We are just happy to be there at all. Being all volunteers, it is a miracle that the show gets on the air every week, fumbling around with all the faders, lavaliers, scoop lights, and other gear outside of our day-to-day experience. Who knows how many people watch? Who knows how good the production values are week to week? But we try. The crew—John, Rory, Tom, Lisa, Gregg, Charlie—and I are happy to give it our best.

One thing we can count on, though: our hosts, Margaret Charmoli and Anita Kozan always do a superb job. They know how to keep the show moving and how to ask guests the right questions. Being a "talking heads" show (a straightforward interview show where one or more guests take the entire half-hour), it is important to move it along and keep it interesting. Anita and Marge also know how to pick good guests. They are both well-connected activists and know who's who in the bisexual community. The show is called *Bi Cities!*, and since it is about bisexuality, the content is always interesting.

On a Tuesday evening, shortly before Christmas, we were happy to have Betsy Warner on the show. Warner is a U.S. patent agent, but that's not why she was on. Warner, a member of the local bisexual organization's board of directors, came to talk about her experience being both bisexual and transsexual.

Warner speaks with an enchanting British accent. Marge asks Warner about it, as well as her life, her transexuality, and her bisexuality:

> I'm American, but I was born and grew up in England. . . . My transexuality and my bisexuality are inextricably linked. Since the transexuality has been there since the earliest times I can remember, that was the beginning of the journey. Realizing I was bisexual came much, much later.

Warner is a tall, attractive redhead, wearing leather pants and a striped shirt. She sits on the half-broken studio chair with her legs crossed and seems quite at ease. I am anything but at ease, running around in the control booth from problem to problem and trying to listen at the same time.

> For some thirty years I tried to live as a boy, as a man, and eventually I got the point I couldn't do it anymore. It just became too hard to keep on doing it. I actually got very desperate. Fortunately I transitioned, began to live as a woman, had sex change surgery, and here I am.
>
> When my body began to change, my perception of my physicality began to change; my perception of myself as a woman was there all along, albeit very buried. But my body began to change, and [the] hormones had an effect. . . . My attraction to men began to develop at that point. Previous to that [point] I was only attracted to other women. I could feel it; it was like a barrier had been lifted. As my body began to develop in a female way, I began to feel a lot more receptive. . . . I found myself more and more attracted to men. It was like a block was removed. That's been a theme all my life: since I've lived as who I really am, it's taken a block off a lot of different things in my life, including that.
>
> It's an extraordinary thing to try to get across to anybody who hasn't been through this experience, who isn't transsexual—about gender identity and how powerful that really is. It's like the whole core of you is hidden. It's so fundamental that everything else sort of rests on it. That's how it feels to me. I didn't go around thinking, "Oh, I'm a little girl." When I was very young, I know that people called me a boy; I knew that physically there were differences, so I called myself a boy. The intellectual part of me always said that. But somehow it was just . . . it was like a discord. It just didn't ring right with me, even though I accepted it as the truth. I would find myself unconsciously mimicking my mother, other girls, and really it was just rather natural for me. I didn't think about being a girl, it was just in my nature. I had this feeling that "Oh,

eventually I'll grow up to be like my mom." . . . I didn't even think about it consciously, it was just there.

Warner's experiences are not unique. According to one estimate, people with "gender dysphoria," defined as being uncomfortable with one's sex, make up from 3 to 5 percent, up to 8 to 10 percent of the general population.[1] Nor is she unusual being both bisexual and transgender. It would seem at least anecdotally many people are members of both communities. It would also seem that a number of connections exist between the two communities, both in their inherent natures and in their place in greater society and in the greater GLBT community. The transgender community and the bi community are allies for good reasons.

WHAT IS "TRANSGENDER"?

In Chapter 3, I described marriages between women in many sub-Saharan cultures.[2] In these cultures, women married other women for several different reasons. If a woman was getting older but had still not secured a male husband, she might choose to marry a woman in order to secure her place in the community and ensure her economic future. The other woman may or may not be married to a man at the same time. Either way, one of the women gains the title of husband and all the rights and privileges thereof and now has the status of a man in the community. Two-spirit people were also mentioned in Chapter 3. Many American Indian cultures recognize more than two genders, some as many as five. They are often held in the highest esteem and are privileged members of the community. In Chapter 3 I draw these two groups into the discussion on bisexuality, but more significantly these cases raise the questions, What is the meaning of gender, and what does it mean to cross between them?

Gender

Gender Education and Advocacy, Inc., defines gender as a "psychosocial construct" used to classify a person as female, male, both, or neither. Gender identity is "a person's sense of their own gender," whether a person considers themselves a woman or a man or something else.[3] Meanwhile, sex is the description of the biological anatomy of a person, as a man, a woman, or intersexed (having ambiguous genitalia). As Betsy Warner says, "Gender identity, gender, is how you feel about yourself. Sex is more of a physical thing." Gender and sex are not the same thing, and for some their gender identity is different from their sex. In the previous example of two-spirit people, a person may have the genitalia of a man, thus their sex is male, but their gender is neither male nor female; it is two spirit.

Just like sexual orientation, gender orientation is a cultural construct. One's culture defines just what genders are available to choose from, their meanings, and their role in the society. As is also true of sexual orientation, people throughout the world express their gender in ways that may not be accepted in their society. Culture defines the rules and the meaning, but, just as with sexual orientation, people are compelled to live their own lives in their own way.

American culture recognizes only two genders, and genitalia is seen as definitive. This view is eroding quickly, if not quickly enough. It is being replaced with the concept of a continuum of gender, with people falling all along a scale à la Kinsey. We can view gender as running from masculine to feminine, with androgyny in the middle. A person who was born a man may be very masculine and at one end of the scale, have a bit of femininity, or more than a bit, or be extremely feminine. The same can be said of a person born a woman. For most people, their gender is close to their born sex, but for some people it is not.

Eyler and Wright have taken Kinsey's concept of a continuum and defined their own gender continuum,[4] paraphrased here and numbered for clarity:

1. *Female:* I have always thought of myself as a woman.
2. *Female:* I think of myself as a woman, but sometimes I feel more like a man.
3. *Gender-blended:* I am both a woman and a man, but somewhat more a woman.
4a. *Other-gendered:* I am not a woman, nor am I a man; instead I am some other gender.
4b. *Un-gendered:* I am neither a woman nor a man, nor am I a member of any other gender.
4c. *Bi-gendered:* I am both a woman and a man.
5. *Gender-blended:* I am both a man and a woman, but somewhat more a man.

  6. *Male:* I think of myself as a man, but sometimes I feel more like a woman.

  7. *Male:* I have always thought of myself as a man.

This is slightly different from the Kinsey scale in that while it is a seven-point scale, one can choose from three genders in the middle: other-gendered, un-gendered, and bi-gendered. This is based on their observations that

> a recent FTM conference convinced us of the need to include the other-gendered and un-gendered options, and to accommodate the "gender agnostic"; that is, the individual who either regards gender as being a very fluid concept, or a notion which is irrelevant to the freely-expressive person.[5]

Once again, much like the Kinsey scale, few things in this world are black or white, fish or fowl.

Transgender Defined

What does the word *transgender* mean? Warner says:

> For me, transgender is a very big umbrella term. It covers a lot of different types of behavior and types of people. For me, someone who is transsexual is someone who strongly identifies with a gender other than the one they were assigned at birth.

According to Gender Education and Advocacy, Inc, "Transgender is an umbrella term used to describe gender variant people who have gender identities, expressions or behaviors not traditionally associated with their birth sex." Gender variant describes those who "cannot or choose not to conform to societal gender norms associated with their physical sex."[6] Gender dysphoria, a psychological condition in which people are unhappy with their bodies and gender expectations, is often associated with transgender people.

    Transgender can also be thought of as an umbrella term for people who are pre- or postoperative transsexuals, cross-dressers (formerly known as transvestites), and/or intersexed people.[7] Warner is a postoperative transsexual:

Transsexual means people who have actually gone on to have a sex change as I have or want to do that.... [A transsexual is] someone who feels the need to change their body to match their own identity and have a sex change. Someone who is transsexual may identify more female than male, if, for example they were born male.

Transsexuals seek to change their sex to match their gender through medical intervention and often surgery. When undergoing this change, they are said to be going through "gender transition." Most transsexuals can be divided into two groups, female to male (FTM) and male to female (MTF), although for many this is changing, as will be discussed soon.

Cross-dressers adopt the dress and often the behavior of someone of a different gender. Drag shows are probably the most famous example but certainly not the most common. Many men cross-dress in private and seldom if ever go outside their homes "presenting" as anything other than a man. Women may cross this gender boundary perhaps more subtly, if no less meaningfully. Although there is now little taboo against women wearing pants, women who adopt an overtly masculine look may well face discrimination. Women's cross-dressing hasn't garnered as much attention as that of men until recently, but this trend is changing; it is growing activity at many gay bars to have not only a show featuring drag queens but also a "drag king" night.

If transsexuals and cross-dressers are about ambiguity of gender, *intersexed people* are about the ambiguity that may exist with physical sex. Warner says:

Intersexed people—it's a preferred term for what might formerly [have] been known as hermaphrodites. People who were born with physical sexual characteristics in between what would be considered "normal" for male or "normal" for female. . . . Their gender identity could be male; it could be female; it could be intersexed. . . . Intersexed people are born with sex organs that are between [female and male.] . . . In extreme cases it can be completely ambiguous. Intersex people have their own issues and concerns to do with forced sexual reassignment at birth.

Intersexed people endure what some consider to be mutilation when doctors and parents, faced with a newborn infant with ambiguous sexual organs, assign a sex through surgery. Sometimes the true sex of the baby is obvious but some physical genital characteristics of the other sex are present, and at other times it is unclear what sex the baby is from visual inspection. Sometimes the difference is minor and goes unnoticed, but other times it is more extreme and the surgery consequently more radical. Sometimes the doctors guess incorrectly and create the wrong sex for the person's innate sense of gender. Intersexed activists want a stop to routine reassignment surgery and to allow people to make their own choice about their genitalia. After all, often the only thing wrong with an otherwise healthy child is that the genitals are not what others expect. Why not let them grow up and decide for themselves?

These three groups make up the transgender community. However, not all people who are transsexual, cross-dressers, or intersexed identify as transgender. Indeed, the number of transgender people is grossly underreported.[8] Not unlike difference between the number of people who have sex with more than one gender and the number of people who choose to identify as bisexual, some who otherwise could call themselves transgender choose not to. For example, a male cross-dresser may reject the label transgender and not consider himself anything more than a man who likes to dress in women's clothing. Or, a transsexual person who was born as a woman may now feel comfortable identifying only as a man. Some transgender people use other identities to describe themselves; "gender outlaws," "gender trash," "gender queer,"[9] "gender variant," "gender bending," and simply "trans" are some of the identity labels one might hear at a GLBT event. Again, paralleling the ambiguity of bisexuality, individual struggles for self-definition create great diversity in what it means to be transgender.

What transgender is *not* is a sexual orientation. People who are transgender can be any sexual orientation—straight, gay, lesbian, or bisexual. As Warner says, "We come in all types of orientation variety, just like everyone else, just like nontransgender people."

TRANSGENDER HISTORY

The history of the transgender community is a short one. Although throughout the world and throughout time people have varied from their assigned gender roles, the term *transgender* itself was coined in the late 1980s. It reflected several different needs. First, cross-dressers objected to the term *transvestite* as describing only their outward appearances and not reflecting their gender identity. Use of the term transgender also included intersexed people in the discussion with the transsexual and cross-dresser communities.[10]

Perhaps most important, however, is that the term transgender represents a sea change in how gender-variant people view themselves and their options. In the past, the choices were to live either as a man or as a woman; people whose genitals didn't match their gender identity had the option of surgically modifying their bodies. By the late 1980s, after two decades of sex-reassignment surgery, two problems appeared. First, the surgery wasn't what some hoped. Even after extensive work, some individuals were not very successful at becoming another sex. Some men were not able to pass as women, and vice versa. They found themselves being neither male nor female. Second, some people didn't want to pass. More and more people were less interested in becoming the "opposite sex" and increasingly interested in defining their gender for themselves. Many rejected the duality of gender in favor of a cafeteria of gender characteristics. For example, a born woman might choose to take hormones to become more masculine (lower the voice, grow facial hair, and change the body shape) but forgo surgery to shape a penis. For these individuals, the older identities of transsexual or cross-dresser were inaccurate, and they needed a word to describe themselves. Enter "transgender."

Transgender people have suffered mightily at the hands of hate. One source estimates that since 1989 an average of one murder of a transgendered person per month occurs.[11] Brandon Teena, whose story is told in the 1999 movie *Boys Don't Cry,* was brutally raped and murdered in 1993. Tyra Hunter died after a car accident when paramedics left her unattended upon discovering she had a penis.[12] These deaths served to outrage people both within and outside the transgender community.

Yet the transgender community has found tremendous success in a very short time in raising their issues and creating community. Four states (including my home state of Minnesota) have civil rights protection for transgender people. Indeed, until recently, a transsexual person was the main advisor for a *Republican* mayor in St. Paul. Organizations have sprung up throughout the country. Several conferences are held each year. Parallel to the bi community, it is now accepted practice in most parts of the country to refer to the lesbian, gay, bisexual, and *transgender* community.

BISEXUAL AND TRANSGENDER

Bisexuality and transgender identities both resist simplification, both cannot be reducible to some simple formula.

Corrinne Bedecarre[13]

You might be asking, this is all good and interesting, but why are we talking about the transgender community in a book about bisexuality? Good question. Although bisexuals in general may or may not be more enlightened about gender issues, there has been, and continues to be, in most places around the country a strong connection between the transgender and the bisexual communities. Indeed, the two communities have been strong allies.

Why is this? One reason certainly is, as I mentioned earlier, the significant number of people who are both bisexual and transgender. As Warner explained, people might find themselves reevaluating the gender of their partners when going through all the physical changes involved in being transsexual. For example, a FTM who previously considered only men for partners might reevaluate that choice after physically becoming a man. The challenges and changes involved in coming to terms with being transgender inevitably lead to reevaluating much of one's life, including sexuality.

Another reason the two communities work well together is that they both have a natural affinity born of living in the gray areas. Both are neither one thing nor the other; both confound the people who view the world in simple either/or, dualist manner. Both communities understand this situation, and they both are more likely to understand each other than are people who don't have a personal relationship to this ambiguity.

One obvious and important cause for an alliance between the two communities has been their exclusion from the lesbian and gay communities, and both groups are excluded for very similar reasons. The transgender community is a thorn in the side of many lesbian and gay people who wish to claim, "We are just like straight people." Many gay and lesbian people, and bi people, too, carry around their share of transphobia. Simply because someone is not straight doesn't mean the person automatically becomes an expert in human sexuality or that all prejudices magically disappear. As bi's fight to be included in gay and lesbian events and in the names of organizations, it is natural for the bisexual community to support the transgender community in its parallel and simultaneous struggles for recognition and inclusion. Perhaps it is an alliance of convenience, but I prefer to think of it as an alliance of understanding.

When I posed the question, "What do you see the relationships are between the bisexual and the transgender community?" to the online support group, they saw their connections (or lack therof) to the lesbian and gay communities as key:

> There does seem to be an alliance between bisexuals and transgenders. As there appears to be an alliance between gays (homosexual men) and lesbians (homosexual women). (Paul)

> I agree, one is an orientation, the other is an actual physical (some would say mental as well) state, but I have noticed that bisexuals and transgenders tend to "link together." One person told me both groups had a lot in common because they were the "bastards" of the GLBT culture. That was a little harsh, but I think some bi and trans people feel they have that in common. (Kimberly)

> Yes, the alliance is that we (bisexuals and transgenders) are stepchildren of gay rights. (Ron)

Stephanie, who is transgender, adds:

> What about the trans people? Well, it so happens that the GL community sometimes look at us as though we changed genders in order to [be] able to relate to "same-gender" partners (partners of the gender we left behind) in a heterosexual manner, i.e., avoiding the . . . stigma of "homosexuality." . . . There's a problem with that. Some of us transition to become trans gay/lesbian/bi people. Gender identity doesn't have anything to do with sexual orientation. I LOVE women, and I can't keep my eyes off them! And I'm transitioning to become a woman physically. Go figure.

Earlier I described the difficult relationship between bisexual women and the feminist community. Many feminists have also ostracized the transgender community, especially FTM transsexuals. In this case, the rejection stems from the belief that women who transition into men are selling out, that they are doing it to obtain male privilege. MTF transsexuals fare little better with the feminist community. They are often scorned as not being "real women" and not having participated in the experience of women in the culture.

Back at the *Bi Cities!* show, Betsy said, "There are . . . some feminists that have strong negative feelings about transgender women in particular. And that's very hard because these are the people, feminists . . . that I regard as my sisters."

Marge answered Betsy with her own experience: "When I was coming out as bi in the lesbian community, . . . I thought [it] would be [more] receptive, [it] was actually the most hostile."

"It hurts more when it comes from women in the queer community and the feminist community," Warner replied.

The two communities have much in common indeed. The transgender and the bisexual communities *are* natural allies. They have many common goals and they tend to understand each other. We are doing each other's work. Stephanie from the support group says it better:

> The trans community is probably the one with the greatest potential for breaking apart effects of sexual division of people. We've been so railroaded into thinking in discreet, limiting boxes of self-identity, whether it's bi, gay, lesbian, tri-sexual, . . . whatever, without thinking about the variations in orientation and gender identity that exists.

The transgender community is a group many bisexuals feel an affinity for, and many people are members of both. Another community also has much in common with the bi community, sharing many goals, struggles, and misunderstandings from outsiders, a community to which many bisexuals pledge allegiance. It is the polyamorous community.

Chapter 7

What Is the Relationship Between Nonmonogamy and Bisexuality?

THE WOG

"We call this a wog." A wog? "Yeah, a wog. A pollywog, get it?"

I came to this meeting, I mean wog, expecting to see some familiar faces. Although I'd never gone to an event organized by the Twin Cities Polyamory Group, I knew several bi activists who were involved.

The meeting was at Anodyne, a cozy coffeehouse located in a rapidly changing neighborhood in south Minneapolis. What was once a small, marginal, neighborhood-oriented business strip is now quickly gentrifying. For example, on the opposite corner from the coffeehouse used to be a little neighborhood Italian restaurant. Now it is a very trendy haute cuisine wine bar. Really, the coffeehouse was the first sign of change when it moved in four years ago; now it is an institution. In the constellation of coffeehouses, this one leans heavily toward the tattoo and body-piercing crowd.

I dragged myself in on a very mild night in January to find, well, no one. Only five minutes to seven, it was way too early for a seven o'clock meeting given that people from my community were involved. By a little after seven, the first people started drifting in. The first there were Dan and Peter. They were friends, I guessed, having met in the group. Dan, a man in his late thirties with short blond hair, told me he had two male partners, one who couldn't be there this evening and the other who had just moved to a small town in Wisconsin. "I miss him, but oh well," Dan said. I asked Dan if he was bi. "I'm gay, but both my partners are bi men."

As more people trickled in, I was happy to see I was at least a little right about knowing people there. Tina, who I've known through the BECAUSE conference and the Bisexual Organizing Project, came alone, leaving her boyfriend at home. I asked what brought her here this evening and she explained, "It's the only time I can see my girlfriend." This Tina is the same Tina from the bi community picnic; she is in her midtwenties and just graduated from the University of Minnesota. Tina is fascinating; she bridges several communities quite successfully.

As more people arrived, I finally figured out this was not a formal meeting with a topic or a facilitator. It was more a social function, a gathering of the community, a wog. Ultimately twelve people came, split evenly between women and men plus some trans folk. Even though it was busy for a Monday night, they didn't sit together as a group but spread out throughout the coffeehouse. It turns out, Anodyne is only one of the coffeehouses in which they meet. "We also like the Riverview, because it has a great children's play area," Darlene says. Darlene, who told me about calling the gathering a "wog" (turns out "wog" was invented by one of their leaders, Robyn), is on the board of directors for the group. "We get anywhere from three to thirty people, depending on the night. But this is only one meeting. We also have a monthly discussion group and a board of directors' meeting." Darlene is there with her partner, and tells me she is a "lesbian and M-to-F transsexual, and I don't care who knows it."

I came looking for clues about the connections between this community and the bi community. The polyamorous community (polyamorous meaning most literally "many loves") is quite similar to the bi community. It has a strong presence in some towns and is nonexistent in others. It has a magazine, a national organization, and regular conventions. The communities are similar in size, politics, and culture. Both communities hold meetings similar to this one: mellow, friendly, utterly nonthreatening, and virtually invisible to the other customers at the coffeehouse. Indeed, I felt right at home there that January night; although it was not my community, it seemed very familiar. It shouldn't be a surprise; after all, according to Darlene, 75 percent of the group is bisexual.

BISEXUALITY, MONOGAMY, AND AMERICAN SOCIETY

Woman in her forties: [I] got married and divorced very young, discovered polyamory and realized I'm also not monogamous, that that was something that's not going to work for me.

Forty-four-year-old woman: I've been married three times . . . to men, and twice to women. So, lots of serial monogamy.

Twenty-nine-year-old woman: I'd like to have a relationship where it didn't matter if the person I was with was male or female; it mattered more that we were compatible and got along and were raising our family together. . . . I think I want to be in a monogamous relationship again. I think that was comfortable for me.

These participants in the Bi History Project offer three different views of monogamy. This range of relationship styles is typical of the diverse bi community. As mentioned in Chapter 4, few good generalizations can be made about bisexuals, and that goes double for the issue of monogamy. As with all other groups, the community includes people who are monogamous, people who are not, people who have more than one partner openly, and others who do so secretly. In this way, bisexuals are just like everyone else. The question is, Are bisexuals more likely than other groups to be nonmonogamous?

We know people in American society highly value monogamy. It is an unspoken assumption that married people are monogamous. It is taught in churches, schools, on television, and in safer-sex education. Most in American society consider monogamy to be an imperative for all relationships, that it shows a greater commitment and maturity. Placing a high value on monogamy is as close to a cultural norm as one can get.

Given its high place in our culture, is monogamy truly the norm? Not necessarily. It is an inconvenient fact that when it comes to the goal of monogamy many people fail dismally. Heterosexual nonmonogamy is well known throughout history, from biblical tales to polygamous societies, from French mistresses to the "free love" of the 1960s. According to the *Janus Report,* 35 percent of married men in the United States have had affairs, as have 26 percent of married women.[1] Humankind is not as monogamous as some would like us to believe.

Although in the eyes of society nonmonogamy is a deviant act, inviting social control ranging from community ostracism to legal sanctions, in some circles nonmonogamy is somewhat routine. In many cultures and subcultures, husbands "running around" bring little or no community sanctions on the cheating man (spousal sanctions may be a different story). Anecdotes (as well as movies, books, etc.) about mistresses and "backdoor men" (as Koko Taylor would say) permeate popular culture and are the subject of uncounted blues and country western songs. Nonmonogamy is practiced by all genders, not to mention all orientations.

Is Monogamy an Orientation?

Scott, who was introduced in Chapter 2, has in the past identified as polyamorous and has led workshops on the topic. His own views have evolved over the course of his life:

> For a while I was anti-marriage. Then I realized, no, there are people in the world who really are heterosexual, who really are monogamous, who really want and need to be married and do best that way. It's not my place to tell them they are avoiding reality. I don't know enough. But I do know where I am most of the time, so I've had to take a very personal stance. I go through changes just like everyone else. And at this point in time, I'm pretty monogamous. So, it can change.

In Scott's view, monogamy or nonmonogamy exists along a continuum similar to sexual orientation or gender.

> I think it's an orientation. I'm thinking that polyamory and monogamy is as much an orientation as gayness or straightness or whatever.

It is a compelling idea. Looking at monogamy this way means acknowledging that some people are very monogamous, and others not at all. Some people are mostly monogamous, and others are mostly nonmonogamous. That we could express an individual's degree of "monogamousness" as a number line á la sexual orientation is certainly true. More problematic is envisioning one's monogamy orientation, if you will, as fixed and somewhat removed from personal agency. Can we say people can't help to what degree they are nonmonogamous or monogamous? I have to admit, I do find it a persuasive argument. Most telling are those who want to be monogamous but do not seem to be able to. Having spent way too much of my free time attending or facilitating support groups, I have heard many, many men talk about their cheating ways as if it was out of their control. Some folks genuinely "can't seem to help it." One could suggest they may be facing issues of sexual addiction, and maybe for some that's it. Instead, it seems to me the major problem these individuals faced was being out of step with our culture, and in a different society one could imagine them being the rule, not the exception. I do know this: similar to the issue of orientation, if these men in the support group could change they surely would. Not one around me has ever rubbed their hands together and laughed about running around; instead, they were seeking help at a support group to stop.

The Complex Relationship Between Bisexuality and Monogamy

Nothing generated more conversation in the online support group than the issue of monogamy:

> In general, monogamy and bisexuality are separate and distinct things. It's relationship orientation v. sexual orientation—not the same thing. For some people, me included, they're closely tied together. I don't necessarily need to have both men and women at the same time in my life, but I feel better, more whole and content, when I have the intimate presence or possibility of the intimate presence of both men and women in my life. . . . I'm not nonmonogamous because I'm bisexual, but it enables me to be healthier as a bisexual person. Could I be monogamous if I had to? Probably not. Maybe gender monogamy. I know monogamous bisexuals and nonmonogamous heterosexuals, and so on. For me, nonmonogamy works, but just like the people who say, "Everyone is bisexual" make me crazy, the people who say, "All bisexuals are not monogamous" make me crazy. (Erika)

> Just because a bisexual person got married to a person of the opposite sex, doesn't mean that they've turned off their bi-ness and are now heterosexual for life. Some people are capable of being totally monogamous, and suppressing their desires, but they still have the desires. Others, like me, want strong, loving and intimate relationships with people of both genders, concurrently, and are working to make that happen one way or another in their life. (Valia)

Many people assume that to be bisexual one must be nonmonogamous. Is it a myth, or are bisexuals really more likely to be non-monogamous than straight or lesbian or gay people? If not, why is the community so closely linked with the poly community and other forms of nonmonogamy?

What Do Researchers Say?

Searching through an academic database will yield very little on the topics of monogamy or bisexuality, and very, very little about the combination. Indeed, in the *Journal of College Counseling,* Janna Horowitz and Michael Newcomb's work on counseling bisexual students begins with the assertion, "There is a relative paucity of research on bisexual identity and counseling issues, as compared to notable research in the areas of homosexual identity and counseling issues."[2]

Kayley Vernallis, in the *Journal of Philosophy,* offers an interesting view of the subject of bisexuality and monogamy. She suggests bisexuals who are monogamous sacrifice a part of themselves: "Monogamy requires bisexuals to sacrifice full sexual flourishing, and that it places no similar demand on heterosexuals and homosexuals."[3] She says of bisexual women: "When she cannot satisfy her desires for sex with the alternative gender, it is not just that she has lost a sexual object: it is as though one half of her sexual self has gone to a nunnery."[4] She goes so far as to suggest a solution she calls bi-monogamy: "In bi-monogamy, an individual commits to one male exclusively of all other males and one female exclusively of all other females."[5]

Other researchers support Vernallis in her view that to be satisfied, bisexuals must pursue sexual relations with both sexes. From the *Journal of Mental Health Counseling:*

> For many bisexual people, the American cultural value of monogamy restricts opportunities for a fully integrated, satisfying life. Some individuals discover they need multiple relationships in order to achieve the emotional, sensual and sexual gratification that heterosexuals often experience with one exclusive partner.[6]

Horowitz and Newcomb, in their guide to counseling, offer some interesting views on the issue of monogamy. They suggest monogamous relationships can present a problem for bisexual students: "Having an exclusive relationship, whether homosexual or heterosexual, led to confusion regarding bisexual identity for both sexes." Having grown up in a society that tells us bisexuality denotes more than one partner, confusion among young bisexuals is of no surprise. Horowitz and Newcomb assert, "Nothing about bisexuality suggests that bisexuals are more promiscuous than heterosexuals or lesbian women and gay men." They suggest that bisexuals can be separated into two groups: one that chooses monogomy and one that does not feel satisfied unless they can be sexual with both men and women.[7]

Are bisexuality and nonmonogamy inextricably linked? What are the numbers?

How Many Bisexuals Are Not Monogamous?

Few data exist about how prevalent monogamy or nonmonogamy is among bisexuals. One study we do have is Martin Weinberg, Colin Williams, and Douglas Pryor's research on the bisexual community in San Francisco during the 1980s. Their book, *Dual Attraction: Understanding Bisexuality,* remains some of the only such research to date. Unfortunately, it would be hard to generalize this data to all bisexuals since the research was conducted at the (since closed) Bisexual Center of San Francisco and is thus geographically and culturally specific. Since their work focused on a community center, these subjects were probably well invested in the bisexual community as I've previously defined it. They found that 23.3 percent of bisexual women in the survey were monogamous, while 12.1 percent of men reported they were monogamous.[8]

Another attempt at research with an even smaller data pool took place in the Twin Cities in 2001 when Outfront Minnesota, a statewide GLBT advocacy agency, undertook a bisexual community needs assessment. The researcher, Dr. Taimur Malik, using interviews and questionnaires, was able to question only a small sample group. The fifty participants were self-selected from a list provided by the local bi group and probably represented some of the most vocal and identifiable members of the community, such as some of the people at BECAUSE and the bi community picnic.

One of the aspects of the community studied was how the participants identified their relationship status. The choices were among no relationship, partnered monogamous, partnered nonmonogamous, and polyamorous. Malik found overall that 31 percent of the subjects were in a monogamous relationship, while 45 percent were in a non-monogamous or polyamorous relationship; the rest were not in a relationship.[9] Therefore, of those in a relationship, about 60 percent were not monogamous.

In the survey for this book, I found a somewhat higher incidence of nonmonogamy: 71 percent of both women and men reported they are not monogamous within their primary relationship. However, an important distinction was revealed when I asked about monogamy and when I asked about relationships. Thirty percent of the respondents who are in a relationship have more than one partner. In other words, about half of those who report being nonmonogamous are in relationships with two or more partners. The remainder could be accounted for with more casual encounters the respondent felt didn't meet the qualification of "partner," or they considered themselves nonmonogamous but didn't have a second partner at this time. Who are the nonmonogamous respondents having sex with outside of their primary relationship?: 31 percent of women reported having sexual relationships with another woman, 41 percent with a man, and 43 percent equally with men and women. On the other hand, men were nearly twice as likely to have sex with another man outside of their relationship than to have sex with a woman.

Conclusions

It is safe to conclude from the available data that self-identified bisexuals are less likely to be monogamous than the general population. But we must also conclude that a significant number of bi's are monogamous. What about the vast majority of bisexuals who will never be found through any of the previous sampling techniques? All three surveys used data drawn from activist groups and, in general, those who tended to be more invested in a bisexual community. Perhaps these numbers reflect that group, but they are unlikely to represent bisexuals at large. We can only speculate as to how prevalent nonmonogamy is among the majority of bisexuals who do not identify with a bisexual community or are otherwise hidden or closeted. Remember the example from Chapter 4: if a bisexual person is happily leading a monogamous life, content in his or her friends and family, he or she would be much less likely to be found by a survey (for example, since such individuals would be less likely to be hanging around the Bi Center, they would have likely been missed by Weinberg, Williams, and Pryor's research). I must pose the following question: If these "invisible" bisexuals were taken into consideration, would bisexuals be any more likely to be nonmonogamous than gay, lesbian, or straight people?

Bisexuality and nonmonogamy are closely associated for other reasons as well. One factor is the uncertainty in the definition of "bisexual," as I discussed in Chapter 3. If researchers choose to define bisexuality as people who have both male and female partners, they can't be expected to find bisexuals practicing monogamy, possibly excluding a good number of bisexuals. If people assume bisexuality equals nonmonogamy, they may choose not to identify as bisexual unless they are practicing nonmonogamy, despite the gender of their past lovers. The more nonmonogamy and bisexuality are linked, the more reinforced this view becomes.

Another reason alluded to when discussing the nonrepresentative nature of the Bi Center is the culture of the bi community itself. As seen with the online survey, within the bisexual community a greater likelihood exists of finding nonmonogamous people living out of the closet than in other communities, perhaps resulting in added visibility and activism. In short, there are numerous outspoken nonmonogamous bisexuals. With nonmonogamy so intertwined with bisexuality in society's view, many people find the bisexual community a safe haven to feel free of judgment and find acceptance for their relationship choices. I would say that more than most other communities, the bi community welcomes such nontraditional relationships.

Perhaps it is time to stop and ask, What is wrong with equating nonmonogamy and bisexuality? In Chapter 4 I broke the bisexual community down into four groups: those who come to the community seeking support, those looking for partners, the politically minded, and those who for whatever reason cannot hide. While an emphasis on nonmonogamy is supportive of those in multiple relationships, some of those who feel part of the bisexual community because of their political activism or came seeking the support of community may be misrepresented and feel unsupported. This could be a significant barrier for some; the vast majority of bisexuals who are not presently part of a bisexual community may not identify with what they are told bisexuality is all about, both by society and by their fellow bisexuals.

STYLES OF NONMONOGAMY

What are the alternatives to monogamy in a relationship? I suggest that five general ways for people in a relationship to express their nonmonogamy are available: cheating, cruising, polygamy and polyandry, open relationships/marriage, and polyamory. What are they, and what does the bi community say about each?

Cheating

Having secret sexual liaisons outside of a relationship is generally called cheating. Few people in America would say cheating is a good thing, yet many people of all orientations are doing it. One reason is that while pretty much judged by all cultures, some are harder on cheating than others. If I may venture a stereotype, a French man and an Amish woman both come from cultures in which cheating is not sanctioned, but I think it would be safe to say if it were discovered by their family and neighbors the consequences would be quite different. On a one-on-one basis, friends who are cheating can find support; a man or a woman may laugh with a friend on the basketball court or over coffee or may have a cohort help cover for them. But at least in the abstract, cheating is generally condemned by our society. The bi community is no exception to this rule:

I don't have much respect or tolerance for cheaters, two of my mottos being "If you are not happy and cannot be yourself, GET OUT," and "Come out before you wed." (Tezza)

Sometimes those who do cheat suffer from guilt and regret long afterward:

I first cheated when I went to college. I started college [with] a fiancé who was back at home, [then] I realized that there was a much bigger world out there, including women!!! I started cheating because I was scared to break it off with him, because I knew he would do something stupid and hurt himself when we broke up—which he did—ran his car into a telephone pole. Luckily I had processed enough to realize that I could not control his reaction to the break up so I did not blame myself when he got hurt. I was an avid cheater on various boyfriends for about a year until I got burned badly when I got caught. (Lori)

Some gender variation may also be involved. The survey found of those in relationships, 90 percent of women said they are open with their primary partner about their other sexual relationships, while 60 percent of men are. Men being more likely to cheat on their partners certainly fits the stereotype, but I wonder how this compares to the general population, or to the gay and lesbian communities?

Also, just because some people are nonmonogamous does not mean they condone cheating. I find many polyamorous people and others in nontraditional relationships have no patience for it. Indeed, even in a nonmonogamous relationship a person may cheat:

> In general, I have always felt cheating went against my personal beliefs about a relationship. Briefly during my early years of college I cheated on a boyfriend with a man who was cheating on his girlfriend. That didn't last long, and I felt very guilty about it. Now I am poly. I am completely honest in my relationships. Based on the agreement I have with my primary partner, cheating is still a possibility, but it doesn't happen. It is a possibility in that if there is dishonesty about a relationship, or if I were to randomly be intimate with someone he does not know or accept me dating, I would be cheating (and the same goes for him). I have been much more comfortable being in a relationship of this style than any other. I trust my partners are being honest with me and they trust I am being honest with them. (Jen)

Yet other bi's accept the conventional wisdom that being bisexual, especially a bisexual male, means being a cheater. Mark, a professional man in his fifties, contacted me when he heard I could be of help in starting a support group. He had decided to start a bi men's group for people, like him, who were married and cheating on their wives. I asked about bi men who were monogamous; would they be welcome? He said, "There's no such thing. All bi men cheat on their wives." I asked Mark how his path would cross with a monogamous bi man. A devotee of cruising, he probably won't be meeting any in the park after midnight.

Cruising

Mark was hoping to get a support group going to reach out to closeted married men, such as himself. As a fan of cruising, he met many men in the past fitting his criteria. It became apparent right away this was not the average support group. Mark had an agenda: he believed in cruising as an acceptable outlet for married men who wanted to stay married. If they would only accept that cruising was okay, he believed, they could keep their marriage and have all the men they wanted too.

I'll define *cruising* as sexual relations with anonymous partners. By *anonymous partners* I mean sex with an individual that one does not really know, just met, and has no intention of forming a relationship with or even seeing again. Cruising often takes place in public at specific beaches, parks, cars, rest rooms (or "tea" rooms), and other such sites that become known as good places to meet someone likeminded. Cruising also takes place in private businesses, such as bars, bathhouses, porn theaters, bookstores, and on the Internet. This behavior is usually confined to men.

Even though I'm discussing a man looking to find sex with another man, men of all orientations cruise for male sex partners, even straight ones. Opportunity, curiosity, denial of one's feelings, and other factors figure into the decision for a straight man to cruise for other men. As discussed in the next chapter regarding HIV/AIDS, we cannot assume the orientation of men who have sex with men. We shouldn't assume those cruising for sex are necessarily cheating on a partner either; certainly some men cruising are unattached and lonely. Also, don't assume that if a man has a male partner that the partner isn't sitting on the other side of the bathhouse steam room.

Nor should anyone be quick to judge. I am talking about consensual sex between adults. Most public cruising areas are by nature secluded and thus unlikely to have unsuspecting citizens happen across a sexual act. With private businesses, men pretty much know what they are getting into. I'm sure someone must have happened into a bathhouse and been surprised to find other motivations to be there besides a good bath, but it can't happen often. Nor can we assume cruisers are practicing unsafe sex and spreading HIV and other sexually transmitted diseases (STDs). Although all varieties of sex acts may take place in a sex business or cruising area, the less comfortable nature of many settings, such as small movie booths or in the woods, often means anal sex is the exception, and thus at lower risk for disease transmission. Besides, nothing about cruising necessarily precludes practicing safer sex.

Often the real argument centers on property values of nearby houses and the problem of traffic. During the 1980s I lived just off Loring Park in Minneapolis, the Twin Cities' gay ghetto and a major cruising area. I would say that it never bothered me; indeed, I noticed it only on the occasions I walked out on my apartment building balcony after 1:00 a.m. After that, which was then bar time, constant traffic filled the streets for several more hours, back and forth, back and forth.

Open Relationship or Marriage

In an open relationship or marriage a couple agrees that one or both of the partners can pursue sex outside of the relationship. Think of it as the opposite of cheating. It may be more common than one might think, but as usual, actual research on the subject is nonexistent.

An open marriage or open relationship implies that some degree of negotiation has taken place between partners and probably some set of rules formulated to govern their relationships. For example, a common plan for a bi man and a straight woman in an open relationship is that the man may have sex with other men but not other women. Several issues need to be put on the table before agreeing to an open relationship: rules for safe sex, keep it a secret or talk about their other partners, how they can meet, where they can have sex, if they can have a fully affectionate relationship or must keep it only sex, if they can have sex only with people they both know or only with people they both don't, and on and on. For example:

Ideally, that's what I want. One man, one woman. . . . However, I am open to loving more than one woman at a time . . . but I will not be open to loving more than [one] man. As trite as it may sound . . . I have found what I consider to be the perfect man for me. What possible reason could I have for wanting to be with other men? Conversely, if I found [one] woman who made me feel that way, then I would stop looking after I found her. (Valia)

It may sound like a significant amount of work, but communication in a relationship is always good, especially when one considers the alternative.

Sometimes it is a challenge to maintain an open relationship in a world having so much judgment for anything but monogamy. For example, from the online support group:

I did get odd looks once from one of my husband's co-workers. He came over one day and I was on the couch making out with my girlfriend. He almost freaked out until he saw that my husband was comfortable with it. Many people seem to feel that if the spouse is comfortable then it's not cheating and therefore nothing wrong. . . . I really don't care any more what others think. It's my life and what happens in my life isn't really anyone else's business. (Jessie)

Swinging

Swinging is a form of nonmonogamy in which partners agree to have sex with other couples or singles. Also known as "the lifestyle," this differs from open relationships in that it often involves couples, is approached planfully ("Hey, sweetheart, lets go to the party Saturday"), and may involve commercial businesses as organizers.

The bi community is often scornful of the lifestyle. Some see it as patriarchal and exploitive of women in that women are encouraged to engage in sex with one another for men's enjoyment. Meanwhile, bi men are all but forbidden in the groups. It may seem logical that the swinger community is part of or connected in some way to the polyamorous community, but in fact quite the opposite is true. Although many people certainly do subscribe to both, in general swingers are oblivious or indifferent to the existence of the poly community and the poly community is often scornful of the swingers.

To help understand this, I talked with three people with considerable experience in both communities. Gregg and his wife, Charlie, are a married couple in their twenties who have been involved in the lifestyle for a couple years and have gone to parties at three different swinger organizations. On the other side of the coin, Tina participated for years in swinger groups but now rejects them in favor of the polyamory community.

I asked Gregg and Charlie about the view that women are exploited in the lifestyle:

Our experience with those in the lifestyle suggests that while the one male–two females fantasy is first suggested (and legitimized, etc.) by the men, females are what drive the scene. If the women are not interested in swinging, then nothing happens. The scene exists (or rather takes the form it does) because women want to get together. This of course is not to say that all swinger women view themselves as bisexual. Bisexuality, and what that term means, is a hot debate. The terms people use for themselves vary widely, including "bisensuous," "bicurious," "bisexual," "heteroflexible," "biplayful," etc. I mainly want to point out that I don't think that women are just doing this to please their mates. I don't think that this is a form of subjugation.

Charlie says:

I agree with Gregg in that women largely call the shots. There is a high level of respect of women's wishes in that if she doesn't want to do something she doesn't have to—"no pressure, no expectations" is the oft-stated mantra. . . . Nevertheless, while women can certainly say when things should stop or not happen in the swinging community, I still often have the feeling that since sex is such a focus and since swingers are . . . a pretty conservative group (or at least no more liberal than any cross section of the community), the overall view of how sex should be or what it should be for is male focused. The attention for physical appearance can be nice for women who aren't used to being affirmed for their bodies, but it also gets a little old, especially for those of us interested in making a mental connection.

Tina has had a very different experience with swinging. Swinging is where she started out, having had her first exposure to bisexuality and the opportunity to explore her attractions to other women in the context of the lifestyle. She got involved in a large swingers' club with her ex-husband:

There were house parties and structured monthly large parties at hotel rooms where they would have a dance and a hospitality suite where people would go off and do all sorts of stuff. I never went into any of those because I didn't want a bunch of people ogling me with someone else. It's not my sort of a thing. I went to a bunch of the house parties because they were more one on one. . . . [Hotel parties were attended by] a hundred to three hundred people. House parties twenty to thirty people. In a hundred people, you'd find five single women and maybe ten single men, and the rest couples.

Tina left dissatisfied, with both the group and her husband:

I was married [for] four years. He was sort of straight. [We split up] because I was polyamorous and he wanted me to be a swinger, and I got involved with who I was with. I wanted to be more involved with the bi community, and I felt guilty for being involved with all this stuff instead of being at his beck and call: the June Cleaver of the swinger community. We'd try and switch partners, but most of the time I didn't want to be with the male partner.

She was especially dissatisfied with the treatment of women at these events:

Many of them have straight males and bi females, and I noticed that a lot of the quote, unquote, bi women are more bi curious [only] if [her] partner was watching. Basically [it's] a show for their partner. . . . I started off in the swinger community basically to be involved with other women, not to do the partner swapping which is more common in the swinger community. I met a lot of wonderful people there [and] had a lot of friendships, but I got treated like a piece of meat. It's interesting how the swinging community views women. [You have to be] tiny and have big boobies, especially now. . . . When I was there in my prime I was the belle of the ball. Now you have to be ninety-five pounds and a double-D before they'll even look at you. Most of the women look like porn stars; that's how sad it's gotten. Oh, they'll take your hundred dollars a year, but you'll sit at the parties and no one will pay attention to you.

And do the men look like porn stars too?

Most of the men are in their forties with their tiny little trophy wives. A lot of doctors, lawyers, white collar, whoever has the bucks, can roll with this crowd. [The men were] average [looking,] too [fat].

Charlie sees different roles for physical attractiveness between the two communities:

Here is where the difference between the swinger scene and poly scene AND the difference between the swinger scene and the "mainstream world" are evident in a kind of curious way. If young, lithe, beautiful women are the ideal in the "mainstream world" they are still the ideal in the swinger world [and they] can enjoy considerable attention and praise in the swinger community. . . . However, it seems to me that in the poly community any focus on how others look physically is seen as shallow. In the swinger community, women get attention (from both sexes) for how they look, but it's always positive attention, whereas in the outside world women can experience a lot of catty negative attention about their age and bodies.

When it comes to bi men, both Gregg and Tina agree that their role in the swinger community is no role at all. According to Tina:

I wouldn't say that the swinging community is really involved with any part of the GLBT communities. They just haven't wanted to be involved with them for the most part. . . . I never found any bi males because they didn't condone bi males. That's part of the reason I got out of there. It just irritated me that bi women could be there but not bi men. . . . It was the unstated rule.

Gregg says:

Like almost everywhere else, bi men scare the hell out of people. Why? Who knows? Maybe thinking of men being intimate, caring, and loving with the intermediate medium of war, hunting, sports, or cars is just not acceptable. If you watch dating shows, . . . the media is still full of images of young men being rough and hard, not only with their women but also with their friends. . . . There are a few of us who are loudly and vociferously pro bi male, but we are the exception.

Polyamory

A subculture that makes up for its small numbers in outspokenness, the Polyamory Society defines the term *polyamory* as "the nonpossessive, honest, responsible and ethical philosophy and practice of loving multiple people simultaneously."[10] As a form of open relationship, the poly community leans toward relationships more than purely sex. Indeed, many poly people would argue being poly isn't an activity but more of an orientation. In other words, a person may be poly without being in more than one relationship, or even any relationship at all.

Many bi people are polyamorous. My survey found 61 percent of bi women and 73 percent of bi men consider themselves polyamorous. According to Tina:

I found out about the polyamorous community and found that more to my liking because that was based on love relationships rather than sexual relationships. The poly community meshes more with the GLBT community, not only in the activist sense but also in a demographic sense. . . . There's quite a few [bisexuals in the poly community]. I think there is more bisexuality there than in the swinger [community], more linked in with the activism part. They are at Pride; you don't see the swinger community at Pride.

I asked Tina to give me a picture of the relationship between her experience with the swinger and polyamory communities:

I would say the polyamorous is more based on the relationship between people. Swinging is a partner swapping, sex only. I was kind of in between there. I was swinging with a group of about twenty people and I was closely linked with them. They were my closest friends. I've talked with a number of people from the poly group and they agree there is a lot of overlap [between the poly community and the swinging community. People in the poly group] are a bit older, I'd say in their mid-thirties.

How would I describe the difference between the poly community and swingers or other open relationships? Both swingers and poly people are organized as communities. For example, the use of the word community is a clue to how important it is to their identity, perhaps even more so with poly people than swingers. Unlike swingers, poly folks tend to approach the topic with more of a philosophical underpinning. After all, the poly community is the one having several meetings each month to talk about issues affecting their community. As for the poly community and the swinger community, I'll put it this way: the difference between the poly community and swingers is like the difference between bluegrass and country music. In many ways they are the same, but not really.

Gregg agrees with this analogy. "That's it. That's it exactly." He adds, "We've . . . noticed that a lot of polys are pagans. . . . This is in opposition to swingers, whose main problem is being conservative. No surprise, they're suburbanites first and foremost." Much like the bisexual community, Gregg finds a polyamorous community heavily allied with the pagan community, something that is a barrier for Charlie and himself. Yet Gregg sees advantages to the poly approach, if only in concept:

Ah, polys, polys! Wouldn't it be nice to have a big house, with lots of potential partners? . . . Most swingers are married couples, many with kids, and houses and complicated lives. It's hard enough to find play partners, never mind another life partner!

Polygamy and Polyandry

Rare in American society, polygamy is marriage between one man and more than one woman. Even more rare is polyandry, or the marriage of one woman to more than one man. This is an interesting topic on its own, but it has little relationship to a discussion about the bi community, other than to say that if it were legal, first in line would be people in polyamorous relationships.

Struggling to Find Definition

These categories I've devised are not the only ones that could be used, but I would argue they are the most common. Indeed, there is a cottage industry of bi people creating new terms to describe their relationships, perhaps in hopes of feeling more comfortable. Some would also reject the one I've used for various reasons, especially the term nonmonogamy, which at least one person in the support group found offensive. The group had much to say on the subject, for example this string of discussion:

You know, with me it's odd. I consider myself somewhat monogamous but that's because I really don't have a better term for it that doesn't make me sound like a slut or a cheat. As far as men go, I'll only be with my husband. With women, when I have a girlfriend there's no other women. I'll just be with her and my hubby. So, in a way it's polygamy but not in the way most people think of it. Maybe dualigamy? . . . Actually, I like the term that someone used as a "triad." It actually fits really well. (Jessie)

How about polyamorous? You seem to have an example of where you are the pivot in the poly relationship, in that you love both people, but the other two individuals may not be necessarily intimate with each other in any way. The one thing they do have in common is that they love you. I don't know if you would see it that way, but that's how some of us in the poly community see that. (Stephanie)

I do not feel that I am polyamorous. To me, that means more than one spouse. Could be of the same gender. Whereas, dual-monogamous has the feeling of one of each. (Ron)

I've heard the term poly-fidelitous too. I think one should call oneself whatever seems best. (Juliet)

There is a term for not dating another person of the same gender as your SO [significant other], it's called gender-monogamy, . . . basically, one is able to date people of the "opposite" gender of their partner. (Areusa)

Polyamory works well for me. However, I've also used the term poly-fidelity, to mean that you have more than one partner, but you are faithful to those partners. Maybe something to consider? (Diana)

I would prefer the term dual-monogamy instead of non-monogamy. Non-monogamy sounds like I go out screwing anything whenever. Dual-monogamy means that I have ONE woman and ONE man. As bi, one could be monogamous or dual-monogamous, or nonmonogamous! (Yes there are some that will screw anything!) (Ron)

LAST THOUGHTS ABOUT MONOGAMY

The bi community continues to struggle to find its relationship to issues of monogamy. It is made more complex by stereotypes that oversexualize them and assume all bi's are nonmonogamous. No one wants to be a stereotype. Indeed, some monogamous bisexuals feel left out of the bi community because they see the community being linked too closely with polyamorous issues. Yet it is clear that many bi people are nonmonogamous and part of various groups such as the polyamorous community. It is a real challenge, but then anything involving sex in our society is bound to be one.

One last visit with the poly community gathering. I asked Tina to tell me about her life:

> I moved to the cities [from a small town in Minnesota] . . . and about two years later got married. Live a quote, unquote, heterosexual life. I got involved in the swinger community. . . . Now I'm dating a bunch of wonderful people. My male partner is a bisexual male, I'm dating a gal from the poly group, . . . and a female artist that I'm getting to know. Courting stuff. Basically [rules are] about safe sex. Anyone outside of our primary relationship has to use protection. When it comes to dating the same sex, we don't talk about it much; it's not as threatening. When it comes to male-female relationships we talk about it, . . . we have extremely open communication. We keep our relationships separate. This way it's more casual, more relaxed. It's amazing: everyone I'm dating Brent knows and gets along with. It's all about respecting the other person. Right now Brent is involved with a woman. That's new. . . . She's bi. But I'm not going to get involved with it. For me, I'm more comfortable keeping it separate. It's new, you know, you don't want to mix the paints.

So although it is unclear whether self-identified bisexuals are any more or less monogamous that lesbians, straights, or gays, it does seem clear that most members of the bisexual community are not monogamous, having found support for more nontraditional lifestyle and family arrangements. Given that, it begs the question, How has HIV affected the community?

Chapter 8

Bisexuality in the Time of AIDS

SAFER SEX SLUTS

A young woman, quite petite with short boyish hair adding to her already androgynous appearance, crawls up onto the makeshift bed where another woman, with blonde hair and a pageboy haircut, lounges in wait. They passionately embrace. Clothes start to come off, revealing flesh-tone sheer body stockings underneath. The smaller woman works her way down the body of her partner until her head is poised between her partner's legs, her partner squealing in pleasure. She pulls out a strip of red Saran Wrap and comments on the color while her lover hands her a bottle of chocolate syrup. The woman on top places the plastic wrap between her partner's legs and smears the syrup on it. Putting her face down between her partner's knees, she begins performing mock cunnilingus, much to her partner's obvious delight. The woman sits up, showing her face smeared with chocolate, and the audience roars with laughter.

The event was a cabaret fundraiser, designed to add to an endowment for future bisexual community projects. Attendance was good even though there were many empty seats, which was more because the space was quite large (I'd guess the old junior high school auditorium held about 400) than poor turnout. All totaled, about 100 people were there that cold winter night to see an assortment of short performances. A fairly typical bi cabaret, the event included spoken-word artists, musicians, more spoken word, a dancer, spoken word, performance artists, and spoken word. As with any such volunteer community effort, the quality was uneven. Still, the weak performances were always heartfelt and the audience encouraged them for their efforts, and the strong ones were truly entertaining and were well appreciated. However, the two women described previously stole the show. They and the rest of their troupe of six performers performed several short skits featuring simulated sex performances. They always steal the show; every time they do their act, they get thunderous approval and the benefit of the after-show buzz.

They call themselves the Safer Sex Sluts. A group of volunteers, the Sluts do a number of performances intended to encourage audience members to practice safer sex. Their main goal is to eroticize latex and make safer sex fun. There is a component of instruction too, but mostly they use sex and humor to get people to pay attention to what is essentially yet another lecture on how not to get human immunodeficiency virus (HIV) and other sexually transmitted infections (STIs).

HIV and acquired immunodeficiency syndrome (AIDS) have been around for over twenty years, and most of the Safer Sex Sluts can't remember a time without it. They grew up with the disease, much like the bisexual community itself has done. The threat of this incurable, catastrophic illness has influenced their entire lives, relationships, and communities. As is true of the gay and lesbian communities, AIDS has helped shape their culture and changed how the larger world sees them. Also like the gay and lesbian communities, they have been the victims of ignorance and prejudice because of it. Bi men are seen as disease vectors between the gay community and women. Similarly, bi women are seen as spreading disease from men to the lesbian community. AIDS has led to many deaths, some at the hands of misunderstanding and misinformation. AIDS has also led to research about the nature of sexuality in general and has challenged what it means to be bisexual. Nothing has made a larger impact on the course of bisexual history.

HIV/AIDS 101

HIV Transmission

My job, the one I actually earn money from, is in HIV/STI prevention. I hold support groups and travel around town to gay bars handing out information and condoms. In many ways I am a poster child for how HIV and AIDS have affected the bisexual community. Although I have not contracted HIV personally, the course of my life has changed because of it. The reality of the disease's effects in my community has led me to activism and eventually a career. Similarly, other bi men and women who are not infected are nonetheless affected.

And many individuals have been infected. As of 2001, over 360,000 people are living with AIDS in the United States and 460,000 people have died. Also in 2001, 11,000 women and just under 32,000 men were newly diagnosed as HIV positive. Suggestions that AIDS has been cured are quite wrong; although people are living longer and healthier with HIV, they are certainly not cured and must face an uncertain future of complex medication regimes with sometimes bizarre side effects. This is not a disease to take lightly.

HIV is the virus that causes AIDS. HIV doesn't kill people; it destroys the immune system to allow other illnesses to do so. When the disease first started to get attention in 1983, no one knew about the virus HIV; only people developing AIDS made the world aware something bad was going on. A person is diagnosed with AIDS when his or her immune system is impaired to a T-cell count of 200 or less, meaning the person is in danger of opportunistic infections. On average, a person will carry HIV ten years before developing AIDS. This is one reason why the disease is so scary and so prolific: for ten years a person could spread HIV without even knowing about it.

HIV spreads in some very specific and well-known ways. We know that four bodily fluids can spread HIV: blood, semen, vaginal fluid, and breast milk. Although saliva has detectable amounts of HIV, no known cases of transmission of HIV have occurred through saliva according to the Centers for Disease Control (CDC). We know the virus needs to get into the body somehow. It is thankfully a fragile little bug and doesn't survive long outside the body. Therefore, a drop of blood with HIV must find an open cut or a sore or other direct entry into the body. Similarly, HIV in semen is looking for a way in via an abrasion or a cut or a sore. Anal intercourse is of particular risk because the rectum is more fragile than a vagina or a mouth. A "handjob" is of low to no risk, because unless the person's hand has an open wound, HIV has no place to enter the body. A person's mouth is fairly resistant to the virus also, unless there is an open cut or sore for the virus to gain entry. Therefore, the highest-risk sex act is unprotected (i.e., no barriers, such as a condom, are used) receptive anal intercourse. The next highest risk is receptive vaginal intercourse.[1] There is risk for the insertive partner also; the "top" in vaginal intercourse has about half the risk as his partner, and the risk for a top in anal intercourse is about the same as with vaginal. Other than anal and vaginal intercourse, all other reports of viral transmission through sex acts have been anecdotal. Although oral transmission has been reported, if it is in the tens or hundreds of people is a subject of debate.* One case of transmission from a woman to a man during cunnilingus has been confirmed.[2]

One solution to the dangers of HIV for those seeking to be sexually active is to practice safer sex. Condoms have been shown to be very effective in stopping the spread of HIV in addition to other STIs, including syphilis, gonorrhea, chlamydia, and, to a lesser extent, herpes, human papillomavirus (HPV), or genital warts. Also, dental dams can be used when performing cunnilingus, as the Safer Sex Sluts demonstrated. Another solution is to perform only sex acts unlikely to transmit HIV. For example, masturbation, hand-jobs, dry humping, watching, kissing, bondage, the sky is the limit.

Yet it must be said that even with safer sex, there is still a risk, however small. A condom can break; you could be the first person to be documented as getting HIV from a hand-job. You need to do the risk assessment for yourself, but I might point out every time you leave the house there is a risk of a car crash or being hit by lightning, two events that in my estimation are far more likely to happen than getting HIV while practicing safer sex. Only you can decide what chance you are willing to live with and if the risk is worth it.

Orientation and Risk

Quiz—Which individual is more at risk for HIV: a gay man, a lesbian, a bisexual female, or a straight man? Okay, it is a trick question. They are all equally at risk because sexual orientation doesn't give people HIV; specific behaviors do. When talking about individuals, we cannot assume they are representative of their group. Although HIV has disproportionately affected gay men as a group, that fact tells us little about any individual and his own risk. As I've explained in this book, the link between sexual orientation, self-identity, and behavior is loose at best. Therefore, when I do a risk assessment for a

---

*However, we can expect that it is underreported. Since researchers can never be sure just when the virus was transmitted, they assume it to be anally (since that is by far the higher risk) if both risks are present, and usually both risks are present.

gay-identified man, I cannot assume he engages in any particular sex act. He may have never had anal sex in his entire life, or he may have anal sex with many different men *and* women. When I see a woman who identifies as a lesbian, I cannot assume she has little or no risk of HIV, because until I ask I don't know if she has sex with men and, if so, what kind of sex they have. When I talk to a straight man I cannot assume he has never had sex with a man; indeed, he may be having high-risk sex on a regular basis. Specific behaviors spread HIV, not a person's orientation.

Unfortunately, the CDC's HIV and AIDS statistics are wrapped up in the language of orientation.[3] For example, one of their *HIV/AIDS Surveillance Report* categories is "heterosexual contact." What does that mean? If they mean penile/vaginal sex they should say so, rather than assume or lead others to assume the only sex heterosexuals have is penile/vaginal, never to venture farther south. Straight people have anal sex too. Lumping all sex acts between heterosexuals together can give a false impression of a person's risk. Another example is "MSM." In an attempt to avoid the use of "gay and bisexual," the term MSM, "men who have sex with men," is used. When I fill out a department of health risk assessment form, there is a bubble for "sex with a MSM" as a risk factor. Sex with a MSM is not a risk factor for HIV; again, it is the kind of sex a person has that solely determines the risk. Of special interest to this book is the unique category of "sex with a bisexual male." Although the CDC reports the number of women who have been infected by "sex with a bisexual male," apparently no man has ever gotten HIV from a bisexual male, since the CDC doesn't report any cases. First, sex with a bisexual male doesn't spread HIV. Anyone can have all the sex he or she wants with a bisexual male, just as is true of any male, and both will stay healthy as long as they avoid specific behaviors that can spread HIV. Second, I would think it safe to say that no reported cases of men being infected by a bisexual male is a bit too optimistic. I'm being facetious of course; what they are trying to get at when they say "sex with a bisexual male" is women infected by "sexual contact with a man who has sex with men." Well then, why don't they say that? Here is my suggestion: instead of "heterosexual contact," "bisexual male," and "MSM," we should refer to receptive anal intercourse, receptive vaginal intercourse, insertive anal intercourse, receptive oral sex on a male, etc.

Preventing HIV in Communities

Given all that, a certain nuance makes the link between risk and prevention complex. As I just explained, when working with an individual, sexual orientation is irrelevant. However, when designing programs on a community scale, we must look at how specific communities are affected and understand the special cultural issues of a community in order to create programs that can reach that community effectively. Whether it is the gay male community, the bi female community, communities of color, or any other group, it is important to know how to reach them and any special circumstances they face. Unfortunately, programs cannot be designed for one individual at a time. So although it tells us nothing about any one person, it is still important to know that, on average, gay men have more receptive anal intercourse than straight men (and thus are more at risk for HIV *as a community*) if we are to target prevention efforts the most efficient way possible. Also, communities can be somewhat insular, so it may be important to know if a particular community has a high number of infected people. For example, if the Belgian community in some city has a high rate of HIV infection, it is necessary to have printed materials in Flemish and to do outreach at Belgian events.

So what do we know about HIV/AIDS and the bisexual community? Unfortunately, we find little research, with bisexuals usually being lumped in with homosexuals. For example, one researcher found in 166 articles mentioning bisexual men over a ten-year time period, only twenty-one pointed out any differences between bisexual men and gay men, and only eight gave information exclusively about bisexual men. In the same ten years, the researcher found only sixty-one articles mentioning bisexual women, twenty-two of which compared bisexuals with lesbians, and only three of which talked about bisexual women exclusively.[4] In fact, even the prevalence of HIV in the bisexual community is unknown. Although 76,075 men with AIDS (21 percent of AIDS cases in men who have reported sex with men) through 1996 report a history of "bisexual behavior," this doesn't mean they are bisexual, since 62 to 79 percent of gay-identified men report a history of "heterosexual contact" and are included in this statistic.[5] We know even less about bisexual women. It would seem there are more assumptions about the role of bisexuals in the HIV/AIDS epidemic than there are facts.

HIV RISK AND BISEXUAL MEN

Overall Risk

It appears that as a group, bisexual men are less likely than gay men to have HIV but more likely than straight men. Related to this is that bisexual men are apparently less likely than gay men to engage in high-risk sex. In fact, our society's perception of the risk of bi men spreading HIV to women may be exaggerated.

The major way men have contracted HIV is through receptive anal intercourse and using hypodermic needles previously used by someone who is HIV positive. There are other ways, of course, as I listed previously, but these two transmission vehicles are responsible for the vast majority of cases.

So how often are bisexual men having receptive anal intercourse? It is hard to say, but Lynda Doll and Ted Myers report in the *Annual Review of Sex Research* that in general, "Bisexual men probably engage in less unsafe sexual behavior than do exclusively homosexual men."[6] However, risky behavior may tend to vary according to whether the man identifies more with the gay community or the straight community. According to Doll and Myers, the stronger the connection to the gay community, the more likely a person is to engage in higher-risk sex.

Although on average bi men's sexual behavior puts them at less risk than gay men's, there is danger from the lack of a bi community. We know in HIV prevention that the less connected a person is to other people and a community, or the greater a person's internalized homophobia, the riskier the person's choices about sexual expression. "Homophobia may also affect the type of male-to-male sexual contact that bisexual men pursue," according to Joseph Stokes and Robin Miller in the *Canadian Journal of Human Sexuality*. "If they have internalized society's homophobic beliefs, men who desire same-sex sexual contact may seek it only in anonymous, highly sexualized contexts, such as parks, cruise zones, adult bookstores, and bathhouses."[7] The solution in HIV prevention work is to create programs, such as support groups, addressing issues for those needing connection and community. The more a part of a community a person feels, the more the desire to be responsible to others and value oneself, and the less internalized homophobia a person feels. Unfortunately for bisexual men, most prevention programs target gay men. The result is that bisexual men tend to drop out of HIV counseling sessions at a higher rate than gay men because they fear a lack of support or sensitivity to bi issues from gay counselors and group participants.[8] According to David McKirnan and Joseph Stokes in the *Journal of Sex Research,* "The sexual risk of bisexual men was high, yet their lack of participation in gay culture made them unlikely to be reached by prevention programs within the gay community."[9]

Are Bisexual Men Responsible for Infecting Women and Spreading HIV to the Straight Community?

Many in society see bisexual men as disease vectors from the gay community to the straight. Bi men are accused of getting AIDS from other men and "bringing it home to their wives." Just read Ann Landers: her first advice to a woman who has sex with a man who also has sex with men is to be tested for HIV and STIs. How justified is this fear?

Of 807,075 people in the United States who have developed AIDS since the beginning of the epidemic, 141,048 have been women. Most women with HIV have contracted it from sex with a man, through what the CDC calls "heterosexual contact" (41 percent); a close second is through sharing needles (39 percent). Of women who acquired HIV "heterosexually," most (38 percent) acquired it from a man who was an injection drug user. Only 3,801 women are reported to have contracted HIV from a "bisexual male," just over 2 percent of all women who are HIV positive. This statistic is an inaccurate picture, because the CDC also reports a large number of women who are positive due to "heterosexual contact, other/risk not reported or identified." But even if we add in all the unknown partner risk (and of course there are bound to be other non-bisexual male routes in this category too, but for the sake of argument), it is now 27,671, or just under 20 percent of HIV-positive women. Studies have estimated 11 percent[10] to fewer than 8 percent[11] of women infected through heterosexual contact were infected through sexual contact with a bisexual man. Everyone can decide for themselves how risky bisexual men are as a group, but I would have to guess this number would be much less than most people would assume. Doll and Myers conclude, "Widespread transmission of HIV from bisexual men to heterosexual women has probably not occurred or has not been detected."[12] This may seem counterintuitive, but not if we look at behavior. As Bruce Bower reports in *Science News,* Ron D. Stall, of the University of California, San Francisco (UCSF), found in a 1990 survey that "[There is] virtually no evidence of men engaging in unprotected anal sex with both men and women—a behavior considered a potential bridge for the transmission of the virus to the general population."[13] As previously discussed, it is harder to transmit HIV vaginally. A healthy vagina, one without STI sores, cuts, or other portals for HIV, does a better job of resisting HIV than a rectum.

All this means little on a person-to-person scale. On an individual basis, a bisexual male partner isn't going to give anyone HIV if they practice safer sex. For that matter, a woman won't get it from a gay man or a straight man or an injection drug user either, as long as they avoid high-risk behavior. Just to hammer it home: we need to be less concerned about orientations and more concerned about behavior.

HIV RISK AND BISEXUAL WOMEN

Similar to bisexual men, bisexual women have been cast as pariahs; in this case, bi women are seen as bringing HIV and STIs to the lesbian community by virtue of their assumed sexual behavior with men. What are the facts?

Little data address the special issues of bisexual women, but when looking at all women who have sex with women (WSW), the picture is pretty bleak. For example, in Los Angeles in 1997, WSWs reported an infection rate of 4.2 percent, and in King's County, Washington, women who were identified as lesbian or bisexual were found to be five times more likely to be HIV positive than straight women.[14] Chris Lombardi of *Women's E News* reports Northern California low-income women had more than four times the HIV-positive rate as the general population, and of that group, the highest-risk behaviors occurred with women who have sex with both women and men. Lombardi's theory is that because they have sex with women they are thought to not be at risk. Add in homophobia, and "the isolation these women feel in society contributes to feelings of worthlessness,"[15] leading to poorer decisions for their sexual health.

Can a Woman Give Another Woman HIV Sexually?

Short answer: maybe. Remember vaginal fluid is one of the four bodily fluids known to transmit HIV. However, the CDC has yet to confirm a case of woman-to-woman transmission through oral sex.[16] On the other hand, it would be difficult to know if women who have sex with women are contracting HIV from each other. Since it was apparent they were not in a high-risk category, the CDC has not been asking the right questions. Simply, WSW doesn't appear on the reporting forms. As Diane Richardson in *Culture, Health and Sexuality* reports, "No specific category exists for female-to-female exposure. Any woman insisting her only risk factor is female-to-female transmission is assigned to the category 'other' or 'unknown' risk."[17] Despite this handicap, upon examination of the data Richardson concludes, "To date only a very few cases of possible female-to-female transmission of HIV during sexual activity have been reported in literature."[18] Of the few having been reported, she says, all have been discounted because of incomplete data and the possibility the women in question concealed other risk factors. More recently, however, a case was reported by Helena A. Kwakwa and M. W. Ghobrial in the journal *Clinical Infectious Diseases,* "A 20-year-old African American woman with no obvious risk factors received a diagnosis of HIV infection, and the genotype of the infecting strain closely matched that of the strain infecting her openly bisexual female partner." They concluded, "The route of transmission was probably use of sex toys, used vigorously enough to cause exchange of blood-tinged body fluids."[19]

So are lesbians safe from HIV? Again, same trick question. Women who exclusively have sex with other women are very unlikely to get HIV, regardless of their orientation. Once again, as Richardson says, "As studies have demonstrated, self labeled identity does not always correlate with sexual behavior."[20] Just because a person says she is a lesbian doesn't mean she never uses injection drugs or never has sex with men. One study, from Sydney, Australia, found lesbians were just as likely to become infected with STIs as straight women and eight times as likely to carry the hepatitis C virus, a disease associated with injection drug use. They noted that women in the study who identified as lesbian were four times more likely to have sex with gay or bisexual men than straight women.[21] Another study found WSWs in general are at the same risk for STIs as heterosexual women, and lesbians have a "significantly higher" prevalence of bacterial vaginosis, hepatitis C, and HIV than heterosexual women. [22]

In conclusion, are bi women the HIV and STI vector to the lesbian community they are accused to be? Apparently not. But they are as a group more likely to have HIV or STIs than either straight women or lesbians. This comes as no surprise, since bi women, along with all other women who have sex with women, are generally ignored by HIV- and STI-prevention programs.

AIDS AND THE BISEXUAL COMMUNITY

I felt like there has been real resistance to the bisexual presence in what we now call the GLBT community for a number of years. I've felt a lot of gay and lesbian folks having difficulty with it, and many times [I've] felt rejected for that reason. And certainly a lot of straight people and ostensibly straight organizations say the same thing like, "Oh, you're weird, you're just doing it to get attention, you've imagined it, it's just a phase," all those standard things. I think one of the things that made the biggest difference was when the AIDS epidemic broke, and it became clear that there were a lot of people who [are] having sex with both genders (or more). And they were undeniable, enough to get people's attention. Certainly the Kinsey studies and everything had shown it, but everybody would dispute that. When the AIDS stuff came up no one disputed it. They all said, "Oh! Those awful bisexuals! Plague vectors! Typhoid Mary!" I thought, well, that's one way to get famous, but at least it put us on the map. I feel like its very hard since then for anyone to say, "No, you don't exist." It still happens once in a while, but that was the big breaking point I think. So I guess out of everything some good must come. (Scott)

Scott, of the Bisexual History Project, expresses the oddity of it all quite well: because of AIDS, bisexuality had to be reckoned with. AIDS brought bisexuality, if not the bisexual community, out of the closet. Even if it is misapplied and misguided, mentioning bisexuals in the CDC surveillance reports raises their profile. Within HIV work, the implications from terms such as "MSM" and "WSW" is clear: there are people who have sex with people of the same gender who do not identify as gay or lesbian. Who are they? One answer is easy: most people have heard the term "bisexual" before, and even if they don't believe it to be real, even if they don't think there really is such a thing, even if they believe people who call themselves bisexual are really gays or lesbians who haven't come out yet, they are still out there. HIV-prevention programs need to be designed to reach them, research needs to be conducted with this in mind, and statistics need to be designed to account for them. Never mind this hasn't happened fully, it *is* happening and there is no denying bisexuals have to be accounted for.

How those in the bi community have come to see themselves and their community in this time of epidemic is unique and personal to each person. I've talked in this chapter about people who are "behaviorally" bisexual, who are sexually active with men and women. Now let me return to the community, the group of people who attend BECAUSE and go to community picnics. What has been their response to AIDS?

First, I can't prove it, but it seems clear to me that in a room full of bisexuals at BECAUSE one will find more HIV/AIDS workers per square inch than anywhere else. Never mind that I work in HIV prevention, within the community I know many people who have jobs working to stop the spread of HIV or helping those who have it.

Second, in my experience, safer sex has become a huge part of bi community culture. In Chapter 4, I told an anecdote about facilitating a workshop in which as an icebreaker I asked people to identify which communities they are a member of. Several people have identified their community as the "safer-sex community." I'm not completely sure whom this community includes, but it does point to how much HIV and safer sex inform many bisexuals' lives. Occasionally, I will hear about someone in the community throwing a mixed-gender sex party. Not very often, but occasionally. Do they or anyone else call it an "orgy"? No. They are called "safer-sex parties." It is no coincidence the Safer Sex Sluts were performing at a bisexual community event.

What Bisexuals Say

On an individual basis many bisexuals have been affected in very personal ways, either having HIV themselves or a friend or relative having HIV. I threw out the question "How have you been affected by HIV and AIDS?" to the online support group and received a number of heartfelt responses:

I'm one of those kids who grew up in the age of Nancy Reagan and "Just say no." I was ten in 1984, and that's when I recall first seeing AIDS on the TV and in magazines. I was in a doctor's office when I was about nine or ten . . . [and] there was an article about AIDS. It was *Time* or *Newsweek* or some other newsmagazine of that sort. I read the article, and at that point had at least gotten enough information about sex to figure out a bit about condoms and how they worked. But I saw "use condoms for oral sex" and couldn't figure out how in the world one put a condom on one's tongue. My childhood mind thought that oral sex equals French kissing.

But it's more than that, more than how I grew up with it. Even after I started having sex, it didn't have much meaning to me. HIV had meaning to me when I was sixteen and met the first person in my life who I knew had HIV. I still don't know why, but it made me angry. And I've fed off that anger for the last eleven years. I've channeled it into a positive source of energy for me. I learn lessons from everyone who comes into my life, but I learn lessons that are applicable to a specific part of my life from the people with HIV who cross my way.

Maybe the awareness of my orientation has made me ultra-conscious of my own safety. Or maybe just the expression of it, and the crowd I've run with for a while have made me conscious. All in all, I work hard at staying [HIV] negative.

But that's not all I do. . . . My job is working with young people who are using, abusing or at high risk for substance abuse issues. I run a six-session program with them teaching basic information about HIV and other STIs, about substance abuse, decision making, negotiation skills, and substance use. I work with gang kids, kids in jail, kids in shelters, all kinds of stuff. It's intense and frustrating and exciting all at once. And some days, it just kicks my butt.

I work for an AIDS service organization. They're quite bi-friendly. . . . My department is about half hetero and half not . . . and there's quite a family environment going on . . . a lot of camaraderie. And so, one of the things they pick on me for is because I'm the only bisexual person. Of course I've also had the opportunity to talk openly about being bisexual, about not fitting in either in gay or straight circles, about the kinds of questions one is expected to answer and so on. And at the same time, I also have had co-workers tell me they didn't believe bisexuality was real before, or that they never knew anyone bisexual before, and all the typical things. I think that's the major intersection of HIV and bisexuality in my life right now.

HIV is something that's hung over my entire experience as a sexual person—I can't imagine not thinking about it. And on one hand, I envy the people I know who had the opportunity to experience their sexuality before HIV, when it wasn't something that you were supposed to be conscious of. At the same time, I don't envy those same people—because I'm glad that I've never had to go through a philosophical change in behavior the way some of them have. HIV will continue to be important to me until it like, totally disappears or something . . . but I can't envision a time without it, simply because it's almost always been there for me. (Erika)

As a bi man who is also HIV positive, I tend to shy away from sexual situations as much as possible because they aren't worth dealing with. I'm fortunate enough to have a lover of many, many years, which makes it possible to avoid sex outside this relationship, even though neither of us chooses to at this point. He tries to encourage me to exercise my straight sexual side, but it's one of the main reasons I choose not to, the other being the insecurity it could cause in our relationship.

I rarely mention this to people, even people I know well. I'd rather keep it a nonissue if possible. I definitely don't want to hurt my family with the news. There's no reason to make them worry. I've been positive for years now and doing okay.

The funny thing is, people will sleep with someone they don't know is negative or positive, yet if you tell them you're positive, they run. It makes me wonder if they are being safe or not when they engage others sexually since safe sex with me sometimes comes across as not being an option. Some gay men don't mind at all, but some freak out. I've always been the first to say something about being HIV positive. Every time I've been with another HIV-positive man, I have always been the first to mention it. Then they will also admit it. Makes me think of how often it isn't mentioned at all.

I don't even approach women. They would be doubly likely to reject me. Gay men can at least relate by having friends deal with HIV or having slept around, been here and done this before. I'd like to find an HIV-positive woman who feels much like I do. Finding an HIV-positive woman, much less one who also is emotionally compatible (that's important to me because if I don't at least like you, I can't go there) seems very unlikely. I live in a very rural part of the world. (Mike)

I was around four when I found out my father was gay (took years to find out he really was bi not gay) and my first thought that still remains is how I told my mom that he was happy and that was good. She went into a brief explanation of what gay can mean if not happy. I would say an open and honest childhood (even with my mother being an open person with all types of friends, for some reason we had to hide our family's issues). I had no shame in who my father was, I was proud. I would let people know without realizing their bias against it. It was in the beginning of the 1980s and from what I can recall AIDS was just really having an impact. My second conversation about this subject with my mother was saddening for me. I was told that I could not let anyone know my father was gay because they would think we had an illness. I was not sure what this illness was but I knew it was serious by my mother's tone. That was the beginning of the lies that followed through my years in school. We never spoke much about it after that time. I knew [that neither] my mother, father, [nor I had] AIDS but we lived in a small town and it can be very hard to grow up with that on your shoulders when people do not understand.

So that is where I learned to not talk about AIDS, just keep my mouth shut. Well, in doing so (before I wised up) I put myself through a lot of close calls. Planned Parenthood was actually a savior for me, not that I practiced safe sex but I could at least get tested after I panicked from not practicing safe sex. I did finally wise up but that was after becoming pregnant at a young age. Then I really started to look at life differently. Realizing you can die from AIDS and get STIs. That I happened to get lucky and the only thing I got was a baby and not a death sentence. I became prophylactic queen at that point. I would carry condoms on me for my friends just in case they did not have one. From reading so many health books on pregnancy I learned a lot about AIDS, STIs, and many other yummy subjects. I would pass that information on to my friends and hope they learned something from it.

AIDS finally came into my life after meeting my husband. We were fine (I still get tested, and he does too, even if we are only with each other), but a family member was not. When I read . . . about people with AIDS looking ill, it made me laugh. This person we had no clue about, no idea, wouldn't have crossed our minds. He was the picture of health, completely fit. I felt overweight and out of shape to even be in the same room as him. My husband would brag about how his uncle was always healthy and working out, ate well and was always getting more and more degrees behind him. So to say the least, when my mother-in-law sat us down and finally told us we were floored. I think our mouths dropped. We just could not believe it. Then to find out his partner was HIV positive too and that they had been living with it for over fourteen years now was just baffling. . . .

Our family members with it are still living, but now you know that you need to see them and visit them because you do not know what lies around the corner. Last time they came to visit my uncle-in-law's partner was not doing as well as he was. He explained the multitude of drugs that he was on, even showed me how many he had to take in the day and evening (it was nothing that I could have imagined) and also mentioned that he thought this was probably the last time he would get out to the East Coast. That kind of slaps ya right in the face! Makes life look that much more precious.

To this day everyone is doing good as can be expected. Taking their lives one day at a time and living it to the fullest. We as family keep in touch and try to see when we can get out to see them now. One day at a time: never thought that statement would mean so much. (Jennifer)

Like Jennifer, I had a gay father. Not bi, really gay. To make a very long story short, my mother left him and my sister and me. I was raised until I was eleven by him and his partner. His partner, my surrogate mother, died in 1986 from AIDS at a time when few people outside the gay community knew what it was. I was very isolated in my grief. Much of my social network died one after the other from AIDS (I've always been a girlfag from way back) and I had to build a whole new one. I took care of my dearest friend Dennis until the hour he died. My father, who also had AIDS for years, died three years ago, ironically not from the virus, but possibly from a secondary effect of his medications.

Like Erika, I worked for AIDS service organizations; except for me it's past tense. I spent thirteen years working out my rage and grief as an AIDS activist. The trenches were filled with angry queer women like myself. Back at the beginning times, we were often the only ones healthy enough and organized enough to get things done. Things changed and became more politicized. . . . [I was] not queer enough (after all I have a child and am bisexual) to be allowed to have a place at the table, despite the fact that I had been working in these organizations since the beginning of the crisis. My time was over, and I left that work.

My experience is that a lot of bi folks really stepped up to the plate from day one. Much of the energy early on came from bi folks.

That's my story, for what it's worth. . . . Sorry it's a bitter one. (Julz)

One could argue the HIV epidemic has retarded the growth of the community or one could say it has increased bisexual visibility, and both would be right. HIV and AIDS have played a huge role in shaping the history of the bisexual community as a movement. In the next chapter, I describe how AIDS, feminism, gay rights, and the free-love movement all played parts in shaping the bisexual community of BECAUSE.

Chapter 9

The History of the Bisexual Community

BOSTON, JUNE 2002

So anyway, I moved here. I was here for less than two weeks, and I was painting my apartment. I *so* remember this. I was in my paint clothes, and I took a paint break. I opened up a magazine, a newspaper called *Equal Time.* It was a women's newspaper; it was one of two in Boston. The other one is still here, but that one is gone. . . . I was reading their calendar, blah, blah, blah, and there's a thing that says, bisexual discussion— . . . no, women's rap, discussion for September (or whatever date it was): bisexuality. And I was there. I was there. I was out of my paint clothes, into the shower, to the women's center in no time. I was there. I felt like I had discovered gold or something. Better than gold. (Robyn Ochs)

I've been to Boston on several occasions; it is one of my favorite towns. The history, the walkable streets, the great restaurants, and the college influence make for a delightful place to spend time. The colleges are very important in this tale. The culture of academia is one reason why Boston is *the* center for bisexual activism in the United States. Colleges are generally good to bi people, tending to have a liberal climate encouraging of personal exploration. The history of Boston is also very important. What San Francisco has meant to gay men, Boston has meant to lesbians. From "Boston marriages" in the 1800s through the women's coffeehouse movement of the 1970s, Boston has been and continues to be a home to feminists, lesbians, and bisexual women. As I mentioned in Chapter 5, in the bi community women have been the leaders, and Boston is the obvious place to foment a new queer politic led by women.

Robyn Ochs, editor of the *Bisexual Resource Guide,* a yellow pages of bi and bi-supportive organizations throughout the world, was and continues to be a leader of the Bisexual Resource Center (BRC) and the Boston bi community, and really the entire United States and the world. She works in the Romance language and literature department at Harvard University and has taught at Tufts University in Medford, Massachusetts, since 1991. I visited with her at her home in an older suburb of Boston, Jamaica Plain, which Robyn describes as "a neighborhood that is about one-third gay, that I call 'Mr. Roger's Gay Neighborhood' because it's so remarkably friendly and wholesome." She strikes me as quiet and settled, with her partner of seven years, Peg, and their cats, named Kiddle, Emma, and Pixel.

The story Robyn told takes place in 1982, after a first round of bisexual activism was already on the wane, before a new wave of community building in which Ochs would play a key role. She met Marcia Deihl at that meeting, leading to a collaboration that created the largest and oldest bi group in the country, the Boston Bisexual Women's Network. In 1982, Deihl was a musician and traveled around the country with her musical group. She also works at Harvard now, in the anthropology library. Having paid more than her share of dues in the 1980s, she is no longer active in bisexual politics. We talked at a bench on the grounds of Harvard University on a beautiful summer day. Deihl talked about that fateful meeting with Ochs:

I saw an ad in 1981 in . . . some paper in Boston, a women's center discussion on bisexuality. And I said, whoa, I am there. And I went. There was a group of about six of us, and we tried to keep meeting, but it petered out. The second year, there was another ad. A discussion about bisexuality, and I have no idea who did it and why. And at that one, Robyn was also there. Robyn and I were the only two that stayed, . . . everyone else left. And we met one more time and a core of six other women came. And I'm pretty sure we are the ones that became the Bi Vocals, a six or seven woman discussion group that clicked, and we just became a consciousness-raising group about being bisexual. There were all different versions of [being bisexual]: there were women deciding they might try it with other women; there was me who just got out of a lesbian relationship and didn't quite know what I would do next.

Anyway, so that's how it started. . . . I didn't fit in as a lesbian, I didn't fit in as a straight woman, and I wanted something in the middle . . . and these six other women did that.

We publicized a meeting in 1983, and that was the clump that became the Boston Bisexual Women's Network. And I think that was the clump that birthed the first *Bi Women* [newsletter]. The first issue was mimeographed; remember mimeograph? Smell that ink. And we had partied; it really kind of blossomed. I would have to say that that was, the Bi Vocals, my spiritual core group. We talked about everything. We met together for about eight years. People got married, got divorced, had kids, slept with each other, broke up with each other. . . . It was a wonderful little education, plus good friends. So

Robyn and I remain friends and I know what some of the others are doing. And that's the story.

Back in suburban Boston, Ochs says:

At that meeting were twenty women, including Marcia. It was amazing. I just remember sitting in this big circle of women on the first floor, and the thing I remember most was grinning. Just grinning so hard my cheeks hurt. . . . There were a lot of us doing that in the room. There was this feeling, "Oh my." So we were all floating above sofas and chairs.

We had this meeting. . . . I think it was Marcia who stood up and said, "Is anyone interested in starting an ongoing support group?" And I was one of the women who said yes. We met, and we called ourselves the Bi Vocals.

The Boston Bi Women's Network story is interesting not only because it is historically important but also because it is in many ways typical of the second wave of bisexual activism. However, before I get too far ahead of myself, it is necessary to examine the beginnings of bi activism in the 1970s.

THE SEEDS OF BI ACTIVISM IN THE 1960S AND 1970S

Bisexuals have been on board, standing next to gays and lesbians and fighting for equal rights for the duration.

Denise Penn, *Lesbian News,* October 2001[1]

The first bi organization started in 1972. But before, during, and since 1972, bisexuals have been involved in the gay rights movement. Any idea that bisexuals were late on the scene is incorrect: bisexuals have always been involved. What changed was that bisexuals began to want their own spaces, for all the reasons previously discussed, including community building.

A good example of this is the story of Stephen Donaldson. He was a national leader of the Student Homophile League and a main organizer for the North American Conference of Homophile Organizations (NACHO) in the 1960s. He was also outspoken about his bisexuality. He says in an essay for *Bisexual Politics: Theories, Queries, and Visions:*

I took a lot of flak from the leaders of other homophile organizations for being bi. For a couple of years I was having an affair with Martha Shelley, leader of the New York Daughters of Bilitis [an early lesbian organization] and later the Gay Liberation Front.

Often they would enter a room arm in arm, much to the chagrin of the other gay and lesbian activists.[2]

Donaldson was instrumental in an early watershed moment for the bi community. He was involved with the Quakers, a religion known for teaching peace and tolerance. He says, "As a bisexual no longer feeling comfortable with the gay liberation movement, I found myself, in June 1972, attending the annual Friends (Quaker) General Conference in Ithaca, New York." There he organized a workshop on bisexuality and was excited when 130 people, fully one in ten of the conference goers, attended. After two days, the group developed the "Ithaca Statement on Bisexuality." This statement may be, as Donaldson claims, "the first public declaration of the bisexual movement." This bi-friendly position statement was not only published by the Quakers in its newsletter but also picked up by the *Advocate,* thus receiving national attention.[3]

This document was revolutionary. It must be remembered that the Stonewall Riot had happened only three years earlier, and acceptance for gays and lesbians was only a dream at that time. Within that climate, discussion of bisexual issues was unheard of. As Merl Storr reports in the journal *Sexualities,* "It is easy to forget, in the present climate, just how hostile academia in general, and lesbian and gay studies in particular, were to the very idea that bisexuality might be considered a serious topic of discussion."[4]

Prior to the Ithaca Statement, and prior to Stonewall, a sort of proto bi activism took place with the Sexual Freedom League (SFL).* Beginning in 1968 and based in a commune in San Francisco, the SFL had a national scope. Their slogan was "If it moves, fondle it," and according to Donaldson the group "staged some memorable orgies."[5] Maggi Rubenstein, a bisexual swinger, helped found the group and

---

*For a very good timeline of bisexual organizing, check out "Appendix A: Brief Timeline of Bisexual Activism in the United States" by Dannielle Raymond and Liz A. Highleyman in *Bisexual Politics: Theories, Queries, and Visions,* Naomi Tucker (Ed.) (Binghamton, NY: Harrington Park Press, 1995).

was very outspoken about bisexuality, as were many people involved with SFL. However, despite her best efforts, Rubenstein didn't have much luck forming a bi group on her own.[6]

The honor of starting the first bisexual-specific group fell to Don Fass, a New York psychologist. In 1972, Fass began the National Bisexual Liberation Group out of his home on the Upper West Side of New York City. He organized social and support programs, and published what has been called the first bisexual newsletter, *Bisexual Expression.*[7]

In 1975, New York psychiatrist Fritz Klein started the Bi Forum. "The whole thing started in 1974 when I wanted to write an article on bisexuality, and there was nothing around," he says. According to Klein, "I created [the Bi Forum] in New York and invited, with a two-line ad, bisexuals to come and talk about bisexuality. And that went on week after week after week until 1978 [when] I published *The Bisexual Option.*" The Bi Forum is long gone, but *The Bisexual Option,* the first book about bisexuality published in the United States, continues to be the most influential work on the subject. This is especially true of its second edition in 1993, in which he added the Klein grid of sexual orientation (as described in Chapter 3). Today, at any given bisexual conference, a "Bi 101" workshop facilitator will likely be leading the group through the twenty-seven rankings. Then and now, Klein is arguably the most important and influential leader of the bi community. In 2002, Klein created the Bisexual Foundation, an agency that gives grants for further research on bisexuality and the creation of resources for the bisexual community. According to Klein, the times have changed quite a bit since he first created the Bi Forum. "The difference is now if I want to I can be going to a bisexual conference every second week somewhere in the world. Then there was no such thing as a bisexual conference. There weren't enough people identified as bisexual who were out."

The 1970s saw the birth of "bi chic" when, in May 1974, both *Time* and *Newsweek* reported that bisexuality was positively trendy. In the *Newsweek* article, "Bisexual Chic: Anyone Goes,"[8] one interviewee said, "But everybody does bisexuality right now. It's really big." The article goes on to warn, according to a psychologist, "Bisexuality is a disaster for culture and society," and "They are selling a phony sex utopia in which the kingdom of the orgasm will supposedly replace the house of the ego." I don't know about the kingdom of the orgasm, but the rise of pop artists such as David Bowie, Mick Jagger, Elton John, and Janice Joplin, not to mention the free-love movement and the disco scene, inspired these magazines to declare it quite fashionable to have lovers of both sexes and blur gender roles. Whether this kind of sensationalism was true or not, the bisexual community seemed on the way up.

The last part of the 1970s saw new bisexual groups forming. For example, Chicago had two bi groups in the late 1970s, Bi-Ways and One to Five. Suburban Detroit had a group called the Bi Married Men's Group. There were bi groups in Southern California, Van Nuys in particular. My hometown of Minneapolis had an early mixed-gender bisexual support group started by Scott Bartell in 1975 as part of Gay Community Services, and later there was the Bi Women Welcome group.[9] Not exactly a flood, but it was perhaps the start of greater things to come. Indeed, that was the case in San Francisco.

The Bisexual Center

If bi activism in the first part of the 1970s centered on New York, the focus soon shifted to the West Coast when, in September 1975, twenty-two people gathered in San Francisco to plan the Bisexual Center.[10] The offspring of the Sexual Freedom League and a sex-information phone line, the Bisexual Center opened in 1976, primarily as a social organization. It quickly became a strong community center offering support groups, counseling, social activities, and a place to drop in. During that time, the center published a very successful newsletter, *The Bi Monthly.* It mostly served people who came out from a married and/or mixed gender/sex experience, but it also aligned itself with the gay and lesbian communities during the Anita Bryant "Save Our Children" crusades.

The center was also the subject of important sociological research by Martin S. Weinberg, Colin J. Williams, and Douglas Pryor. Their work remains the most comprehensive sociological research done about the bisexual community. Weinberg, Williams, and Pryor painstakingly gathered data on many aspects of the lives of the bisexuals who participated in the Bisexual Center, including partner choices, sexual practices, and the stability of self-identified orientation. The results were published in their book *Dual Attraction: Understanding Bisexuality.*[11] The work could be seen as salvage anthropology (documenting a culture, society, or other group of people that is disappearing), as the center closed its doors for good in 1983, a victim of internal politics and the rising toll of the AIDS epidemic.

With the closing of the Bisexual Center in 1983, we see the end of the first period of bisexual activism. It was a period defined perhaps most by the sexual liberation movement of the 1960s and 1970s and a society-wide liberalization of sexual mores. Although that is a sweeping generalization, as different groups had different needs and motives, it is also a good generalization. Also important to note is that the groups of the 1970s were generally dominated by men. As author Lani Ka'ahumanu, who was involved with the Bisexual Center beginning in 1981, says, "These groups were mainly social support groups for and organized by married bisexual men. Most of the organizing in the 1970s was done by married men and tended to social and support aspects." This was a situation about to change.

THE 1980S AND THE SECOND WAVE OF ACTIVISM

As discussed in the previous chapter, AIDS hit all of the GLBT communities hard. The free love, disco, and drug era was over. It was replaced with the fear of contracting a fatal illness that for quite a while no one was sure how you got, other than it had to do with sex. Bi men died throughout the country but especially on the coasts, coincidentally where the centers of bi activism were. Some bi men fled back into the closet, fearful of the disease and the added stigma of being suspected of being a modern Typhoid Mary; others simply withdrew from the bi community. Some became AIDS activists. In any case, suddenly a lot fewer men were available to pursue bi activism.

AIDS had a huge impact, but it wasn't the only change in the 1980s. Before the epidemic, Ronald Reagan, once ridiculed and considered by many to be an unrealistically ultra-right-wing demagogue, won the presidency by a landslide. The country was moving to the right, a trend that continues today. There was a sea change toward a quieter time, a time of getting on with careers, a time of nesting in bigger and bigger houses, a time scornful of the idealism of the past decade, seeing ideas such as "free love" as hopelessly utopian and hedonistic.

But bisexual community activism didn't disappear. The Bisexual Center in San Francisco may have closed, and bisexuality may not have been chic anymore, but the bi community had been given a taste of success, and it couldn't just disappear as if all that was learned and achieved had never happened. Bi activism not only didn't disappear, it changed, it adapted. Over the course of the 1980s, it refocused many bi groups toward a more political mission of community building and fighting the spread of HIV/AIDS. "The first bisexual feminist political action group BiPOL founded in 1983 in San Francisco was expressly focused on visibility, . . . building the bisexual community and to educate about AIDS," according to Ka'ahumanu. The changing times also led to a change in leadership.

Feminist Bisexuality

In the 1980s, women in the bi community took the lead, putting a very different stamp on the movement. Bi women brought not only different experiences and needs to the effort; they brought different skills born of the culture of feminism. In the 1970s, feminism led to the creation of a new women's community, complete with institutions such as women's centers, shops, and coffeehouses and resources such as magazines and newspapers, curricula at colleges, and visible, outspoken leadership. This change brought a new approach, thinking in terms of "systems of oppression," which, as explained previously, focuses on the connections between privilege, power, racism, classism, able-ism, sexism, homophobia, and so on. Feminists brought a particular style of leadership, scornful of Robert's Rules of Order as patriarchal, instead favoring flat or no hierarchy in organizational governance. Feminist bi women learned from that experience and brought these unique and well-honed skills to the task of bi activism.

As discussed in Chapter 5, for some women, bi activism was born of a reaction against ostracism from the feminist and lesbian communities. This rift must be seen in the context of the time. In the beginning of the 1970s, many straight women in mainstream feminism rejected lesbians as threatening to their chances of success. Lesbians were accused of selling out because they were seen as fleeing the fight, not engaging it. The counter argument arose that lesbians elevated women and their interests over men, which was exactly what feminism was all about. Enter into the equation bisexual women.

Many straight feminists saw bi women as no different from the lesbians they didn't want tainting the movement. Meanwhile, many lesbian feminists saw bisexuals as sellouts, tourists, trend chasers, and, at best, fair-weather friends. All of the factors discussed previously came into play, meaning bi women often found themselves unwelcome in the feminist bookstores, coffeehouses, etc. This was especially painful, because many had put their whole lives into that scene, until they came out as bisexual, perhaps complete with a new and unacceptable partner.

Bi men simply didn't have any experiences to parallel the problems faced by bi women. As Amanda Udis-Kessler says in *Bisexual Politics:*

> Tensions between lesbian and bisexual women are understood as much more problematic than tensions between gay and bisexual men. . . . Life before AIDS in the baths and discos, at the bar or the opera, did not exclude bisexual men in the same way that lesbian space came to exclude bisexual women.

The consequence was that bi women were both trained *and* motivated to build the bi community. "Bisexual organizing in the early 1980s, like feminist organizing ten years earlier, was primarily a task undertaken by women."[12]

The Boston Bi Women's Network discussed earlier by Ochs and Deihl is a fine example of the changing shape of bi activism. What was once primarily the province of bi men in New York and San Francisco was soon refocused on the Boston bi women's community. Robyn Ochs explains the genesis of the Boston bi scene this way:

We had this little party, and we expected twenty women to show up, and we ended up with twice that number. Then we thought, maybe we are on to something! We had a summer retreat in Provincetown. A bunch of us went to Provincetown and spent the weekend. That fall, September of 1983, we had our first meeting of the Boston Bi Women's Network. It was at the Women's Center, again in that same room. What was amazing was that we expected thirty, thirty to forty women. I think there were about eighty women who showed up. The room was not capable of handling even half that number. There were women stacked up on the couch. There were women standing outside in the garden beds looking in the window. They were going up the stairs in the hallway. There were other women who were just walking by and saying, "Oh my God, what's going on? Look at all the cute women; what is this group and how do I join it?" There was this amazing feeling of euphoria.

So that's how the Boston Bi Women's Network was born. And it's been going now for nineteen years, yeah, since 1983. And what's amazing about it for me is that it's an organization that has never had any kind of formal leadership. There's no president, no vice-president, no board of directors; it's kind of anarchy at its best. The only formal roles are the newsletter editor, the post office–box picker-upper (whatever that is called), the mailing list maintainer, the treasurer, which has been me for a long time, and that's it. Everything else just happens or it doesn't. What's amazing is that we've actually managed to put out what I say is a high-quality newsletter for nineteen years with no structure, no steady income. We just do it somehow and it just goes; it's really interesting. And for me it's an important model; it goes because people care. And sometimes less people care, or they care but they don't want to do anything. And sometimes it's a lot of energy. But I think it's the oldest bi women's group in the world, and perhaps the second-oldest bi group in the world.

Men have been involved in bi organizing in the Boston area from the beginning, if not as effectively. Ochs remembers:

Well what happened . . . was that the women did all this stuff, started this group. There were some bi men . . . who were [saying]: hey, what about us? And that happened in Seattle too, interestingly, and they formed what they jokingly called the "Men's Auxiliary" for a while. And then they formed the SBMN, the Seattle . . . Bi Men's Network. [Also], the men in Boston formed the Boston Bi Men's Network. It was never near the size of BBWN. But it was its own thing and it was successful in its own right. But what started happening in a couple of years was the men started saying, "How come the groups have to be separate? We want to have the groups together. Why are the women insisting on being separate?" Blah, blah, blah. And I think there were really good reasons why we needed [the] two separate. I think there is a value to groups together and there is a value to separate space, given the history of sexism and all the stuff we were dealing with. And also most of the women in BBWN came from a very feminist background, and most of the men in BBMN were not. The leaders were wonderful feminists. The rank and file, as it were, were sometimes—they just hadn't thought about politics at all. And there were questions about were the men coming just to pick up women, and we didn't want that. So we were holding out, we want our own space.

What happened was a group started to form called Biversity, this is down the road, and Biversity is a mixed social group. And BBMN, the men's network, I think, got folded into that. At least that's my recollection. And this was in the, I don't even know when this happened, maybe the end of the 1980s, sometime around that time period.

Elsewhere in the 1980s

The effects of AIDS and the changing times on bi activism varied depending on what part of the country people were in. As Ka'ahumanu says, "In general, . . . cities initially not as hard hit by AIDS had more social and support groups." Other cities were moved to more political action. As the Bisexual Center in San Francisco faded away, BiPOL emerged as a group dedicated not only to political action but also to fighting the spread of HIV. The group organized a first: a bisexual rights rally at the Democratic National Convention in 1984, held in San Francisco.[13] Shortly after, in 1985, Seattle gained the large and popular Seattle Bisexual Women's Network (that Ochs mentioned earlier). New groups started up in other cities too, including Bi Unity in Philadelphia, the Bi Connection in Minneapolis, the New York Area Bisexual Network, and a group in Miami.

The 1987 March on Washington for Gay and Lesbian Rights was another key moment for the bisexual community. Bisexuals were not included, which not only enraged bi activists around the country but also sensitized many non-bi people to the challenges faced by bisexuals within the greater GLBT community. It had an effect: the 1993 march was called the March on Washington for Lesbian, Gay, and Bi Equal Rights.

In 1990, BiPOL organized the first national bisexuality conference, featuring a city proclamation of Bisexual Pride Day. Held in San Francisco, it became the springboard for the creation of a national bi organization. At first called the North American Multicultural Bisexual Network, it eventually changed its name to BiNet USA. BiNet made gains through political action and connecting bi groups throughout the country. At its peak, BiNet had organizers in most of the country and helped support bi groups in many locations. Indeed, several groups in the country still use the BiNet name, including BiNet Atlanta, BiNet Houston, BiNet Los Angeles, and BiNet Arizona.

Shortly after the 1990 national conference, a group from San Francisco began publishing a national magazine about bisexuality, *Anything That Moves*. The magazine, whose title was intended to be more ironic than literal, spoke almost entirely to the established, core, bisexual activist community. *ATM,* as it was affectionately called, was published for the next ten years. The main significance of the publication was less the import of its content and more that it featured the opportunity for bisexual voices to be heard from the magazine rack at the local bookstore, a highpoint in bisexual community visibility to be sure.

The Bisexual Resource Center

In 1993 the Bisexual Resource Center (BRC) opened in Boston, Massachusetts, ten years after the Bisexual Center in San Francisco closed. Part community center and part national organization, the BRC has worked steadily to support the bi community through programs such as support groups, discussions, and social activities, while reaching out to other communities with informational brochures. However, the organization's major influence may be via the Internet. From its Web site at <www.brc.org>, it is reaching out to bisexuals throughout the country, from big cities to the tiniest of towns. Here they offer their informational brochures for downloading as well as links to groups throughout the world. Indeed, their very existence supports bisexuals everywhere, because merely knowing somewhere in this world a resource center exists for bisexuals gives hope to bisexuals in communities without any bi resources (which are most communities).

I met Wayne Bryant for the first time on my visit to Boston in 2002. An affable, calm sort, Wayne is the author of *Bisexual Characters in Film: From Anaïs to Zee*.[14] He is also one of the main leaders of the Bisexual Resource Center. Wayne says:

The Bisexual Resource Center started in 1983, under the name East Coast—Northeast Regional Organizing Committee, or something like that. I can't remember the exact name, but something like that. It happened after a bisexual conference, the very first bisexual conference in this country, held at the University of Connecticut at Storrs, Connecticut. And there was some money left over from the conference; it turned a profit. A committee was organized to decide what to do with the money. They decided to use the money to help fledgling bisexual groups get off the ground and to organize further conferences. And that group evolved over the next couple of years into the East Coast Bisexual Network, because by that time we had groups as far north as Portland, Maine, and as far south as Washington, DC, who were all coming together to organize loosely these conferences and later some retreats.

The Bisexual Resource Center is located in the Back Bay neighborhood of Boston in a nicely restored old building owned by the Boston Living Center, an HIV/AIDS organization, and is shared with other nonprofits. It is nothing to look at: a small office with two rooms, crammed with materials; boxes of T-shirts, racks of informational brochures, file cabinets full of archives, and the like; and it shares a conference room with other groups on the second floor. Bryant continues:

The East Coast Bisexual Network got its first office in 1989 on Newbury Street. In 1990 they incorporated as a nonprofit group. In 1993—because BiNet USA had formed and organized the country in different regions than the East Coast Bisexual Network was set up—we changed our name and mission and became the Bisexual Resource Center. We've published the *Bisexual Resource Guide* (it's in its fourth edition now), published a series of pamphlets about bisexuality. We keep an international archive of bisexual newsletters, articles, pamphlets, video tapes, anything that might be of interest to future researchers. And we've organized a number of regional conferences and one international conference. I was the main organizer for the fifth international conference, held at Harvard University in 1998.

THE 1990s AND CONFERENCE CULTURE

I don't know what it is about conferences that attracts bisexuals, or why the bi community is so interested in conferences as community-building vehicles, but it is. There are certainly models in gay and lesbian organizing; Minnesota, for example, has an annual statewide GLBT conference. Perhaps part of it is the number of science fiction fans in the bi community. Since there is usually more than one science fiction convention annually in any large town, people who are in both groups have a good model of how to gather a community. Both the pagan and the polyamorous communities have traditions of regular gatherings also. Perhaps it is merely a lack of other institutions that drives a need to create opportunities to gather the community. Regardless, conferences like BECAUSE are how many bisexuals interact with their community, and, indeed, many times it is the only way.

Boston and New England set the model for bisexual conferences. Robyn Ochs tells the story:

In 1983, [The University of Connecticut] organized the first regional conference on bisexuality, and Boston went en masse. And we had a very good turnout there. And we were inspired. And I don't know how they came up with the idea or where it came from. It was held at the University of Connecticut School of Social Work. I don't know, even to this day, I don't know how that happened and who organized it. I'm hugely impressed. We ended up, the following year, organizing the second regional conference in Boston. And it was actually really big. I don't remember exactly how many people, but there were a few hundred. And it was in Cambridge, in old Cambridge Baptist Church. It was a huge success and it was the first time I organized anything. It was scary!

And then, the next year, we basically tried to establish a rotating, not rotating, but a traveling road show of annual conferences with the idea that whatever city it was in would, number one, have to put out a huge amount of energy, number two, hopefully get back a community base as a result of organizing a conference, because the conference both burns out a community and creates a community. So we had one in Connecticut, Boston, New York next, I think Boston again, and then Maine, we did one in Portland.

In 1991, the First International Conference on Bisexuality was held in Amsterdam, the Netherlands. Fritz Klein, who was living there at the time, played a role by convincing the planners to think larger than a local conference. His vision worked, with 250 people attending. A second international conference took place the following year in London,[15] and since then an international conference has been held every other year. In 1994, New York was the host, with 350 attendees, followed by Berlin in 1996. In 1998, Boston hosted the most successful conference to date, with over 900 people attending. Held at Harvard University, it featured more than 100 workshops. Since then, the conference has had less luck. In 2000, the conference was held in London after Rotterdam canceled (due to problems with securing a site), and 265 people attended. In 2002, it moved to Sydney, Australia, where it was held during their famous annual Gay and Lesbian Mardi Gras celebration and coincided with the Gay Games athletic competitions. However, due to travel problems, difficulty securing a suitable site, and perhaps a late start, the conference drew only about eighty people.

I mentioned earlier the first national bi conference held in San Francisco in 1990. A second national conference was held in Washington, DC, in conjunction with the 1993 March on Washington and drew 600 people. Meanwhile, regional conferences popped up in many parts of the country. In the Midwest, BECAUSE was first held in Minneapolis at the University of Minnesota in 1992. It has been an annual event ever since. BECAUSE has always been framed as a regional, Midwest conference, but for its first nine years it was in the Twin Cities. In 2001 and 2002 it moved to Milwaukee, Wisconsin, where a strong bi community has grown. Drawing anywhere from eighty to 200 people, BECAUSE has been a focus for the bi community from Ohio to Kansas, Winnipeg to St. Louis. In the East, a Mid-Atlantic conference is held in Washington, DC, in additon to a South Eastern regional bisexual conference. In the West, conferences have been held in Seattle and in Austin, Texas. More recently, the first North American Conference on Bisexuality was held in Vancouver, British Columbia, in 2001, and the second was held in San Diego in August 2003. These are just a few of the conferences that have been offered across the United States. Add in bisexuality conferences happening in Europe—Great Britain has held a national conference every year since 1984—plus the international conferences, and it is clear how important they are to the development and culture of the bisexual community.

Other Developments in the 1990s

Meanwhile, the late 1990s saw the development of the Internet, and the bi community was quick to exploit it. National and local bisexual organizations and individual Web sites and electronic mailing lists began reaching into people's homes. No longer did bisexual people need to live in one of the few towns with a bisexual community to be connected; they could now find their community right there at their desk. I take a closer look at this phenomenon in the next chapter.

The Internet begat another interesting item: a bi flag. In 1998, Michael Page, with his very popular Web site <www.bicafe.com>, introduced a flag design. Much like the ever-popular rainbow flag adopted by the greater LGBT communities, it was offered free from copyrights or other restrictions for bisexuals to use at events such as GLBT Pride celebrations and, as mentioned briefly in Chapter 4, bisexual picnics. It is important to note that the bi community was hardly alone in introducing its own flag for these sort of events; the leather community and the group known as the Bears, both subcultures within the greater LGBT communities, also introduced their own flags.

Meanwhile, books about bisexuality began to be published with greater frequency. In 1991 Loraine Hutchins and Lani Ka'ahumanu edited *Bi Any Other Name: Bisexual People Speak Out,* a compilation of essays by bisexual writers.[16] In 1995 another compilation, *Bisexual Politics: Theories, Queries, and Visions* by Naomi Tucker, Liz A. Highleyman, and Rebecca Kaplan hit the bookstores.[17] Several other such sets of essays by bisexuals and about bisexuality have been published since, as well as a handful of more academic books, such as *Bisexuality and the Eroticism of Everyday Life* by Marjorie Garber.[18]

In the 1990s, clearly bisexuality became a little less invisible.

WHERE DOES THAT LEAVE THE BI COMMUNITY TODAY?

In the 1990s more bi groups began while others ended. In San Diego, Houston, Dallas, New Jersey, St. Louis, Memphis, Minneapolis, Atlanta, and Milwaukee groups have come and, sometimes, gone. At the same time, Chicago and Seattle, among others, have experienced a kind of organizing fatigue and now have little activity. *Anything That Moves* quit publishing in 2001. Most dramatically, BiNet USA went from a fast start, to entropy, to all but gone as it struggles to find a mission and volunteers to pursue it. Even with the impressive gains for bi visibility in the 1990s, the growth of bisexual organizations seems to have stalled. I look at possible reasons why and what this may mean for the future in the next chapter.

Clearly the bi community has made some steady gains over the past thirty years, and especially over the past fifteen. Ochs has the perspective of someone who has been there over the long haul:

When I started doing activism around bisexuality, we were fighting to be acknowledged as existing. We were fighting to have our existence recognized, to have our names spoken out loud, because a lot of people didn't want to say that word. In the 1987 March on Washington one of the bumper stickers being distributed said, "Dot, dot, dot and Bisexual, come on, you can say it." It was gay and lesbian this and gay and lesbian that, so we were almost fighting for our existence, I guess symbolic existence. Largely because of student activism, the "B" word did get included with the "T" word. And it's really pretty, [if] not universal, . . . common now those words are spoken out loud. I have [known people] who would have completely dismissed "bisexual" ten, twenty years ago who [now] say GLBT . . . regularly without prompting, and have friends who are out bisexuals. It's a world that, I don't know, I never could have imagined it, we would have been, embraced is not the right word, but acknowledged.

I asked Ochs if this is what she imagined when she began her work:

We've gone way beyond what I ever thought was possible. We're not anywhere near where I think we should be, but we've gone way beyond what I imagined was possible.

Just as the second wave of bi activism supplanted the first, some would argue that a new wave of activism is beginning. Some have suggested that a shift has occurred away from organizations made up of refugees from the lesbian-feminist community to more and more men and women who are sex radicals, former activists for other issues, and polyamory community members.[19] Others have argued the bi movement has shifted to college campuses and younger people, and now centers more on discarding identity politics altogether. I'm not sure I agree with either of those two opinions, although both could be true. In the next chapter I examine the direction the community is going in and what the future may hold.

Chapter 10

The Future of the Bi Community: GLBT Identity versus Cyberspace

THE COLLEGE WORKSHOP

As I listened to Kathy give her portion of our workshop, I had a chance to reflect on where we were. The short answer of course was we were in Morris, Minnesota, at the University of Minnesota campus. Morris is a small town almost dead center of the state on Minnesota, near some good fishing, surrounded by excellent farmland, and smack dab in the middle of nowhere—not a place most people would willingly go in February. But go we did, as we had been invited to give a workshop on bisexuality at their annual LGBT Pride celebration. This was, for both Kathy (from Chapter 4) and me, our first time (as it turns out first of many) for giving such a workshop. The U of M–Morris has small but vocal GLBT communities, and they put on quite a Pride celebration, featuring workshops, speakers, a dance, informational tables, and generally high spirits. So here we were on a Saturday morning in a meeting room in the student union, with about twenty-five young college students, a few transparencies, and butterflies in our stomachs.

That's still the short answer to the question of where we were. The long answer is more complex. First, we were a long way from where we were only thirty years ago. GLBT communities in general have made incredible progress in securing basic human rights and in building a strong, supportive community. Second, we were attending not a Gay Pride celebration, not Gay and Lesbian Pride, but a LGBT Pride celebration. The U of M–Morris LGBT organization, like many other LGBT organizations around the country, was now just that: LGBT. Bisexuals, not to mention transgender people, are now officially included. That was a long road to travel, and I don't mean I-94 from Minneapolis.

But as I watched Kathy, I didn't reflect on this progress for long; my needs were more immediate: we were bombing. I had that sense when I was talking, but sometimes I'm so busy flailing around in front of an audience that it's hard to get a good read. Now that she was on, it was clear: tank city. What was wrong? We were prepared; we had an audience full of bi people; and we were cute up there. What could it be? Then it hit me: I was talking about my experiences as a (at the time) forty-year-old man, of bi activism, and of identity politics. I was talking about my reality and what informed it. For most of them, it was meaningless. As twenty-year-old college students, they have had an experience completely different from mine. They grew up with "GLBT." Kathy and I were talking about battles fought before they were born. They are under less pressure than we were to pick an identity, or, for that matter, to remain in any identity they do pick. They are influenced less by oppression and more by the desire to deconstruct orientation and identity to make sexuality relevant for them. Although most of the workshop participants identified as bisexual when asked, most also identified as queer. As I was talking about fighting for the right to claim my identity as a bisexual person, they were so far past this milestone that Kathy and I must have looked like dinosaurs.

What does this foretell for the future of the bisexual community? Will the bi community go the way of the dinosaur?

INTO THE FUTURE

The future is the future. I will write this chapter and someone will read this in twenty years and find me to be akin to either Kreskin or the guy in the patent office a hundred years ago who declared everything that could be invented had been invented. Even with this uncertainty, it is still interesting to see which direction the signs are pointing right now. To be sure, the work of the past and the efforts of the present shape the future. David, speaking at BECAUSE to the Bisexual History Project, commented on this:

I have high hopes, moderately high expectations. And you know, there are a couple of kids here [at the conference, if I can] call them kids; they're in high school. It's a different world. People view bisexuality differently than they did ten, fifteen, twenty years ago, and I think that, I hope, what I'm doing now is helping make that happen.

It *is* a different world. Although homophobia remains a powerful barrier, many cities now offer the opportunity to find a supportive community of, if not fellow travelers, accepting and encouraging peers. Publicly identifying as bisexual not only carries less stigma, but also, as I explained in Chapter 5, is in some circles popular or even trendy. There is a new freedom to explore sexuality and consider possibilities that were once taboo and unacceptable. Youths are now facing fewer barriers to being openly gay, lesbian, transgender, or bisexual than in the past.

With a considerable number of youths able to identify as bisexual, does that translate into a stronger bi community? So far, I would have to say no. As I pointed out in the previous chapter, no more, and perhaps even fewer, bisexual community organizations exist in America in 2005 than did in 1993. This doesn't make much sense until considering again the lesson of the workshop: If I am not talking about issues relevant to the youths, if I don't understand what their goals are, if I don't see how what it means to be bisexual is changing, I have lost them. Robyn Ochs in Boston works with college students every day:

> Most of the people I work with are now under twenty-two. I love it. I learn so much from them. There is a resistance to labels. If you were talking academically, you would call it this post-identity politics phase. There's a lot more discussion and acceptance of the idea of sexual fluidity. And a lot more acceptance of the idea of resistance to the mainstream norm of queerness, saying, "I don't have to follow the rules, you can't tell me what to do." But at the same time, often a resistance to saying, "Well I am this specific label, I am a lesbian, I am bisexual, I am gay." So there's this whole other thing going on that is new.

Perhaps one reason bisexual institutions aren't growing is because they are losing the youths.

BISEXUAL INCLUSION

So has the community reached its peak? Dr. Fritz Klein doesn't think so:

> I don't know. If you would have asked me five, ten years ago, I would have said the bisexual movement would be going nowhere, but I've been proven wrong in the last five, ten years; [it's] grown tremendously; [it's] gotten stronger.

Dr. Klein is right if we consider the progress the bisexual community has made in its relationship to the gay and lesbian community. In many areas of the country, organizations once called "gay" or "gay and lesbian" are now "GLBT." Klein has lived through this transition and seen its impact, and it gives him encouragement this is the right place to put the community's energy. Klein says:

> One thing that has changed is that bisexual was invisible, and in some cases still is, in many gay and lesbian institutions. [But now,] in San Diego, what was the Gay and Lesbian Center is now the GLBT Center, Gay and Lesbian Pride is now GLBT Pride.

Often the change is only cosmetic; after all, simply adding a "B" to the name doesn't mean an organization won't continue to do things the same old way. For example, a formerly "gay and lesbian" newspaper becomes a GLBT community newspaper but continues to ignore the bisexual community, or a so-called GLBT organization's brochure, Web site, or newsletter refers only to lesbians and gays. On the other hand, some organizations that do not include bisexuals in their name are very supportive of the bisexual community. For example, in the Twin Cities (if not nationally), Parents, Families, and Friends of Lesbians and Gays (PFLAG) has been very supportive of the bisexual community. Nationally, the National Gay and Lesbian Task Force (NGLTF), one of the largest and most influential gay and lesbian organizations, and the media watchdogs at the Gay and Lesbian Alliance Against Defamation (GLAAD) are both very supportive of the bisexual community. In some ways it is irrelevant what the name of the group is, as long as it is welcoming and actually works for the entire GLBT community.

On the other hand, having "bisexual" in the name of gay and lesbian groups does make a real impact. Seeing the bisexual community as important enough to overtly include is meaningful to a community previously excluded. It is good for outreach and education, too, since in the past many people never heard the word bisexual until late in life, and now it's right there on the masthead of formerly gay newspapers. Also, having "B" in the name gives bisexuals real leverage; after all, if "bisexual" is encoded into the organization's name and mission, it is harder to ignore the community now and in the future.

These changes have real ramifications for the future of the bi community and, more specifically, for the mission of bisexual organizing. Klein says:

> So I don't know where it's going to go. . . . Do you create a rainbow coalition with the gay groups? Do you go off doing your own thing? Do you do both? . . . I have a feeling that's what's going to happen: you do both. You are a part of the gay, lesbian, and transgender community because you're not straight, so you belong there.

This then is an important question for the future of the bisexual community: Will bisexuals be part of a larger LGBT community, will they exist as a community of their own, or will there be some combination of the two? There is one more choice, one I would guess to be very appealing to the college students attending my workshop in Morris: the label "queer."

Queer?

"Queer" has much going for it. It can be seen as a rejection of an either/or, straight/gay paradigm, blending all those who feel different by virtue of their sexuality. It is inclusive of bisexuals, lesbians, gays, people who are transgender, as well as leather, levi, B/D, and S/M people of all orientations, and just about anyone else who feels "queer." Many people, including myself, find having one word uniting all these communities compelling. Indeed, it seems to be getting support: an annual Queer Film and Video Festival is held in Vancouver, the Deaf Queer Resource Center operates in San Francisco, and cable television offers *Queer Nation, Queer As Folk,* and *Queer Eye for the Straight Guy.*

But queer is much more than sexuality alone. It implies a politic, a radical sexuality rejecting traditional labels. For example, Cheryl Dobinson, in her essay "Beyond Bisexuality," says, "I have not only given up on, but now actively reject any attempt to fit myself neatly into current models of sexual identity. . . . I maintained my ambiguous and uncertain sexual status, perhaps best described as queer—the current anti-identity." Yet, Dobinson claims, "My sexuality is infinitely more complex and dynamic than a single word allows. . . . I refuse to be classified and understood."[1]

Unfortunately, I don't see the term working well for most GLBT people. For some it is too soon to recover the word; the childhood taunts are still too fresh, the wounds too deep. I hear the pain, but I would think if this were all that stood in the way of *queer,* sooner or later time would heal the wound.

Instead, I think two bigger problems stand in the way of *queer* gaining acceptance. First, some individuals don't like *queer* for the same reason I do like it. As a lesbian *ex*-friend of mine once told me, she didn't like *queer* because it *did* include bisexuals. Many members of GLBT communities have no interest in a united B, T, G, and L.

To better illustrate the second reason, I want to tell a story about a party. Now, I knew no one at the party save the man who brought me. It would be an understatement to mention the cultural gap between the other partiers and me. Frankly, they were ten of the loudest, biggest rednecks you'll ever meet. Never mind they were all gay. They wore wraparound metallic sunglasses and belched for one another's amusement. If Nader wins in a landslide at BECAUSE, Pat Buchanan wins here. The topic turned to the use of "GLBT." One man asked, "What's with all this glbtxyz crap anyway? What's wrong with just gay?" To which I replied, "For me, I like 'queer.'" All ten men turned to me and stared. They didn't say anything, just stared. Then I knew: these men were not queer. They may be gay, but they will never be queer. Queer implies an embracing of one's status as the Other. I strongly suspect these men have no desire to embrace being "the other."

That all said, a significant number of bi people do identify strongly with a queer identity. For many such as myself, the calling to build a true unified community is strong, whether those men I met at the party come along or not. People are deciding right now with their feet whether they want a queer, GLBT, or independent bisexual community. Far more bisexuals are found within GBLT and lesbian or gay communities than are in a bisexual community. In addition, many bisexual people have adopted *queer* as their identity and are not seeking any other community. Considering how small the bisexual community is and that most bisexuals are not participating in it, one might conclude that the majority has spoken: the future does not lie with a strong bisexual community.

HERE COMES THE INTERNET

Perhaps, however, that conclusion would be premature. The 1990s saw the creation of the greatest organizing tool since the invention of the printing press: the Internet. The entire world, and any subject you might be interested in, is available now at the touch of a few keys right there on your desk. Dr. Klein has seen and joined in the changes. When he started his work on bisexuality, he found, "The New York Public Library had nothing on bisexuality, only two cards, and I had to find out." The early support group he founded, the Bi Forum, was "a very lonely cause." Now we have "the Internet, where the bisexuals now can communicate with hundreds and thousands of other bisexuals." Hundreds of thousands? Yes, indeed. The Bi Men Network at <bimen.org>, managed by a man in Long Beach, California, claims over 200,000 participants. "What I thought was a very small community, when we had 150 people in a room we were doing good, it ain't so," Klein noted.

Bisexuals are very big on the Internet, both as consumers and hosts of Web sites. The Web has three main features making it so valuable for bisexual organizing. First, it is anonymous. Online, people can find any information or resources they want and no one will find out. There are no accusing stares in the bookstore; no chance of getting caught in the gay bar; no fear of being seen going into the local gay and lesbian center. The Web gives its users true freedom to explore. Second, the Web facilitates finding obscure information and resources. Searching online for the word "bisexual" is just as easy as searching for "grocery," whereas in the real world it is much easier to find a grocery store than to locate bisexual resources. You may find there aren't many bi resources around your area, but in a few hours you will become an expert on what resources there are. Third, the Web is democratic. Bisexuals may be silenced in American society, but they cannot be silenced on the Web. For example, the gay and lesbian press may ignore the bisexual community, but any Jane can put up a Web site. If someone in Waterloo, Iowa, creates a great site with great content, that voice will be heard by hundreds of thousands of people, regardless of what any of the old gatekeepers of the gay and lesbian press may think.

The result is an incredible growth of information and connection for bisexuals—not just cyber connections either; if I knew nothing about the bisexual community, I could find out in a matter of a few minutes if a bisexual group has formed in my town. Juli from the support group says:

> I can honestly say that if I didn't seek things out first on the Web that I never would have connected to my local bi community. It was a safe way for me to have a look around and see what was out there. I have learned of books, resources, movies, and events from the Web. I don't think it should replace human contact but enhance it. I don't do a lot of e-mail with other bi folk, but I have met some wonderful people in person because of Web calendars. It has been a great starting point for me. (Juli)

To find out what the bisexual community is up to in any town, go to Klein's site <bisexual.org>, click on local resources, and there they are. Indeed, thirty years after looking at those two cards in the library, Klein is a leader in using the Internet with a Web site getting 25,000 hits per week. That is just one; thousands of bisexual Web sites (not counting the porn sites) are giving expression to individuals and groups and hope to isolated bisexuals in all corners of the world.

What the bisexual community in most cities lacks in institutions it has, at least to some degree, made up for by creating a community on-line. For example, I used the online support group as a resource in writing this book. They have never met in person and exist as a group only at Yahoo. Yahoo groups, a free resource for anyone seeking to find other people who like to fly-fish or tango, for example, has scores of bisexual discussion groups, some on a national scale and some for a particular geographical area. What I find most appealing is the local aspect: I can find, and if not, create, a Yahoo group for any location I want. Can I "talk" with bisexuals in the Twin Cities? No problem. For example:

> I would have to say the Web is my lifeline to the bi world. When I got on-line in [1996] . . . I had only met one other person like myself. I figured this new medium would be just the thing to reveal the others that I hoped were hidden in plain sight all around me. Every same-sex relationship I have had has started right here in front of my computer screen. In 1999 I started an on-line group like this one for bi women in my area and have since talked to at least a hundred of them about their lives, experiences, relationships, desires, thoughts, etc. Even if I could have met them all off-line in a group of some kind I doubt I could have gotten so much candid information from so many. . . . There are now real world links to the GLBTI community that I probably would have eventually stumbled upon, so I happily have both. But it still

upsets me that this is about the only place we have every day to be ourselves en masse. (Tezza)

I joined [Tezza's] group in January and since then have felt more connected with the local bi community than ever before. Other than on-line I've never really found any sort of bi community. We are always joking about how bi people are hidden in plain sight and how we wish there was a way we could identify each other when we meet off-line. Of the relationships I've had with bi individuals, the majority were initiated on-line, including the one I'm in currently. Thank goodness for the Internet! (Juli)

The Internet's impact on bisexuals, if not the bi community, has been enormous. Again, from the online support group, Kimberly says:

Wow, . . . I can say I wouldn't know ANY bi people if it wasn't for the Web. I went to the Internet to really find out what bisexuality was. I went there to meet other bisexuals; I made all of my bisexual friends on-line. I'd be lost and confused and who knows what else if it wasn't for the Internet.

Or Glenn:

The Web is my only connection to the bi community. I have some gay and lesbian friends, but I know only one other person who is bi. . . . Being able to connect with other bisexuals via the Web keeps me from feeling isolated in what is, for me, a relatively new community.

So the Web is wonderful. The Web is powerful. The Web connects communities. Why then has the past ten years seen a decline in bisexual community building?

DO WE WANT TO HAVE A COMMUNITY?

One person who thinks bisexual activists have been going at it all wrong is Rich Woulfe, the vice-chair of the Bisexual Foundation. He is very outspoken about his belief that we won't get anywhere thinking in terms of "bisexual" as a sexual identity. He believes we need to talk about bisexuality as an orientation. In other words, he is less interested in who calls themselves bisexual as getting people to accept people who are attracted to more than one gender, regardless of their self-identity. Woulfe would like his organization and other bisexual organizations to move more toward teaching about bisexuality and not be as concerned with building a community for bisexuals. For example, in his view a conference should be about studying bisexuality and include professionals and anyone interested in the topic, not a conference for only members of the bisexual community. Woulfe says, "I don't have this vision of a bisexual utopia. What I have is a vision of a world where people are comfortable with their own sexuality." He feels he gets better reception from the general public when bringing a message of tolerance for all sexual minorities rather than one of identity politics. Woulfe describes an encounter with a doctor, "When I talked with him about bisexual, he says, 'No. No way.' When I talk to him about bisexuality, he listens." Less interested in a bisexual community per se, "We are about creating an environment that makes it safe to be yourself," he says.

The same barriers to building bisexual community complicate teaching about diversity of sexuality: invisibility within and resistance from the lesbian and gay communities. He sees name inclusion as where the work needs to be done:

> We are at war with an element of the gay and lesbian body politic. There is a segment who gets it, there's another segment needing to be educated, and there is a third segment, I'd say 20 to 30 percent, who consciously or unconsciously want to erase bisexuals. They are no different than the far right; they are about ignorance and fear.

Is this the shape of things to come? Are bisexuals less interested in building a bisexual community and more interested in educating about sexuality in general? Has working toward bisexual community become a barrier to greater gains in understanding and accepting bisexuality? Will bisexuals now be better served by fighting for their acceptance into other communities rather than building one of their own?

The Third Wave

If Klein's Bi Forum and the Bisexual Center in San Francisco represent the first wave of bisexual activism, and Robyn Ochs and the Boston Bisexual Resource Center represent the second wave, are we now in a third wave? Certainly Woulfe's ideas, if implemented, represent a sea change. While the second wave, based in feminist politics, sought to fight systems of oppression (as I talked about in Chapter 5), Woulfe's model of activism is focused more narrowly, only teaching tolerance for variation in sexuality. The second wave featured groups organized in a more feminist or anarchist system of low to no hierarchy. For example, Robyn Ochs said of the Boston Bi Women's Network, "It's an organization that has never had any kind of formal leadership. There's no president, no vice-president, no board of directors. It's kind of anarchy at its best." Now we have "vice-chairs." One prominent bisexual leader and proponent of this new, traditional, hierarchical approach told me, "Why continue the mistakes of the past?"

The second wave made some impressive gains for bisexuals and the bisexual community, but at the same time, the feminist nature of the movement may indeed have become a barrier for some who would otherwise want to participate. As Stephen Donaldson, in *Bisexual Politics: Theories, Queries, and Visions*, says,

> This imbalance of gender is a problem. Bisexual leadership at all levels must reach out to men, and men in the movement must take responsibility for developing remedies. The intellectual discourse of the bi movement, which often appears to be dominated by "women's issues," must be broadened, or the movement may be perceived by men as primarily a vehicle for arcane intra-feminist controversies.[2]

Is this then the third wave of bisexual organizing? Discarding the feminist, anarchist, oppression-based approach to community building and replacing it with a more traditional organizational model working to encourage acceptance for bisexuality and thus lessen the need for separate communities?

WHAT IS THE FUTURE OF THE BISEXUAL COMMUNITY?

I think it is time to go to the source, bisexual people themselves, and ask what they see as their future. When the question was posed to our Bisexual History Project participants, there seemed to be a common thread, one that may support Woulfe's activist goals. Few spoke of a big, happy bi community. All spoke of living in a world where sexual orientation is irrelevant, where everyone is accepted, and sexuality is simply no longer a big deal.

To me the ideal situation would be more personal than political. It would be that people think more about their feelings and attractions and less about their own labels. . . . I'm attracted to who I'm attracted to. Whether that word "bi" and an actual sense of duality actually work, doesn't matter. I've known too many straight people or gay men or lesbians who've been attracted to somebody who is not their usual gender list and [have] not done anything about it because they thought it didn't fit their label and their category— which I've lived through myself and it's a lousy feeling, it's a frustrating feeling of regret. I'd like to see people function more on their feelings and attractions and less on their label. (Rob)

I'd like to have a relationship where it didn't matter if the person I was with was male or female; it mattered more that we were compatible and got along and were raising our family together. . . . An ideal situation would be: everyone in my neighborhood could know that I was bisexual and it wouldn't matter. It wouldn't matter if I hung rainbow flags out my window or not. My daughter wouldn't be teased about her mom being gay or bisexual.
Sometimes I wish that people could look beyond the orientation issue a little bit and just see each other as people, and you know. . . . You do end up meeting people, hooking up with them, and you might decide to date or not date, but why can't you just be friends first and see where it goes? Why does it always have to be, "Well, how do you identify?" You know, I've gone to lesbian events, dances and things identified as women-only events, and the first question is, "Well, are you lesbian or bisexual?" And it's like, "It depends." It's like, "Do you want to go out with me? If you want to go out with me maybe I'll be lesbian, maybe I'll tell you later. If you have a partner, then maybe I'll tell you I'm bisexual. Why? What does it matter?" I don't think it should matter. My daughter says it doesn't matter if you're black or if you're gay. What matters is your friendliness. That's what I think, too. I think what matters should be your friendliness. (Kathleen)

I guess I'd like to be able to be more interactive, more open with people about who I am and have that be just a normal part of life. And that's a big piece of me, but it's the whole culture, too, the overriding culture to have that be opened up a little bit more. I don't care too much for categories and labels, so a worldview that I would prefer would just be one of acceptance of people and their affinities and their love. (Elizabeth)

In some ways I'd like to see a world . . . where sexuality is no more of an issue than anything else. It should be less of an issue than food preference. I know people get in fights about whether they're vegetarian or not or vegan or whatever, and I'm sure for a long time there will be that same sort of stuff around sexuality. . . . I think we need to build bridges. . . . I think there're also links between other communities like the pagan community and the leather community, other communities of people who are made to feel different. . . . I think we need to form broader alliances if we are to bring into being a world where we can be ourselves. (Magenta)

I have a vision of if a kid, on finding out that [they] were bisexual thought, "Oh, okay, cool, and I know who to call and who to talk to, and if I say that at school it's not going to cause a problem for me." That's where I think it ought to start. And I don't think it's quite at that point yet. I think it's moving toward it, better than it was when I was fifteen or younger, but that's where it has got to start. There ought to be publicly identified space and place, and reputation [for bisexuality] . . . other than just an AIDS carrier infecting the unsuspecting world. (Scott)

I think ideally it would just be nice if people could be open . . . and society wasn't so judgmental about things. I think it's sad we have to have all of these isolated fringe communities, and I really wish people would just get over the idea of . . . women's rights and blacks' rights and gay rights; . . . the real issue is just human rights. Why can't we just treat everyone equal? You know, I think it just really comes down to psychology, and people always have this hang up and have to divide everything into us and them. Well, I think bisexuality is . . . so hard to define [that it] has forced the community to be more inclusive. (Brian)

Is the Bisexual Community Working on Mutually Exclusive Goals?

In these stories I hear people calling out for acceptance and for inclusion. I hear people calling out to be themselves, to love their partners and their children. What I don't hear is the demand for a bisexual community.

In Chapter 4, I talked about the challenges to creating a bisexual community, such as invisibility. One last barrier is the bisexual community itself, or, more accurately, the conundrum at the heart of bisexual activism: How can a population both work to build a community based on identity and put an end to the need for identity? One of the implicit, and in some cases explicit, goals of bisexual conferences, picnics, groups, workshops, and organizations is to build a larger, more complete bisexual community. The desire is to create a bisexual space to feel at home, to feel whole, to be with one's own. Yet, as can be seen in the comments from the Bisexual History Project, all longed for a world where it doesn't matter what the gender of one's partner or partners is, a world where they can feel accepted, a world where their orientation doesn't matter. Only one had as a goal a large and successful bisexual community. Now, if the question of community was raised specifically, some would probably say sure, they'd like to see such a community, but I think the omission is significant. Is the goal of bisexual activism to create and brand a bisexual identity complete with community and institutions, or is it to tear down the entire construct of sexual orientation as something artificial built to divide us and deny our fundamental sexual nature as humans? I would argue we can't do both.

Here It Is: The Future of the Bisexual Community

Herein lies at least some of the questions needing to be answered if we are to divine the future of the bisexual community. First, is the bisexual community speaking to the issues and experiences of the next generation of potential activists? Second, is "bisexual" as a separate identity a thing of the past, to be assimilated into a true LGBT community or possibly replaced by "queer" or some other inclusive identity? Or is sexual orientation itself a bankrupt concept, ready to be replaced by an acceptance of sexual fluidity and diversity for all people?

Although I don't have answers to any of those questions, I'll pull out my crystal ball and give it my best shot.

As I talked about in Chapter 3, I believe the bisexual community is the product of ostracism by the gay and lesbian communities. When all sexual minorities were fighting for even the most basic rights and acknowledgement by society, the gay community was a united community for lesbian, gay, bisexual, and transgender people. With the beginnings of success for the gay rights movement this alliance fractured. The goal for many gays and lesbians became making it not only okay to be straight, but also okay to be gay or lesbian. I would argue the better and more inclusive goal is that it is okay to be whatever orientation a person is or wants to be; everyone has the right to love whomever and however they please with other consenting adults regardless of gender.

I believe this is the direction America is now going. Mike from the online support group says:

I'd think general acceptance for bisexuality isn't too awfully far away—or at least a strong movement in that direction fueled by younger and younger people being more accepting. . . . Within thirty to fifty years, bisexuality should be fairly well accepted. Within 100 years, accepted as the norm.

According to Wayne Bryant, in the future the community will be "obsolete, because everyone will be fine with how everyone else is [and then] why would we need a bisexual community." As objectifying and tacky as it is, the story of women kissing on television[3] I related in Chapter 5 is a sign of this greater acceptance of sexual fluidity. The college students at Morris got it; most saw little connection between my tales of bisexual community and their lives of sexual exploration. I think we are starting to see increasing casualness about sexuality and the boundaries of sexual orientation. In the long run, you can put me firmly in the sexual orientation deconstructionist camp.

In the short term, I think we are seeing the rectifying of an old wrong, in that the lesbian and gay communities are increasingly accepting bisexuals back into the fold. LGBT is becoming a reality. As haltingly and irregularly as it has been applied, a united LGBT community is the future. Or not. The future may indeed lay with "queer," but either way, the communities are united. In other words, I think success in encouraging recognition of the fluidity of sexuality will lead to the demise of the bisexual movement. I believe that is what we are seeing right now with the dwindling energy for separate bisexual spaces; remove the anger at the lesbian and gay communities for their lack of support, and there is much less reason to seek out a bisexual space. According to Robyn Ochs:

> If you had asked me ten years ago I would have said, oh yes, in ten years there will be a lot more bi groups. And what I am seeing instead, much to my surprise, is there's not as much need for separate bi groups. And if you look at younger people, most of them don't see the need for separate groups.

Ochs is on the front lines of change not just with the Bisexual Resource Center but also in working with college students where she teaches:

> Gay, lesbian, trans, allies; they're working together. There are a few schools where separate bi groups have formed as well, such as Brandeis, which has as group called Bi Space. . . . Bi Space is not a separate community; it's a separate meeting space and time. . . . Even there, where they have decided there is a need for some separate space, it's not because they feel completely outside of the mainstream, it's not because they feel completely unwelcome, but it's because they want to talk once a week or once a month about being bisexual.

Ochs's last point is important because if bisexual activism folds into a greater GLBT movement, some need for bisexual spaces will remain. Says Marcia Deihl:

> Since we succeeded so much (for me, that means seeing "GLBT" in place of "gay and lesbian," the difference between 1980 and now), we don't need to exist. But we may choose to do so for, one, historical archiving; two, support of bisexuals in outposts whose peers ARE back in the 1980s (or even worse, the 1950s); three, resource places and lists for coming out bi's . . . and four, cultural festivals and conferences for bonding and inter-generational exchanging of ideas.

I agree.

Nevertheless, the future for a bisexual community is dim. While it is sad to think of this little, iconoclastic community dwindling away until all that remains are a few old activists from the past keeping the light on, I also think it is hopeful for all people coming next, that they will have a chance to not live a life of invisibility and ostracism. This was everything any bi activist ever hoped for. As Robyn Ochs said:

> It's such a different world now. It's great, but in a way it's frustrating because it's like, I did all this work to make bisexual space and now you're saying you don't need it as much? But that's great! That really means that we've succeeded. That we've done a lot. . . . What I said . . . that things have happened that I could never really have imagined, that's what I'm talking about: we've succeeded in a way I never thought was possible. Our success has reduced the need for us.

Chapter 11

BECAUSE Reprise

BACK TO THE WORKSHOP

Now that I have looked at bisexuality and the bisexual community, I want to go back to BECAUSE on that sunny afternoon in April and examine the list of thirteen myths about bisexuals from Chapter 1:

1. Bisexuals are easy; they are indiscriminate about whom they have sex with.

On average, people willing to call themselves bisexual probably do have more sex partners than people who identify as straight. A male friend of mine once observed, "People think because I'm bisexual I must have more sex than nonbisexuals since I have a larger pool to draw from. I rebelled against that for years until I realized, hey, I'm married and I have a male lover. Yeah, I have a lot of sex." However, having more sex partners hardly means a person is "indiscriminant" in the choice of partners. As I discussed in Chapter 2, bisexuals are oversexualized in the public's view.

2. All bisexuals are swingers.

Chapter 7 introduced the swinger community, a group within which bisexual women were prized and bisexual men were ostracized. Although certainly some bisexuals do take part in the swinger community (after all, most communities have some bisexual people), it is largely a straight institution. Perhaps bisexuals are more visible there (bisexually behaving women to be sure), but the overwhelming majority of bisexuals are not swingers.

3. Bisexuals have the best of both worlds and are twice as likely to get a date.

Twice as likely to get a date? Many people, straight, gay, or lesbian, swear they will never date a bisexual. For an out bisexual, the dating pool may actually be quite small. As for the best of both worlds, recall that Aaron said in Chapter 5, "Best of both worlds? I don't think I get the best of either." Being bisexual can be a wonderful life, but it can also be a challenge; so it is not realistic to romanticize it.

4. Bisexuals are unable to commit to either gender.

Bisexuals come in all levels of commitment, just like straight, lesbian, and gay people. The survey for this book found about 30 percent of bisexuals are monogamous in their primary relationships, which is certainly a significant number of bisexuals. However, the group surveyed did not consist of average bisexuals, but instead those who are part of the bi community. What then can be said about all those who identify as bisexual and how monogamous they are? This question remains unanswered. My intuition says the 4 percent of the population that identify as bisexual are probably about as monogamous as lesbian, gay, or straight people are: not very.

5. Bisexual women are all wives just trying to please their husbands and bisexual men are all married guys cheating on their wives.

Probably a large number of "situational" bisexual women do have sex with other women for men's enjoyment within, and bordering, the swinger community. Chapter 5 reprinted some ads from personal sections of alternative papers. How many of these women identify as bisexual is anyone's guess, but as I mentioned previously, few bisexuals are swingers.

Certainly a number of bisexual men cheat on their wives. As an HIV/STD prevention educator, I lead a discussion group every month for married men attracted to men, many of whom fit that description. But again, most bisexual men are monogamous. Many bisexual men live quiet lives with their same-sex or opposite-sex partners and wouldn't think of cheating. Some bisexual men are nonmonogamous by agreement with their partners. As with all myths and stereotypes, people can always find examples to reinforce their preexisting beliefs, but the variation within the bisexual community is so great as to defy generalizing most anything to bisexuals as individuals.

6. Bisexuality is just a phase on the way to being lesbian or gay.

For some people who call themselves bisexual this is true. For many, it is not. Similarly, some people who call themselves lesbian or gay are in transition to being bisexual. As discussed in Chapter 3, sexual orientation is fluid. The reason this stereotype stays around is because it does such a good job of making bisexuals invisible, denying their very existence.

7. Bisexuals are unable to be happy, have low self-esteem, or are mentally ill.

In fact, my survey found that 82 percent of respondents were happy with being bisexual. Once, at a workshop, I employed a favorite facilitation device of mine to loosen up the crowd and encourage them to ask hard questions. I handed out index cards and pens and asked the participants to write questions for our panel of five; the cards were collected and anonymously read aloud. One of the questions was, "Do you think you could ever be truly happy as a bisexual?" I thought this question was interesting: What would give the questioner the impression that I or any other members of the panel were unhappy? Bisexuals have neither more nor less problems than anyone else, other than their being a target of such a great deal of misunderstanding, ostracism, and discrimination.

8. Bisexuals are disease carriers.

In Chapter 8, I discussed how this view is both popular and wrong. Bisexuals are not a hot spot in the HIV epidemic, which is surprising considering they are left out of so many services and prevention efforts.

9. Bisexuals are a very small part of the population.

I have heard bisexual activists describe anywhere from 25 to 80 percent of the population as bisexual.* Bad news; it's not true. I prefer the *Janus Report,* which says 4 percent of the population is bisexual,[1] which is a higher figure than is given in most other studies. I don't know if most people would say that is a small number, but I think 11 million is still a lot of people!

10. Bisexuals are just trying to maintain heterosexual privilege.

"Trying" is where this myth falls apart. As discussed in Chapter 2, bisexuals in opposite-sex relationships are afforded the privileges of American culture, such as marriage, automatic approval from relatives and society, not to mention near freedom from being beaten up for the choice of who they hold hands with in public. Although I'm sure some bisexuals choose to hide and not come out or not openly date people of the same sex, so do gay and lesbian people. Bisexuals in same-gender relationships face exactly the same problems confronting lesbians and gays. When it comes to the topic of privilege, no G, L, B, or T person invented this mess, and all would end it if they had the power.

11. Bisexuals can't be feminist.

As I discussed in Chapter 5, the idea that "bisexual women are traitors to feminism" is completely false. Women who own their sexuality and demand a place at the table despite ostracism because of their partner's gender are the ones who are truly liberated.

12. People call themselves bisexual to be trendy.

This myth first started in the 1970s, when it appeared in articles in *Newsweek* and *Time.* Bisexuals may be cool in some circles, but it is a long way from being true for the vast majority of the world. Instead, what little bit of popularity bisexuality holds is used to "prove" bisexuals don't really exist: "You're not bisexual; you're just trying to be cool."

---

*The 80 percent comes from the mistaken belief that if 10 percent of the population is gay (wrong in the first place) then 10 percent is straight, leaving 80 percent as bisexual. Nonsense.

13. Bisexuality is a choice.

If bisexuality is all about a woman pleasing her man, if it is about being trendy, if it is about seeking privilege by denying one's homosexuality, then it must be a choice. If bisexuality doesn't really exist, then those who choose to call themselves bisexual are doing just that: choosing. But we know people do not choose their sexual orientation; orientation exists on a feelings level, and we can't control how we feel. Some people are simply attracted to both men and women, and thus bisexual, whether they like it or not. Besides, why would someone "choose" to put themselves in the way of abuse, ridicule, and societal sanction?

If this list is what the bisexual community is not, what then is it? What I hoped to show throughout this book are individuals within a community, embattled from all sides, stubbornly holding onto their belief in themselves and their right to live and love consensually whomever and however they see fit. A large number of people behave bisexually in that they have or had lovers of more than one gender in their lives, but those who decide to take up the mantle of a bisexual identity are a special lot. Of those identifying as bisexual, a minority form a small, very small, community of like-minded individuals who share, among other things, an undying belief that they deserve a full place at the table, coupled with a wonder why more people are not joining them. This is an interesting group of people in an interesting time in history, for them and their community.

But we must keep in mind that whatever the bi community was in the past and what the bi community is like in the present are surely not what the community will be in the future, if there even is a future for the community. The lives and efforts of Kathy, Brent, Tina, and Becky at BECAUSE, Mike, Kimberly, Ron, Lori, and Stephanie of the online support group, and Magenta, Scott, Brian, and Anita of the Bisexual History Project all need to be remembered. I asked in Chapter 3 if in a hundred years Pashtun historians in Afghanistan will remember to write about the *halekon*, the "pretty young men" whom up to half the male population take as lovers.[2] Will history remember this plucky little bi community, pushing their boulder up the hill?

SUNDAY MORNING BREAKFAST

A quiet time after the storm would describe early morning breakfast at BECAUSE that Sunday. While most people slept off the previous day's excitement of workshops, entertainment, dancing, and late-night partying, some of us made it to the hotel restaurant early for the breakfast buffet. Seven of us shared a large, round table in an out-of-the-way corner and talked about the past and the future. At the table was Dr. Fritz Klein, whom I discussed while looking at the history of the community in Chapter 9, as well as Gary Lingen, a Twin Cities bi activist for the past twenty years. Dr. Marge Charmoli was there, a leader in the fight for Minnesota's 1993 Human Rights Amendment, which was the first such law to include bisexuals and transgender people with gays and lesbians. Her partner was with her, Dr. Anita Kozan (from Chapter 4), a board director of the Bisexual Organizing Project who has made major gains for bisexual visibility on a national stage in her professional speech pathology association. Rich Woulfe, from San Diego, was there. He is involved with the Bisexual Foundation and appears to be Dr. Klein's protégé. He has been very outspoken throughout the weekend about his vision for the direction of the bi movement in the future. And there was Mary Hoelscher, a teacher in Minneapolis and future star in bi activism who soon after this conference was chosen to co-coordinate the Eighth International Conference on Bisexuality.

As we relaxed in the glow of our shared community, and Rich elaborated on his ideas for the future, it struck me that three generations of bi leadership were here. The changes Fritz, who is in his seventies, has seen are no greater than the changes Mary, only twenty-three, will see in her own time. The people at this table have had a hand in defining what it means to be bisexual in America and the shape of the bi community. For some here, their work is largely in the past; for others, the work is just beginning. When Mary assumes leadership, where will she choose to go? The bi community is at a crossroads; I know this to be true because the bi community is always at a crossroads. History will decide if we chose well, and if the community is to have a future, or if we are to be remembered at all. All of which was too heady for a Sunday morning, so instead I chose to enjoy the all-you-can-eat breakfast buffet and the company of old friends.

Appendix A

The Survey

In the summer of 2002, I published a survey on the Internet as part of the online support group. The Web site gave information about this forthcoming book and asked the viewer to help by taking the survey and then joining a book advisory group. Ultimately, the book advisory group evolved into the online support group.

To gain participants, I e-mailed every bisexual group listed at the Web site <www.bisexual.org>. This is a very significant detail to keep in mind while perusing the data, because it means the results cannot be assumed to represent bisexual people in general but rather a small subset with some connection to a bi community, if only online. To be sure, they do not in any way represent all those people who may "behave" bisexually. Perhaps more accurate would be that the survey is somewhat representative of the bisexual community as defined in Chapter 4. Still, this too is imperfect, as four in ten respondents do not feel they are part of a bisexual community.

Also important to remember is that those people who are active on the Internet may not represent the other half of the population who are not. In 2004, a significant portion of the population was still not online, and these people were therefore missed. Also, participants in the survey were self-selected, and it cannot be assumed people who are willing to help out by wending their way through a Web site and a survey are representative of the general population.

All totaled, 270 people—151 women, 114 men, and five people who chose "other" for their sex—participated in the survey. Of those, about ninety people chose at one time or another to join the online support group. Perhaps, then, it can be surmised the survey data are most representative of the support group, a group seen earlier to be thoughtful, articulate, often isolated, sometimes closeted, sometimes not, if not fully involved in the bi politics of the day at least generally aware of the shape of the community and its relationship to the greater society.

SURVEY RESULTS

TABLE A.1. How old are you?

Age (years)	Total % (n = 268)	Women % (n = 151)	Men % (n = 112)	Other % (n = 5)
<18	1	1	1	0
18-20	3	5	1	0
21-30	35	50	14	40
31-40	35	32	39	20
41-50	17	11	24	40
51-60	9	2	19	0
61-70	1	0	2	0
>70	0	0	0	0

Note: The average age of the women participants is 30 years old, while the average age for the men is 40 years old.

TABLE A.2. Where do you live?

Area type	Total % (n = 269)	Women % (n = 151)	Men % (n = 113)	Other % (n = 5)
Rural	12	7	16	40
Suburban	43	47	38	40
Urban	45	46	46	20

TABLE A.3. What is your income?

Income	Total % (n = 262)	Women % (n = 145)	Men % (n = 112)	Other % (n = 5)
<$10,000	15	18	9	60
$10,000-20,000	10	17	1	0
$20,000-30,000	16	17	16	20
$30,000-40,000	18	19	16	0
$40,000-50,000	13	12	13	0
$50,000-75,000	13	8	21	0
$75,000-100,000	11	6	18	20
>$100,000	4	3	6	0

TABLE A.4. What is your education?

Education level	Total % (n = 269)	Women % (n = 151)	Men % (n = 113)	Other % (n = 5)
Did not graduate from high school	2	2	1	20
High school graduate	7	7	7	0
Some college	39	39	39	20
Bachelor's degree	30	30	31	40
Advanced degree	22	23	22	20

TABLE A.5. Are you transgender?

Response	Total % (n = 268)	Women % (n = 150)	Men % (n = 113)	Other % (n = 5)
Yes	4	2	4	80
No	96	98	96	20

Note: Here some in the survey identify their sex as either male or female but also identify as transgender.

TABLE A.6. Do you identify as "queer"?

Response	Total % (n = 270)	Women % (n = 151)	Men % (n = 114)	Other % (n = 5)
Yes	47	54	37	80
No	53	46	63	20

Note: 50 percent of those 30 and younger identify as queer, while 45 percent for those 31 and older identify as queer. Therefore, adoption of the label "queer" in this survey is more gender based than generation based.

TABLE A.7. Whom are you more *visually* attracted to?

Gender	Total % (n = 270)	Women % (n = 151)	Men % (n = 114)	Other % (n = 5)
(1) Other sex only	0	0	1	0
(2) Primarily other sex	10	3	20	0

TABLE A.7 *(continued)*

(3) More other sex, but some same sex too	28	20	39	20
(4) Both sexes equally	27	34	16	60
(5) More same sex, but other sex too	26	33	18	20
(6) Primarily same sex	9	11	6	0
(7) Exclusively same sex	0	0	0	0

Note: Bi women's average "visual attraction" on a 1 to 7 scale is 4.29, while men's average visual attraction is 3.47. In other words, both the men and the women in the survey were slightly more attracted visually to women.

TABLE A.8. Whom do you enjoy sex with more?

Gender	Total % (n = 185)	Women % (n = 83)	Men % (n = 98)	Other % (n = 4)
(1) Other sex only	3	0	5	0
(2) Primarily other sex	7	10	5	0
(3) More other sex, but some same sex too	32	34	32	0.25
(4) Both sexes equally	32	33	32	0.5
(5) More same sex, but other sex too	18	13	22	0.25
(6) Primarily same sex	6	11	3	0
(7) Exclusively same sex	1	0	1	0

Note: On a 1 to 7 scale, bi women's average for "enjoyment of sex" is 3.82, while bi men's is 3.74, meaning both enjoy sex slightly more with the other sex than the same sex.

TABLE A.9. Whom do you fantasize about more?

Gender	Total % (n = 197)	Women % (n = 106)	Men % (n = 87)	Other % (n = 4)
(1) Other sex only	1	2	0	0
(2) Primarily other sex	7	8	7	0
(3) More other sex, but some same sex too	27	23	33	0.25

TABLE A.9 *(continued)*

(4) Both sexes equally	28	27	28	0.5
(5) More same sex, but other sex too	19	21	16	0.25
(6) Primarily same sex	15	17	14	0
(7) Exclusively same sex	3	3	2	0

Note: On a 1 to 7 scale, bi women's average for "fantasies" is 4.20, while bi men's is 4.03, meaning bi women fantasize slightly more about women, and bi men fantasize about men and women equally.

TABLE A.10. Whom are you more interested in romantically?

Gender	Total % (n = 194)	Women % (n = 91)	Men % (n = 99)	Other % (n = 4)
(1) Other sex only	11	0	21	0
(2) Primarily other sex	19	10	27	0
(3) More other sex, but some same sex too	19	19	18	0.25
(4) Both sexes equally	28	41	15	0.5
(5) More same sex, but other sex too	14	18	11	0.25
(6) Primarily same sex	8	11	6	0
(7) Exclusively same sex	2	2	1	0

Note: On a 1 to 7 scale, bi women's average for "romantic interest" is 4.08, while bi men's is 2.90, meaning bi women are equally romantically interested in women and men, while bi men are significantly more romantically interested in women.

TABLE A.11. How long have you identified the way you do now?

Years	Total % (n = 265)	Women % (n = 148)	Men % (n = 112)	Other % (n = 5)
<1	4	3	4	0
1-2	9	10	7	0
2-4	16	19	12	40
4-6	14	17	11	0

TABLE A.11 *(continued)*

6-10	20	22	18	0
10-15	14	13	14	20
15-20	8	7	9	0
20-25	7	3	12	20
>25	9	5	13	20

Note: Participants have identified as bisexual for an average of 10.3 years.

TABLE A.12. How did you identify your orientation before you began identifying as you do now?

Orientation	Total % (n = 264)	Women % (n = 147)	Men % (n = 112)	Other % (n = 5)
Asexual	4	5	2	0
Bisexual	8	5	10	20
Straight	81	81	82	60
Gay/lesbian	8	8	6	20

TABLE A.13. How comfortable are you with your orientation?

Comfort level	Total % (n = 187)	Women % (n = 89)	Men % (n = 95)	Other % (n = 3)
Very comfortable	52	57	46	100
Mostly comfortable	30	27	34	0
So-so	14	15	14	0
Mostly uncomfortable	3	1	5	0
Very uncomfortable	1	0	1	0

Note: Both bi men and bi women in the survey tended to be very or mostly comfortable with their bisexual identity, with a combined total of 82 percent.

TABLE A.14. In the past year, how many women have you had sex with?

Number of women	Total % (n = 172)	Women % (n = 85)	Men % (n = 83)	Other % (n = 4)
0	30	35	24	50
1	35	34	39	0
2	15	15	16	0
3	6	5	6	25
4	4	5	4	0
5	5	4	6	0
6-10	3	2	5	0
11-15	0	0	0	0
16-20	0	0	0	0
21-30	1	0	1	25

Note: Bi women had sex with an average of 1.3 women in the past year, while bi men on average had sex with 1.9 women.

TABLE A.15. In the past year, how many men have you had sex with?

Number of men	Total % (n = 173)	Women % (n = 84)	Men % (n = 85)	Other % (n = 4)
0	21	17	26	25
1	24	31	15	50
2	14	19	9	0
3	11	11	12	0
4	4	6	2	0
5	5	7	2	0
6-10	11	7	15	0
11-15	2	1	4	0
16-20	2	0	5	0
21-30	3	1	4	25
31-40	1	0	1	0
41-50	1	0	1	0
51-75	1	0	1	0
76-100	1	0	1	0
100-500	1	0	1	0

Note: Bi women had sex with an average of 2.6 men in the past year, while bi men on average had sex with 10.6 men.

TABLE A.16. In the past year, how many times have you had sex with someone who doesn't identify as a woman or a man?

Number of times	Total % (n = 173)	Women % (n = 67)	Men % (n = 85)	Other % (n = 4)
0	94	98	93	25
1	5	2	7	0
2	0	0	0	0
3	1	0	0	50
4	1	0	0	25

TABLE A.17. In the past five years, how many women have you had sex with?

Number of women	Total % (n = 174)	Women % (n = 84)	Men % (n = 86)	Other % (n = 4)
0	16	17	14	25
1	28	23	34	25
2	11	18	3	25
3	11	15	7	0
4	6	10	3	0
5	6	6	6	0
6-10	11	10	14	0
11-15	4	1	7	0
16-20	2	1	2	0
21-30	2	0	3	0
31-40	1	0	2	0
41-50	1	0	1	0
51-100	0	0	0	0
>100	2	0	2	25

Note: Bi women had sex with an average of 2.6 women in the past five years, while bi men on average had sex with 10.6 women.

TABLE A.18. In the past five years, how many men have you had sex with?

Number of men	Total % (n = 172)	Women % (n = 83)	Men % (n = 85)	Other % (n = 4)
0	15	11	20	0
1	18	23	12	50
2	9	13	5	25
3	10	8	12	0
4	4	5	4	0
5	9	16	4	0
6-10	13	14	12	0
11-15	5	2	7	0
16-20	7	4	11	0
21-30	5	2	8	0
31-40	1	0	1	0
41-50	1	1	1	0
51-75	1	0	1	0
76-100	1	0	1	0
100-500	1	0	1	25
>500	1	0	1	0

Note: Bi women had sex with an average of 5 men in the past five years, while bi men on average had sex with 20 men.

TABLE A.19. In the past five years, how may times have you had sex with someone who doesn't identify as a woman or a man?

Number of times	Total % (n = 172)	Women % (n = 83)	Men % (n = 85)	Other % (n = 4)
0	87	89	88	25
1	6	6	7	0
2	2	1	2	0
3	2	2	0	25
4	0	0	0	0
5	1	1	0	0
6-10	2	0	1	50

TABLE A.19 *(continued)*

11-15	0	0	0	0
16-20	0	0	0	0
21-30	1	0	1	0

TABLE A.20. When did you first have sex with a woman?

Age (years)	Total % (n = 149)	Women % (n = 73)	Men % (n = 75)	Other % (n = 1)
<18	19	8	29	0
18-20	34	27	40	100
20-25	27	36	19	0
25-30	11	15	8	0
30-35	3	4	1	0
35-40	1	3	0	0
40-45	4	7	1	0
45-50	1	0	1	0

Note: The average age the bi women in the survey first had sex with another woman was at 24, while the bi men in the survey first had sex with a woman at age 20.

TABLE A.21. How many women have you had sex with?

Number of women	Total % (n = 162)	Women % (n = 81)	Men % (n = 79)	Other % (n = 2)
0	10	15	4	50
1	13	12	14	0
2-5	33	46	20	0
6-10	20	20	19	50
11-20	11	6	16	0
21-50	6	1	11	0
51-100	3	0	6	0
>100	4	0	9	0

Note: On average, bi women in the survey have had sex with 5 women. Although the men have had sex with an average of 27 women, the average drops quickly if one removes the top twelve individuals who have had sex with 50 or more. Indeed, the mode is the same for male and female participants, with 2 to 5 female partners.

TABLE A.22. How many women have you ever been "in love" with?

Number of women	Total % (n = 170)	Women % (n = 82)	Men % (n = 85)	Other % (n = 3)
0	12	20	5	33
1	24	28	20	0
2-5	54	48	60	33
5-10	9	5	14	0
>10	1	0	1	33

Note: 81 percent of bi women have been "in love" with another woman.

TABLE A.23. When did you first have sex with a man?

Age (years)	Total % (n = 160)	Women % (n = 75)	Men % (n = 83)	Other % (n = 2)
<18	17	21	13	0
18-20	34	45	23	50
20-25	22	21	23	0
25-30	13	8	18	0
30-35	5	1	8	0
35-40	4	3	6	0
40-45	4	0	7	0
45-50	1	0	0	50
>50	1	0	1	0

Note: On average, women first had sex with a man at age 20, while men first had sex with a man at age 25.

TABLE A.24. How many men have you had sex with?

Number of men	Total % (n = 173)	Women % (n = 79)	Men % (n = 90)	Other % (n = 4)
0	9	8	10	0
1	10	13	7	50
2-5	24	24	26	0
6-10	13	22	7	0

TABLE A.24 *(continued)*

11-20	17	19	16	0
21-50	17	11	21	25
51-100	5	4	7	0

Note: Bi women in the survey have on average had 12 male sex partners in their lives, while bi men have had 28.

TABLE A.25. How many men have you ever been "in love" with?

Number of men	Total % (n = 169)	Women % (n = 79)	Men % (n = 88)	Other % (n = 2)
0	34	11	56	0
1	21	20	20	50
2-5	40	59	23	50
5-10	5	9	1	0

Note: 44 percent of men have been "in love" with another man.

TABLE A.26. Do you have someone you consider yourself in an intimate partner relationship with?

Response	Total % (n = 169)	Women % (n = 74)	Men % (n = 91)	Other % (n = 4)
Yes	65	68	63	75
No	35	32	37	25

TABLE A.27. How many intimate-partner relationships do you currently have?

Number of relationships	Total % (n = 120)	Women % (n = 53)	Men % (n = 64)	Other % (n = 3)
1	64	70	61	33
2	21	19	23	0
3	8	6	8	33
4	2	2	2	0
5	1	0	2	0
>5	5	4	5	33

Note: 30 percent of bi women and 39 percent of bi men have more than one intimate-partner relationship.

TABLE A.28. What is the gender of the first or primary partner?

Gender	Total % (n = 136)	Women % (n = 63)	Men % (n = 70)	Other % (n = 3)
Female	57	17	91	67
Male	43	83	7	33
Transgender/intersex	1	0	1	0

Note: When this is triangulated with the partner's orientation (see question 30), 55 percent of bi men's first or primary partners are a straight woman, while 47 percent of bi women's are a straight man; 23 percent of the men's first or primary relationships are with a bi woman, and 18 percent of the women's are with a bi man.

TABLE A.29. How long have you been with this partner?

Number of years	Total % (n = 131)	Women % (n = 61)	Men % (n = 67)	Other % (n = 3)
<1	8	13	3	0
1-2	16	16	16	0
2-3	11	10	12	0
3-5	11	11	10	0
5-10	21	28	13	67
10-20	22	18	27	0
>20	11	3	18	33

TABLE A.30. What is the orientation of this partner?

Orientation	Total % (n = 120)	Women % (n = 55)	Men % (n = 62)	Other % (n = 3)
Straight	57	56	58	33
Bisexual	37	31	40	67
Lesbian/gay	6	13	0	0

TABLE A.31. Are you legally married to or had a commitment ceremony with this partner?

Response	Total % (n = 123)	Women % (n = 56)	Men % (n = 64)	Other % (n = 3)
Yes	52	38	64	67
No	48	63	36	33

TABLE A.32. Do you consider yourself polyamorous?

Response	Total % (n = 114)	Women % (n = 51)	Men % (n = 59)	Other % (n = 4)
Yes	68	61	73	100
No	32	39	27	0

TABLE A.33. Are you monogamous within the above relationship(s)?

Response	Total % (n = 115)	Women % (n = 56)	Men % (n = 56)	Other % (n = 3)
Yes	29	29	30	0
No	71	71	70	100

TABLE A.34. If you are not monogamous, do your partners know?

Response	Total % (n = 82)	Women % (n = 39)	Men % (n = 39)	Other % (n = 3)
Yes	76	90	62	100
No	12	8	18	0
Some do	12	3	23	0

TABLE A.35. Who are you usually sexual with outside of relationships?

Gender(s)	Total % (n = 160)	Women % (n = 72)	Men % (n = 84)	Other % (n = 4)
Women	24	31	20	0
Men	30	21	39	0
Both men and women the same	34	43	29	0

TABLE A.35 *(continued)*

Transgender people	2	0	1	50
Transgender and women the same	1	1	1	0
Men and transgender the same	1	0	2	0
Men, women, and transgender the same	7	4	7	50

TABLE A.36. Where do you meet partners to be sexual with?

Place	Total % (n = 168)	Women % (n = 81)	Men % (n = 83)	Other % (n = 3)
Friends, work, relatives, church	70	86	52	100
Sex/swinger parties	18	10	27	0
Bi or poly community events	37	44	29	67
Cruising for sex	13	2	23	0
Prostitutes	2	1	4	0
Internet	24	15	33	33
Pagan community	2	1	1	33
Sci-fi conventions	2	1	2	0
Queer spaces	1	1	0	0
BDSM community events	1	2	0	0
Bars	7	7	7	0
Other	6	2	12	0

TABLE A.37. Have you ever attended a bi event, support group, dance, etc., and if so, how many?

Number of events	Total % (n = 196)	Women % (n = 92)	Men % (n = 100)	Other % (n = 4)
0	35	28	42	25
1	12	15	9	0
2-5	20	22	18	25
5-10	5	9	1	0
>10	29	26	30	50

TABLE A.38. How many bisexual people do you know personally?

Number of bisexual people	Total % (n = 179)	Women % (n = 81)	Men % (n = 94)	Other % (n = 4)
0	6	1	11	0
1	8	6	10	0
2	6	6	6	0
3-5	24	25	23	25
6-10	16	21	13	0
10-20	15	20	10	25
>20	25	21	28	50

TABLE A.39. Do you know of a bisexual group in your town?

Response	Total % (n = 173)	Women % (n = 79)	Men % (n = 90)	Other % (n = 4)
Yes	64	59	68	75
No	36	41	32	25

TABLE A.40. What community do you *most* feel a part of?

Community	Total % (n = 186)	Women % (n = 84)	Men % (n = 98)	Other % (n = 4)
Straight	38	35	42	0
Bisexual	51	55	48	25
Lesbian	3	7	0	0
Gay	6	4	8	0
Transgender	3	0	2	75

TABLE A.41. Do you feel part of a bi community?

Response	Total % (n = 199)	Women % (n = 95)	Men % (n = 100)	Other % (n = 4)
Yes	61	62	59	75
No	39	38	41	25

TABLE A.42. What has been your experience with the bi community?

Experience	Total % (n = 126)	Women % (n = 65)	Men % (n = 57)	Other % (n = 4)
Welcoming/accepting	79	75	86	50
Only fair	18	23	11	50
Not welcoming/accepting	2	2	4	0

TABLE A.43. What has been your experience with the straight community?

Experience	Total % (n = 159)	Women % (n = 79)	Men % (n = 85)	Other % (n = 4)
Welcoming/accepting	58	59	52	25
Only fair	37	41	29	50
Not welcoming/accepting	5	0	8	25

TABLE A.44. What has been your experience with the transgender community?

Experience	Total % (n = 65)	Women % (n = 31)	Men % (n = 30)	Other % (n = 4)
Welcoming/accepting	75	94	63	25
Only fair	8	3	10	25
Not welcoming/accepting	17	3	27	50

TABLE A.45. What has been your experience with the lesbian community?

Experience	Total % (n = 122)	Women % (n = 67)	Men % (n = 51)	Other % (n = 4)
Welcoming/accepting	26	25	29	0
Only fair	40	40	39	50
Not welcoming/accepting	34	34	31	50

TABLE A.46. What has been your experience with the gay male community?

Experience	Total % (n = 137)	Women % (n = 59)	Men % (n = 75)	Other % (n = 3)
Welcoming/accepting	59	59	60	33
Only fair	31	29	31	67
Not welcoming/accepting	10	12	9	0

Appendix B

The Bisexual History Project

The bisexual community seems to be disappearing. Not that there won't always be people around who like to have sex with people of all genders, the community, as I've discussed in this book, is a different matter altogether. With this in mind, at the BECAUSE conference in 2000, I started the Bisexual History Project—a big name for a small effort to record for posterity the history of the community and its printed materials, and, most important, the everyday voices of those who make up this interesting group of people. With the help of Sean Kinlin on camera and Mark Schuller doing the interviews (and eventually Dawn Pankonien transcribing the tapes), we were able to film and document the stories of fourteen people. Twelve individuals' stories are printed in their entirety, as no efforts were made to edit out the conversational tone or limit the discussion in any way. The entire project is available at the Minnesota History Center's GLBT collection.

I think what you will find as you read these stories is a group of people who, be they a witch or into leather or transgender, are merely going through life like everyone else, trying to gain some meaning and perhaps even contentment along the way. In that way, you are assured of finding here twelve people just like any other twelve people. One difference you will find, however, is these are twelve people who were willing to bare themselves in front of a camera and reveal their personal struggles with sexuality in an effort to let people in the future know what it meant to be bisexual in America in 2000. In that way, these are twelve highly unusual people.

SCOTT

SCOTT: Well, I'm Scott Bartell. I'm fifty-one. I live in Minneapolis and work there, and I have identified as bisexual since I was fifteen; but probably I was aware of it—without a name—for all of my life.

INTERVIEWER: Are there other important aspects of your identity, and how do they relate to your bisexuality?

SCOTT: There's a lot of levels to that question. Within the current GLBT community I also identify as transgender. I think that does tie in, very much, for me. I'm also a polyamorous pagan, and those tie in and seem to be part of the community spectrum at the moment, for which I'm glad. I'm a writer, therapist, a lot of other stuff that's part of identity. But back to bisexuality, they all fit in with it; they don't feel incongruent.

INTERVIEWER: How has being bisexual changed your life?

SCOTT: Well, since it never was different, it hasn't changed my life, but I think being bisexual in this culture is a gift and a curse. It gives you—it gives me—a certain flexibility of thinking, and I don't know that it does that same thing for everyone, but I think it's forced me to work outside the box in many ways. And then, of course, that makes things a little more difficult sometimes. I've been married and divorced and had many different relationships both with men and women. I'm in one right now, and I think it's been harder to get kind of overall community support for relationships that include and recognize bisexuality.

INTERVIEWER: You mention community. Do you feel connected to a bisexual community? And describe what that community looks like.

SCOTT: Well, very much so, because I came out publicly—I mean, most of my friends knew, but my parents didn't—when I was twenty-five. And that was in the city newspaper here. In the course of an interview that wasn't focused on that, but it was just natural to me, and then I realized, whoops! I just put it as clearly and finely as I could. And that was okay with me, but I, from that moment on, realized that if I didn't want to be alone I had to do a lot to find and create community, and so I've been working on that ever since. I did the first bisexual support group in the Twin Cities in 1975. And it's kind of gone on from there. I helped build the Men's Center; I was one of the first board. And they do a lot to help bisexual people find community. I'm working with the Bisexual Organizing Project now, and I think I've been at all of the BECAUSEs except one, presenting at most of them. And I work a lot with bisexual people in my practice as a therapist. So I try to do what I can to build community.

INTERVIEWER: You've been around for a while; you've been a leader in the movement for a while. So how have things changed over the years?

SCOTT: I know a lot more people who are bi than I did before. That's been one of the greatest things. I mean, what BECAUSE is now is wonderful and due to many, many other people who, if this hadn't happened, I wouldn't have known probably. And I do get the feeling in the Twin Cities these days that saying you're bi doesn't bring on immediate raised eyebrows and disapproval—at least in any of the parts of the world I travel through, whereas twenty-five years ago it often raised questions.

INTERVIEWER: Describe an ideal situation. What should the bisexual community be all about?

SCOTT: Well, that's a tough one. I mean, I guess it's nice to operate from a vision, and I guess I have a vision of if a kid, on finding out that they were bisexual thought, "Oh, okay, cool, and I know who to call and who to talk to, and if I say that at school it's not going to cause a problem for me." That's where I think it ought to start. And I don't think it's quite at that point yet. I think it's moving toward it, better than it was when I was fifteen or younger, but that's where it ought to start. There ought to be publicly identified space and place, and reputation or mythos other than just an AIDS carrier infecting the unsuspecting world.

INTERVIEWER: What do you see as the challenges, other than the educational institution? What are the challenges that lie ahead for us?

SCOTT: Well, I think there's still a lot of entrenched turf thinking on portions, like of the gay or the lesbian community. And certainly in the straight world, people that want to have theirs be the best and nobody else, and bisexuals get kicked around in that equation a fair amount. What else? This is such a default monogamy culture that assumes you can only have one partner so you better only have one interest and that's one of the sticking points. I know that politicians have been using that one the last year or two to push for legislation that tightens up a lot of things for fear that bisexuals will get more freedom or recognition or something like that. They use us as the boogey man a lot of the time.

INTERVIEWER: Do you have any other things you'd like to say to the history project?

SCOTT: Well, here in the Twin Cities there is a GLBT history project going on. I don't know if you're allied with it or know about it. There is an overall umbrella thing being led by Leo Treadway to compile a better history of the whole GLBT community in Minnesota working in combination with the Minnesota Historical Society. So I'm hoping this will link into and be used as part of it. Thanks for doing it.

MAGENTA

MAGENTA: My name is Magenta. I've probably identified as bi since I first heard the word; I don't remember how long ago it was. I realized in my early teens I was attracted to both women and men, and it was very confusing because I didn't even know what it meant to be attracted to women. I read some novels of Collette and immediately asked my mother if I could go away to boarding school, which she didn't know what that was about. And then I found a psychopathology book and read the chapter on homosexuality and said, "Oh, I guess that's what I am." And that kind of scared me. And I couldn't understand why, well, I'm attracted to women, but I'm also attracted to men, and it was several years later before I found the term bisexual and thought, "Okay, there's a word for it; I'm not the only one; I'm not completely sick and twisted."

INTERVIEWER: Tell me more about that—realizing you weren't the only one. Was that opening doors for you?

MAGENTA: It did in some ways. I'm in my forties and I started to explore my sexuality before Stonewall. And the first gay bar I went to was like this storefront with totally black windows, and you didn't know it was there unless someone took you there, and it was really kind of scary. And I kind of retreated into heterosexuality for a few years. Got married and divorced very young, discovered polyamory and realized I'm also not monogamous, that that was something that's not going to work for me. And then discovered the women's coffeehouse. I'd moved to Minneapolis at that point—that was mid-seventies—and I started going to women's coffeehouse, but I wasn't quite correct to be a lesbian. I had long hair—I've always had long hair. I'm a witch. And one of my teachers said witches don't cut their hair. Which is not true, but I've always had long hair and I really like long hair. And I like long hair on other people—I really admire your hair; it's beautiful. So I wasn't going to cut my hair to be a lesbian, and I got a lot of grief over that. And I didn't have any plaid flannel shirts, and I didn't really want to wear plaid flannel shirts, and for all kinds of other reasons I didn't seem to fit into the mold of being a lesbian. And I really had no respect for bisexuals. It was like, "Oh, you're just sitting on the fence, or you're just immature, and you'll be a lesbian," and it made me feel really bad. And so I hung out in the lesbian community for a couple of years, and then I drifted away, and it's only relatively recently in the nineties that I really came back to identifying with bisexuality even though I knew that's what I was.

INTERVIEWER: Do you feel connected to a bisexual community, and if so, what does that look like?

MAGENTA: Not really. I've been very, very active in the pagan and Wicca community in Minneapolis. I'm actually one of the leaders, one of the people who founded a lot of things, and my primary identity has always been as a witch; my sexuality has always been in the context of my sacred spirituality. And my sacred sexuality. And it's only relatively recently that there've been organizations I've felt comfortable with that recognize bisexuality is a possibility, that polyamory is a possibility, that didn't have these hard lined agendas the lesbian community I was in contact with in the seventies and early eighties had. This is the first BECAUSE Conference I've been at.

INTERVIEWER: What made you decide to come here?

MAGENTA: A friend of mine twisted my arm. Not very hard, obviously. But I know somebody who was here last year and really liked it and said, "Oh, you've got to come this year." So here I am. I'm really enjoying it. I really feel comfortable.

INTERVIEWER: Describe an ideal situation. What would the bisexual community or movement be all about?

MAGENTA: In some ways I'd like to see a world where it isn't necessary, where sexuality is no more of an issue than anything else. It should be less of an issue than food preference. I know people get in fights about whether they're vegetarian or not or vegan or whatever, and I'm sure for a long time there will be that same sort of stuff around sexuality. But it shouldn't be something where someone realizes when they're thirteen or fourteen or fifteen that they're attracted to the opposite sex or the same sex or both sexes or either sex or whatever that they say, "Oh, that's a new part of me that I've discovered," and that they wouldn't be scared and they wouldn't need a specific group more than any other thirteen- or fourteen- or fifteen-year-old—I mean, at that age you really need support groups anyway. I'd like to see something where sexuality isn't such a determining factor, people don't have these assumptions and prejudices and baggage.

INTERVIEWER: Anything you want to say to history?

MAGENTA: Hi, history! One thing I see is I think we need to build bridges. I think we need to build bridges. The bisexual community—fortunately it's now lesbian, gay, bisexual, transgender, and it wasn't for a long time. And I think there're also links between other communities like the pagan community and the leather community, other communities of people who are made to feel different now and whose difference is in who they are, not in the fact that they do anything that is primarily "bad." I mean, of course my values are such that I consider doing full moon rituals and loving women and a lot of these other things to be who I am and who many of my friends are, and the people who say that we're wrong or we're immoral and there should be laws against people like us, are themselves the ones who are wrong. But I think we need to form broader alliances if we are to bring into being a world where we can be ourselves. Thank you for doing this.

CAREY

CAREY: My name is Carey. I grew up in Rochester, Minnesota, and I live in Minneapolis and have for quite awhile, in Powderhorn. I think I identified as bisexual since I was about twelve, and I think understanding and accepting myself as bisexual came as part of understanding and accepting myself as female. When I was twelve I ran away from home for a weekend—and it ended up being for a week—I didn't want to run away from home forever, but when I was twelve it was going to be this, "I'll show you; I'll go away and do something else for awhile," you know. And so I ran up—I had a cousin who was living up here, and she had been someone I had really enjoyed having contact with, and she's given me a copy of *Our Bodies, Ourselves,* so I'd been reading that since I was eight. And she had told me, well, if you ever want to come visit, go ahead. So I hopped on a bus and came up from Rochester to Minneapolis, knew enough to get off at the airport rather than going downtown, and showed up on a Saturday morning and said, "Here I am; come get me." And so, she came out to me as a lesbian in the car when she came to pick me up. And I ended up spending the whole week here just being immersed in basically working-class, lesbian culture—urban culture—big switch. And it was actually a huge growth experience for me in a lot of ways; you know, considering that I was the scapegoat of my family and everything that I did was wrong, it was good place for me to stay sane about a lot of things. But it also helped me decide, well, you know, Beth, my cousin Beth, this big dyke, could be a woman, then I could be a female, too, because I grew up feeling like female was something I didn't want to be because I didn't like how women were treated in society. I didn't necessarily want to be male, but I didn't like how women were treated and I didn't like a lot of things about a lot of the girls I knew.

INTERVIEWER: So being bisexual really opened up being a woman in a different way.

CAREY: It was a kind of joint opening one might say. The irony of that story, if anybody's heard this before, is that that cousin who opened me up to the possibility of being female is now male and identifies as a transgendered male. So, what does that make me? That's the big question.

INTERVIEWER: Are there other identities that seem to be important?

CAREY: It's not so much centrally now, but I think now it's more about kind of breaking down the gender barriers. I do identify as transgendered, transgressively gendered in the Kate Bornstein kind of sense [a transgender writer and author of several books including *Gender Outlaw: On Men, Women, and the Rest of Us*]. I'm also pagan. I'm also a feminist. Those things are crucial.

INTERVIEWER: How has being bisexual changed your worldview, your look on life?

CAREY: I think that it helps flavor, kind of, my view about everything. I think it can lend itself to not seeing the world in such either/or kind of terms and thinking about transcendent third or fourth or sixth options, you know, that are out there.

INTERVIEWER: Do you feel connected to a bisexual community?

CAREY: I do, in a sense, feel connected to a bisexual community. I feel connected to people here. I haven't been as active in the bisexual community recently; I used to be very involved. I helped organize BECAUSE for several years. I've been very involved in the Bi Women and Friends group. Even though that hasn't been my focus lately, it's still home to me; it's kind of like I've gone off into other things, but this is still the place I come back to, and it's not quite as much about bisexuality per se but it's about people who are really open to different things and have a different view of the world than mainstream culture, people who tend to be active and present and caring.

INTERVIEWER: So a big part of the community you see is a support network where you can feel comfortable with who you are?

CAREY: It's partly that, but it's also about—it's a place to feel normal, but it's also a place to feel connected with other people who—to feel responsibility for what goes on in the world, you know, whether we agree or disagree about specifics of how it should be, it's people who feel concerned and connected to what's going on in the world and feel like it's important to be an active participant in the world.

INTERVIEWER: Is there a bisexual movement?

CAREY: Oh, I think there are many bisexual movements, and actually think that—I really enjoy how I see the bi and transgender movement together. I think that we have, kind of—I think that one of the things I'm really proud of, actually, is here in the Twin Cities and Minnesota that the bi-trans movement has really been pretty cohesive compared to a lot of other parts of the country, and that, you know, we'll come out sisters and brothers, and our gender flows through in a lot of ways. So yeah, I think there is a movement, and I think it's infiltrating kind of a lot of other movements.

INTERVIEWER: Describe an ideal situation—or what should a bi and trans community be all about?

CAREY: Umm, taking over the world. [laugh] I think it's about, you know, people being able to be who they are and respecting people for who they are and about creating an end to all kinds of oppression. I think that's crucial. I think, you know, gender and sexuality oppression are just more of many, many pieces of oppression, and I think it's important to force us to be allies with other people in their struggles against oppression.

INTERVIEWER: What other challenges lie ahead for us?

CAREY: I think that it's seeing ourselves as part of the Earth in that way, you know, connecting with the living, breathing organism. That is our planet and I think when we feel that connection—maybe we need to find that boundary between ourselves—before we feel that resolve. Or maybe we need to develop boundaries with the Earth. Or maybe it's kind of just a synergistic kind of a thing.

INTERVIEWER: Anything you want to put down for history?

CAREY: It's happening, you know; it's happening. I'm actually just reading about the French Revolution—Marge Piercy's fictional account of it [*City of Darkness City of Light* (Fawcett Books, 1997)] and it's so rare that I think of history as being about people and their connection and their community, and it's not just a kind of made up persona kind of thing, it's real people doing the work. And so we're here, and we're doing it, and this is real.

BRIAN

BRIAN: I'm Brian. I'm your stereotypical, polyamorous, bisexual, pagan from St. Paul, Minnesota. I kind of do that—a lot of times everyone's so hung up on labeling things, I find if I hit people with four or five labels at one time, no one's able to define more than two of them anyway, so . . .

INTERVIEWER: Could you give them again? You did it kind of quickly.

BRIAN: Bisexual, polyamorous, solitary, eclectic figure—that all fits together. I mean, pagan is a broad general heading. If you ask ten different pagans how to define it, you'll get twelve different definitions. For solitary eclectic it's really just—I don't follow any one written tradition. I have kind of assembled my own religion over the years through my own experience and things I've found that communicate to me.

INTERVIEWER: How does that relate to your identity as a bisexual?

BRIAN: Well, see, I don't have a separate identity as a bisexual and as a pagan. I identify who I am, and who I am is always going to mix together. There's really no way to separate them out.

INTERVIEWER: Do you think you see things differently than someone who is not all the things that you are?

BRIAN: I think I probably have a rather unique worldview; I probably see things differently from anyone else. When it gets to certain topics I can relate to different people on different levels. There are some issues that if I know someone is bisexual, I know at least we'll have a similar angle to it, a similar viewpoint to it.

INTERVIEWER: Do you remember the first time you realized you were bisexual?

BRIAN: Well, everybody always asks the question. For me I had my first serious relationship with a girl when I was fourteen and got involved with a guy less than a year later. And for me it wasn't really realizing I was bisexual, it was realizing that at some point I had been expected to choose. But by the time I realized that everyone else wasn't bisexual, it was too late for me.

INTERVIEWER: Do you feel connected to a bisexual community?

BRIAN: I'm aware there's a community out there. I don't really feel I'm very connected to it. This is my fourth year at the BECAUSE conference, and it's like I run into people here and there, but I'm pretty much overwhelmed just dealing with my day-to-day life and I don't have enough time to participate on any particular level. I think the main thing is—of course, to give out information on different things—but the main thing is really just a place where I can be open about everything and socialize. And that is one thing I find unique with the bi community; it is more encompassing, more allowing of a lot of different things, because I found that, even with the other groups I've tried to participate in, that, well, when I've been around groups with gay men, that, it's like, I kind of have to keep bisexuality undercover. It's like it's okay for them to have sex with me, but they don't want their friends to know I'm bi. And with different groups I have to keep different things undercover, and it really just seems like the bisexuals are the only ones that are really willing to accept everything and willing to accept the polyamory and the pagan—all of it in one place.

INTERVIEWER: You said you don't have time to go to groups and lots of functions. Do you feel connected to any community?

BRIAN: Well, I feel I'm holding threads to things, mostly. The Internet has been nice. At least I can keep connected to a lot of different people that way. But I'm an at-home dad; I have a full-time job raising a ten-year-old and taking care of two teenagers, and my part-time job's taking care of another woman's toddler. And whenever it happens that I'm not watching kids, I have to go out and try to make money as a handyman. So I'm pretty well filled up.

INTERVIEWER: What's the ideal situation for you? What should a bisexual community be all about?

BRIAN: I think ideally it would just be nice if people could be open about things and if society in general wasn't so judgmental about things. I think it's sad we have to have all of these isolated fringe communities, and I really wish people would just get over the idea of their, you know, women's rights and blacks' rights and gay rights, and you know, the real issue is just human rights. Why can't we just treat everyone equally? You know, I think it just really comes down to psychology, and people always have this hang up and have to divide everything into us and them. Well, I think bisexuality is—just by the nature that it's so hard to define—has forced the community to be more inclusive.

INTERVIEWER: Is there anything else you'd like to add?

BRIAN: I don't have any specific things. One of the things I do think just seems to always get lost is the idea that everybody's also part of families. Another thing I found unique about BECAUSE is you're actually seeing children here—people bring their kids. Last year my teenage daughter and her girlfriend helped me host a workshop here—I'd like to see more of that. The communities have to involve the families. You're not dealing with individual people because you have got to deal with the people they live with too.

ALIX

ALIX: My name is Alix. I identify as a transgendered man, F to M and bisexual. I was actually married in my twenties, had a son, came out as a lesbian for twenty years, came out as a transgender a couple years ago, am in transition right now, just had chest surgery last year, hormones for a month, so I'm brand new. I realized I was bisexual last year when I started meeting the trans community, some of the trans men, and realized I had an attraction for both, M to F and F to M. So it's been probably less than a year that I've had that.

INTERVIEWER: How has that awareness changed you?

ALIX: Actually it's offered me a whole new community to network with because I was not even aware of the bi community, so that's been pretty exciting.

INTERVIEWER: What do you think about this new bi community?

ALIX: I think that they're pretty much the leaders; I think that their thinking and the action they take and how they embrace the community is pretty phenomenal, pretty impressive.

INTERVIEWER: Do you feel connected to a bisexual community?

ALIX: I'm starting to feel connected. I know quite a few trans men who are bi and am meeting some M to Fs who are bi, and they've always been very welcoming, and I haven't done too many things, but I probably will do more and more.

INTERVIEWER: What brought you to the conference?

ALIX: This is my first year. I just thought it would be another support system for me and I was really interested in the topics and the willingness to really go out there and think about things that are out of line for a lot of people.

INTERVIEWER: Do you feel like you're in a movement?

ALIX: Oh, yeah, absolutely. Like I said before, I'm just aware of it, so I don't know if I can really say much about it. It's exciting that other people are thinking and pushing the envelope because I don't think we have enough of that. We need people to push the envelope, people that are willing to do it out in the open.

INTERVIEWER: "Pushing the envelope"—what does that do for you?

ALIX: For me? It gives me permission to be who I am completely, and it also helps me to make connections with other people who have some depth.

INTERVIEWER: What do you think is the ideal situation for how you relate to the world?

ALIX: I don't know. I think the bi community should just keep stirring the mud and try to keep taking the risks they're taking to get peoples' confidence level to come up a little bit.

INTERVIEWER: You're taking a risk?

ALIX: Um-hmm.

INTERVIEWER: How do you feel about that?

ALIX: Oh, I feel great about it.

INTERVIEWER: What challenges lay ahead for you in your transition and your journey?

ALIX: Um, quite a few. I have a twenty-year-old son, so all of my relationships are changing. I consider myself polyamorous. However, I am in a nine-month relationship with another woman so that's something I have to look at. I'm in a Jewish community that has viewed me as female and so they will have to waive the consequences a little bit.

INTERVIEWER: How does being Jewish and being bisexual and being trans relate to each other?

ALIX: Actually they remind me of the same thing because Judaism, they have always been leaders about embracing other cultures and taking things to another level and debating and questioning. So it's almost the same.

INTERVIEWER: What kind of challenges lay ahead for us pushing the envelope?

ALIX: I think, of course, to keep including the transgendered community and, I don't know because I really think the bisexual community is doing a pretty good job. Maybe networking with other communities.

KEVIN

KEVIN: I'm Kevin, happily married bisexual man. I've been married for twelve years. We were lucky, my wife and I were lucky, in that we both knew that each of us was bisexual before we got married. I see a lot of couples kind of struggling with that later as they realize, you know, "Well, maybe I'm not what I thought I was," and so it hasn't been too much of a struggle for us.

INTERVIEWER: You're married. How does that relate to being bisexual?

KEVIN: Well, I think it's good for the straight community, maybe for everyone; not that I'm holding myself as a great role model for the world. But—swipe the halo away—but I think that it's good for people to see a married couple as one example of a bisexual couple. In our case we happen to be a man and a woman who are married, madly in love, very, very, very close, and we're so close we're practically the same person, and adventure outside the marriage doesn't hurt anything. In fact we can get together over details and giggle.

INTERVIEWER: What is a bisexual marriage like?

KEVIN: We're ecstatically happy. I don't know about other bisexual marriages. I do see other bisexual couples discover that later and struggle. I know that's hard. We're floating on a cloud.

INTERVIEWER: Do you think you see things differently than straight couples?

KEVIN: Yeah, probably. I think that we're a little more aware, perhaps, if I can pat myself on the back, of—I think the bisexual community and the gay community resist a very unjust system, and I think that's part of why we have a community; in that, we're resisting the ridiculous system of one gender oppressing another or straight sexism oppressing bisexual or gay sexuality. We're holding out.

INTERVIEWER: Do you feel connected to the bisexual community?

KEVIN: I do. I have to say I feel a little more connected to the gay community because I am very interested in gay activism. I feel fine about the bi community being, maybe not a part of, but being very closely connected to the gay community. I know that—you know there are [bisexual] separatists who—that's fine, whatever.

INTERVIEWER: When was the first time you felt you were bisexual?

KEVIN: I was born bisexual. And I think I knew it, and I think that awareness became more front-brained as I got older, probably in my twenties.

INTERVIEWER: When did you realize that the rest of the world wasn't bisexual?

KEVIN: Oh, I was aware that I was different when I was a kid, though I probably couldn't explain it.

INTERVIEWER: What was that like?

KEVIN: Um, I was really okay with it. I was surprisingly untraumatized by it compared to lives that I've seen and read about. And I read a lot of Paul Monette. He's one of my heroes, and his "becoming a man" struggle [*Becoming a Man: Half a Life Story,* Reprint edition (Harper San Francisco, 1993)]. There's this tremendous, just, redefining of self and butting his head against life. And then he had this magnificent career as a writer. I think that I was lucky in that there was this brief period of confusion in my twenties where, "Gee, maybe I am gay. Why do I want to have sex with women? Oh, okay."

INTERVIEWER: Do you feel like it's more of an option now to be bisexual?

KEVIN: More of an option? No, I think we're born who we are. It's more of an option to be out. I feel like sexuality, and I will say for me, because I'm not going to define sexuality for other people, for me it's a natural alignment. It's part of my cells, part of my genes.

INTERVIEWER: What brought you to this conference?

KEVIN: We, my wife and I, were here last year, and what made us notice BECAUSE or come to BECAUSE? I cannot remember. We saw it in the paper or something; I just don't remember. And then we came, we had a lot of fun, we met some wonderful people, and thought, let's go back, so we are back.

INTERVIEWER: Is there a bisexual movement?

KEVIN: Yeah, I've met bi activists. Like I said before, I think in general, if I can say the "queer movement" as an umbrella for us all, I think that we're resisting an unjust system. I feel happy to be a part of that. Whether it's the gay movement or what, I don't much care.

INTERVIEWER: What would the end product of a queer movement look like?

KEVIN: Gosh, I don't know. I really don't know. It seems to me that I hear a lot of straight people and an increasing amount of, "Oh, just, I don't want to talk about it; I don't want to hear about it; it's not important." And I think it is important, and I think we do need to talk about it. I love talking about sexuality. I think it's very interesting, and I don't know where we're headed. I have no idea.

INTERVIEWER: Being married, there's always an issue of, are you visible? When people see you gardening are you a bisexual, married couple? Do you have those kinds of concerns?

KEVIN: Well, specifically when we garden we do carry the sign. We have a rainbow flag on our house, but as people get to know us, obviously very soon after they get to know us, they realize that we are bisexual. In con-

versation it becomes pretty obvious. And they see a very, very close couple who have trouble sometimes even realizing that we're separate people really, because we're very, very close.

INTERVIEWER: Does she have a beard? [laugh]

KEVIN: Fortunately not. [laugh] She's much better looking than I.

INTERVIEWER: Anything else?

KEVIN: No, I don't think so.

ROB

ROB: My name is Rob, and I'm forty-two years old, and I'm a misplaced
Easterner living in Minnesota at the moment. Let's see, when did I first
identify as bisexual or realize I was bisexual? That's hard because I was a
kid and then an adolescent in the hippie era. You know at eleven I was
pissed off I couldn't go to Woodstock. So when I started to realize I was
attracted to lots of different people I just assumed I was really open-
minded. "Peace, love, happiness, let's all love one another, and wow,
aren't I really beautiful and open-minded, I can love boys and girls." And
so I was open-minded and really horny. Then when I was about twenty, I
was at a college that had a very gay-supportive atmosphere, and literally,
on my twentieth birthday I woke up and realized, "Gee, I'm not just
open-minded, I like this sex with guys thing; I must be gay." So I identified as gay for ten years—sometimes I identified as gay with a footnote,
"I'm gay, ah, some women I like." I did that for a good decade. I identified as gay until I was interviewed by a young Minneapolis activist
named Joe Duca, and he was doing a "needs assessment" of bisexuals in
the Twin Cities probably nine or ten years ago. And we made an appointment—he said the interview would take a half of an hour, maybe forty-
five minutes if we were gabby, he came over at seven thirty in the evening
and left at one thirty in the morning. I had never talked to anyone who
identified as bi before and had been through so many of the same things
as I had, and literally that night, that's when I started identifying as bisexual and realized that was the appropriate word for me.

INTERVIEWER: Why did you identify as gay?

ROB: Because I was in a gay-supportive atmosphere and not a bi-supportive
atmosphere. Bisexual was seen as what you called yourself until you
were ready to say you were a lesbian and there was no support for it
around the campus where I was and the people I knew, even to the point
of walking away from mutual attractions with women—duhh—that I'm
still kicking myself for, because I thought I wasn't supposed to. So bisexuality wasn't presented to me as an option, a viable option. That's why I

said I was gay. It was years later that I realized no, this was a more appropriate term for me. And now I'm not sure that it fits because I'm attracted to so many genders that bi doesn't necessarily do it.

INTERVIEWER: How are things different now? Is there a bisexual option?

ROB: Oh yeah, I know lots of options now. No, very few, actually, come to think of it. I find at this point in my life I'm primarily attracted to butch dykes, very few of whom will actually date guys, oddly enough, and genuinely, sincerely, feminine men. So I have a dating pool the size of a Dixie cup. [laugh] I'm attracted to people who either barely exist or who aren't interested in dating me. That's not who I'll be sexual with because, let's face it, I'm a big slut. [laugh] So there are lots of people I'll be sexual with, but the people I actually want to date and be in a relationship with I'm getting choosier and choosier about. The past year or so I've been completely fascinated with F-to-M people, female-to-male transgendered people, because I'm getting all of this butch masculine energy and none of the "I'm a male raised in America" bullshit. So it's a wonderful combination to me.

INTERVIEWER: Is that something the bisexual community is ready to embrace?

ROB: I'm not sure. I'd like to think the bisexual community is more open-minded, but I think we've got just as many barriers and stumbling blocks as everybody else. Gender categories are still so rigid for a lot of people, and certainly in the bi community we're breaking down a lot of those barriers and looking past them. One of the positive stereotypes about bi people is when people treat you like you're really noble. I've had both gay and straight people say this to me: "Oh, wow, you're bisexual"; you just like the true inner person for their soul; you don't care about the genitals—you don't have standards, yeah, you don't have standards; you just care about inner soul. It's like, "No, sometimes I want dick; sometimes I'm in the mood for pussy, okay." That's it, you know. I like tits: male tits, female tits, I don't care but I love tits, and so it's not just about the soul or just the inner being. I'm not that noble. [laugh] That I think is a stereotype we need to get past which is healthy to get past because there's a lot of boundaries we need to break down, and for me, that's what being bisexual is about: it's about breaking down the categories and breaking down the boundaries, and stop feeling inside that there are these artificial walls that somebody else placed in there, where I'm supposed to go and who I'm supposed to be attracted to and what I want to do and who I want to be.

INTERVIEWER: Do you feel connected to a community?

ROB: Yes. The queer community in general, the bi community specifically, yes. Maybe largely because of how I've been involved in it. I was one of the first co-founders of the BECAUSE Conference. As I mentioned before, I was interviewed by Joe Duca who was doing a needs assessment of bisexuals in the Twin Cities; he asked me to be on a panel discussion with several other people that was explaining bisexuality to people who worked on crisis lines and in gay organizations. From that panel that night, literally the group of us talking out in the hallway about how we need to do something more than this, and that's how the BECAUSE conference was formed. So yeah, I feel very connected locally and nationally because I've done things both locally and nationally in terms of bi activism.

INTERVIEWER: A conference is a concrete way to feel community. Is there other ways you feel connected, other avenues . . .

ROB: In some media, some publications, like *Anything That Moves,* and that sort of thing. *Taste of Latex* was a great, a polysexual porn that doesn't exist anymore. In ways like that I feel connected. Outside of conferences, no, conferences and meetings and groups, it tends to be pretty structured in that sense. In terms of who I'm involved with, no I don't think about it that much, I'm not all that concerned—except politically I'm concerned with how people identify themselves, personally I'm not that concerned with how people identify themselves "Look at me, I'm this kind of a person, and I'll be Rob." Help me out. Maybe t-shirts will be nice or a pin, maybe a symbol or ribbon.

INTERVIEWER: What would be an ideal situation [for the bisexual community]?

ROB: To me the ideal situation would be more personal than political. It would be that people think more about their feelings and attractions and less about their own labels, and there are people who will identify as bisexual or straight or gay or lesbian or dyke or you know fag or whatever—my current is an extremely queer big old bisexual fag, that's what I call myself today. But I'm attracted to who I'm attracted to. Whether that word "bi" and an actual sense of duality actually work, doesn't matter. I've known too many straight people or gay men or lesbians who've been attracted to somebody who is not their usual gender list and [have] not done anything about it because they thought it didn't fit their label and their category—which I've lived through myself and it's a rotten feeling; it's a frustrating feeling of regret. I'd like to see people function more on their feelings and attractions and less on their label. Keep whatever label feels good to them fine, you know, whatever identity, but go ahead and process, if only internally, their feelings they have for any other person.

INTERVIEWER: So what other challenges lay ahead besides breaking down rigid labels?

ROB: Breaking down rigid labels, be continuing to get gay and lesbian communities to recognize us, especially in the media. The *Advocate* recently did a story on queer youth who were starting groups in high schools, you know, against much opposition. [There's] very important activism going on in our community right now, especially among the youth. In an eight-page article the word "bisexual" appeared twice; once was by the right wing or citizens alliance, so the right wingers remembered us, and once was by a young lesbian who recognized that the gay-straight alliances that are being started in schools need to be inclusive in welcoming bisexual teens because so many teens are using the term now and not wanting to pin down to one or the other. So we need to get the community, especially our community's media in line with recognizing that we exist, looking for the bisexual aspects of stories, stop lumping Ani Difranco in with gay and lesbian artists. You know, there are so many bi-identified artists now that just get lumped in with gay/lesbian artists, and there needs to be more respect for people's self-identification.

INTERVIEWER: Dare I ask, is there anything else you want to add?

ROB: I think the only thing I want to add is, "Thank God I'm queer." You know, the thing I don't want to hear is when queer people say, "Well, obviously if I could choose not to be born this way I wouldn't because I go through so much oppression and discrimination." Well, bullshit. That's made me who I am today. That's made me as strong as I am today. It's brought so many beautiful people into my life, so many beautiful ideas into my life that I might not have looked at if I were straight. So I'm just thrilled to death that I'm queer or bisexual or pansexual, or, I'm not a slut, I'm a sexual opportunity technician; whatever I am, I'm just glad that I am.

JODI

JODI: I'm Jodi. I grew up on a farm in West Central Minnesota, but I now live in Minneapolis.

INTERVIEWER: How long have you identified as bisexual? Or do you?

JODI: Oh yes. Yes, I do, though now I'm kind of questioning that because right now sleeping or dating with men just isn't very appealing. Although, I was involved with a man for a very long time and ended that relationship because I just really wanted to explore dating with a woman and have found out that it's a lot better, and I'm really happy, and I really like that. I'm very attached to the bi label because the bi community helped me feel very safe. And I'm not one of those people who grew up like "Well, when I was nine, I knew I was different and it really freaked me out." I was, like, really a girl, really heterosexual, you know—nothing untoward.

INTERVIEWER: What changed?

JODI: What changed was I moved to Manhattan and all sorts of things opened up for me. I nannied for this family who were labor lawyer activists and [it] exploded a lot of things that I believed about the world. And [I] also met some lesbian and bi women and began to think, "Oh, wow, just like I can challenge everything else, I'll challenge my sexual orientation!" And so it just came about that way, and then, shortly thereafter I met my male partner that I was with for so long, and so it all happened kind of at once. And looking back I think I should have put the brakes on that relationship until I figured out what was happening in my head, because it was hard, it was very hard, to leave, but there was such a huge part of me that was so unhappy staying that I just couldn't.

INTERVIEWER: So a bunch of ideas opened up to you. How did that change your world?

JODI: It opened up my eyes to a lot of experiences that are very different than mine and about a lot of the injustice and oppression that exists. You know, one of the first things that I read when I was there was Emma Goldman's autobiography [*Living My Life*, Volume 1 (Dover Publications, 1930)], and so I really take class into account when I look at the world, and race and gender and orientation and ability, that stuff too. It's kind of always been like a running commentary in my head, how I see stuff and how I'm always analyzing stuff.

INTERVIEWER: You said you're not interested in men anymore, but you still identify as bisexual. Tell me more about that.

JODI: Well, because I was for so long, you know, and it's got I think to do with that fluidity of, you know, right now I'm not attracted to men but I can't guarantee when I'm fifty I might not be—I kind of doubt it, but who knows? So there's that part. But also, I found the bi community and once I actually met bisexual people—and I have an anecdote about that—like it didn't happen for a long time that it's just been a very accepting, very warm place to be, so I think it's out of sheer loyalty that I always will [call myself bisexual]. Because calling myself a lesbian just doesn't fit. It just doesn't fit at all.

INTERVIEWER: Tell me about that anecdote.

JODI: Well, the anecdote, and the reason why I avoided seeking out other bi people was—this would have been probably in about 1990 or so—I was really struggling with this mother stuff. So I go to see a therapist—because that's what you do, especially when you're a social work major—and I was talking to the therapist about being bi, and I assumed, like any good therapist, she would have gotten over her own crap and been able to deal with it. And I was saying, "I know there's a bi group here on campus," and she said to me, "Oh, I wouldn't test that out, they'll probably just encourage you to experiment." "Oh, okay." And so for a long time, and I've lived in Madison till 1993, till I moved here, and I did not seek out any bi people. Until this feeling got so strong I was just going crazy because the only person I was out to was my male partner, and of course I couldn't tell him everything. And I really needed other women to talk to, so by sheer willpower, I managed to track down Bi Women and Friends, and that's how I got involved in here.

INTERVIEWER: Do you feel connected to a bisexual community? What does it look like to you?

JODI: Well, what it looks like to me is my friends and, you know, because I heard other people answer this question, it's kind of touch and go. I mean, most of my friends are bi or very comfortable with that, and I'm really glad that the Bi Women and Friends brunch is opening up—or it started again. But I'm just kind of living my life. There are not enough hours in the week, you know, to do everything and see everybody that I want to.

INTERVIEWER: What brought you to this conference?

JODI: Well, it's my second year, and last year it was an amazing experience. For me, this is so validating. I had just separated from my male partner and so I felt free that I could finally just really be who I wanted to be. And so I just wanted to come back and reconnect with everybody and hear about the workshops and just learn about things that I don't know about yet.

INTERVIEWER: Is there a bisexual movement?

JODI: Well, obviously there is; this is it, today, you know, with the people seeking out and organizing and working everything from—and education, you know, trying to make the "B's" and "T's" get included with the "L's" and the "G's." Whatever it is, you know, with the legislative stuff that happens, a lot of times "B's" and "T's" get, kind of, traded off so the field will be more palatable. And so, I think there are obviously a lot of bi activists working.

INTERVIEWER: Well, so we're kind of left out.

JODI: Well, we're trading chips, you know. I don't know, I'm probably going to get this all wrong, but there was some bill where transgendered was just part of the bill and there was talk that the people who are pushing for the right bill, "Well, we'll lop off of transgender because then it will be more palatable to the mainstream politicians, and we can get it passed." So I think sometimes by the quote unquote mainstream lesbian-gay movement we're expendable.

INTERVIEWER: How does that make you feel?

JODI: Pissed off! For example, like at the workshop this morning, at some national conference, the people in the room were asked to stand up if they were bi or transgendered—the National Gay and Lesbian Task Force thing—and over half the room apparently stood up and were still not part of the title, were still not included more than as tokens, and lip service. We've helped build this movement; we've always been there.

INTERVIEWER: What is the ideal for you?

JODI: Well, that people don't get hung up on, like, who you're attracted to. You know, that litmus test, "Are you really gay or really lesbian." I've heard it all, "Oh, you haven't made up your mind yet, blah blah blah." And unfortunately, the worst things have come out of the mouths of the lesbians. All of my straight friends, you know, have no problem when I've come out to them: "Oh, okay, no big deal."

INTERVIEWER: Why is that?

JODI: I think it might have to do with what—with power. I think lesbians as a group in the mainstream society don't have a lot of power, and so it's much more threatening for someone to come and mess with your identity and your power if you don't have a lot, whereas straight people, they feel pretty comfortable, they have that privilege, so they can afford [to be] more generous. I don't know, ask them.

INTERVIEWER: Are there other important aspects of your identity?

JODI: Oh, absolutely. As I mentioned, I went to school to be a social worker, and so it was lovely, it just kind of encompassed all of my worldview, because social workers are allegedly all about empowerment and oppression, and that's kind of our official saying, and that's why I went into it because it's a much more "systems" view than psychology. And also, I've been really influenced by a lot of Buddhist thinking which really merges with this because it's all about nonattachment and forgetting about labels in a way and on a very profound level, cherishing and being in awe of the connection that we all have. This winter I got totally obsessed with this series of articles on cosmology and natural history, and one thing that I remember from that which kind of sums up everything here is that we are all literally stardust and born of one star. We all started—everything you ever laid eyes on—comes from the same star that exploded about fifty million years ago. And that's what gives me hope that things will improve, that people will understand a very deep connection, and that in a very mini sense there is no separation between you and me.

INTERVIEWER: Any other thoughts?

JODI: I want to encourage people to be brave and to take risks and to be vulnerable because I think why people cling to dichotomy and their power, you know, if they're not disabled or if you're white, why you cling to that is you're afraid. What will happen if I give up my little piece of power? And what I've found out, when you open your heart up and take the risk, you have more power because of the synergy that happens. So be brave.

ELIZABETH

ELIZABETH: I'm an everyday gal. I'm Elizabeth. I'm forty-four. I grew up here, in Minneapolis, lived a couple other places.

INTERVIEWER: Do you identify as being bisexual?

ELIZABETH: Yes, I do.

INTERVIEWER: When did you first realize you were bisexual?

ELIZABETH: I think . . . I didn't get a name for it until I was in my twenties, but I acknowledged the feelings for it from a very early age and had my first girlfriend when I was fourteen, about the same time I had my first boyfriend. And it seemed normal to me, but I knew that—but I didn't talk about it.

INTERVIEWER: Why didn't you talk about it?

ELIZABETH: Because although it felt right to me, I assumed that I wouldn't be accepted in my community.

INTERVIEWER: Why did you assume that?

ELIZABETH: I suppose messages. Got pretty direct messages that I was supposed to be a certain way. I come from a family—my mom's a teacher, my dad's a preacher, and I was the only girl, and I was supposed to be frou-frou—they had very predetermined ideas about who I was supposed to be, and I just never fit them. I'd try, and I'd be so uncomfortable and unhappy, and I'd sort of slide back, and that's been most of my life. I've tried to meet other people's expectations, but really, I always knew it wasn't quite me, and I'd give up for awhile and be myself, and then I'd go back to trying to please people. I also went to a church school. It was pretty clear about gender roles and people's behaviors. However, it was in that school that I met my first three girlfriends and we were lovers on and off for many years, and I felt—I mean it was fine, it was like we could do that, felt great about it, but I couldn't talk about it. Which is why it took me sitting here, listening to everyone else for so long. It's like, no, I've got to talk about it. When I was in my early twenties, one of my roommates came out as a lesbian, and she was very open about her experience and we talked a lot, and I told her, "Well, I've always had boyfriends and girlfriends. What does that make me?" And she said, "Oh, there's a name for that, it's bisexual!" And I just will never forget that. It was like, "Oh, I have a name. Wow!"

INTERVIEWER: Did it give you a feeling that part of you was fulfilled?

ELIZABETH: Well, it felt more comfortable. It was nice that there was some-thing—it felt normalizing. And then, I've been married three times.

INTERVIEWER: To men or women?

ELIZABETH: To men, and twice to women. So, lots of serial monogamy. And what has happened is that I have been—again, you know, when I'm with women, there was a certain amount of people who would just leave me, not be close to me, and I would never make a fuss about it, and then a whole different group when I was with men. And I just accepted that; I just thought, you know, that's the way it is. It certainly wasn't my vision, but it still doesn't make sense to me. It just seems like because of how I might be interested in others, I'm just attracted to some people and other people—and roles don't have a lot to do with it—body parts do, but roles don't, and gender stereotypes don't.

INTERVIEWER: Was your father conservative?

ELIZABETH: Yes, still is.

INTERVIEWER: Would you consider that an important part of identity, being a preacher's kid? And how does that relate to being a bisexual?

ELIZABETH: I guess I brought it up because it was fairly restrictive and a dogmatic kind of upbringing, and who I was clearly didn't fit. It was a counterpoint for me because if I was going to love myself I had to face that it didn't fit. So maybe it pushed me along my path a little bit better.

INTERVIEWER: Are there important parts of your identity that relate to being bisexual?

ELIZABETH: It's hard for me to separate it, because it's just who I am. On the one hand there's sexual preferences and likes and dislikes, and another big part of who I am is the spiritual aspect that's not about organized reli-gion. Another part is having a great affinity to healing. And so, those three things are pretty connected for me, and I don't know if they fit into what you think should be connected to bisexuality or not—it doesn't matter. I don't know how to answer, but they are connected for me.

INTERVIEWER: It's all connected, not just little chunks of identity.

ELIZABETH: Absolutely. Yes, it's so connected. It's part of how I approach being a mom and a grandmom, and it's part of how I approach folks in my work. And intellectually I know that being quiet about my affectional preference is in conflict with that fluidity. Does that make sense? But I'm not quite there yet.

INTERVIEWER: What brought you to the conference?

ELIZABETH: I just happened to see a little blurb in a local paper and I was so excited! I just wanted to come and be with other bisexuals when I feel most comfortable. A couple years ago I was working in a different situa-tion for a short period of time, and it was a much more open situation than my general job, and so I had the opportunity and almost the expectation to be more out there than I was in my general job. And I felt very uncomfortable until I met another bi woman, and it normalized it for me, and I felt an immediate connection, and it was real exciting. And from then on I felt more comfortable about sharing who I was.

INTERVIEWER: What's holding you back?

ELIZABETH: I think, chicken shit. Chicken shit-itis. It's some bad experiences I've had in the gay community, and I'm a little gun-shy about—and I wouldn't expect it in the bi community, but I'm a little gun-shy about someone else deciding what my sexuality is. I've felt it more—I'd expected more from gays and lesbians to be accepting of me than I had straights, and because of that, when some people aren't, or challenge, and think, "Oh, you're a fence sitter, that sort of thing."

INTERVIEWER: Besides the name-calling, besides being called a fence sitter, how do you feel like you're not being respected? How do you feel like you're not being affirmed by gay and lesbian people? Can you think of an example?

ELIZABETH: Well, the example of my lesbian friends not being near me when I'm with a guy, but that happens to me in the straight community, too, and maybe I need to pick better friends. I don't know. That's another example. And I think, too, that the whole chicken shit piece again is that I anticipate not being accepted and so, what goes around comes around. It's like if I'm sitting here, white knuckled, thinking, "Well, they're not going to like me because I'm bi," then why would they? Or they have to work twice as hard to show me that it's okay.

INTERVIEWER: What's an ideal situation for you? What would you like to be in your own life?

ELIZABETH: I guess I'd like to be able to be more interactive, more open with people about who I am and have that be just a normal part of life. And that's a big piece of me, but it's the culture, too, the overriding culture to have that be opened up a little bit more. I don't care too much for categories and labels, so a worldview that I would prefer would just be one of acceptance of people and their affinities and their love.

INTERVIEWER: Anything else you want to say to history?

ELIZABETH: No, this was a big enough chunk for me. Thank you for the opportunity.

ANITA

ANITA: My name is Anita. I just turned fifty-three. I live in South Minneapolis, Minnesota, and I have identified as being bisexual, officially sort of chosen that word, since early 1994. And this is 2000, so that's six years. But I have known my whole life that I was attracted to both boys and girls, men and women. Growing up I sort of thought everyone felt that way.

INTERVIEWER: When did you realize that not everyone felt that way?

ANITA: Well, I guess probably as the feelings continued. And maybe I should say that I just thought it was part of growing up that you did experimenting with your girlfriends, and that that was sort of in preparation for having relationships with boys. But the feelings continued. And then I saw people being, become embarrassed about them in college when some situations happened. And so the way I looked at my own self was that I was attracted to both men and women, but emotionally I felt that a relationship with a man was more what would be satisfying to me emotionally. And so I never used the word bisexual even though I told a partner that I had sixteen years ago, when we started going together, that I was attracted to women as well, but I really didn't see it as being an issue.

INTERVIEWER: Why wasn't it an issue?

ANITA: I guess because I saw there being a difference. I did not feel attracted to women in a way I would want to have a long-term relationship or committed relationship with them. So I didn't see it as being a threat to our relationship in anyway.

INTERVIEWER: And you say this all in past tense?

ANITA: Yeah.

INTERVIEWER: So now what's it about?

ANITA: I think it was just all part of my own personal growth journey, that as I did some family work in terms of my own history and really cleaned up some issues, that I felt free in my level of attraction, and that it was as strong to women as it was to men. And it has pretty consistently stayed that way now for six years.

INTERVIEWER: You feel different now?

ANITA: I think that there continues to be an evolution in terms of my comfort with who I am. Definitely went through a phase of, "My gosh, if I'm this attracted to women does this mean I'm a lesbian?" And no, it didn't. I'm less attracted to men and have continued to have those experiences, so—but it just seems consistent, you know. In one of the workshops, someone said, "Do you tend to look more at, when you see someone walking toward you on the street, do you look more at the men or at the women?" And I flashed back to, probably to twenty-five years ago walking across the skyway between Dayton's and the IDS, and teenage boys walking toward me saying, "What is she? She looks at both men and women," and it was sort of like an interesting observation on their part. And I do; I look at everybody. People are interesting to me.

INTERVIEWER: Do you think being bisexual gives you a different outlook?

ANITA: Definitely. I feel that I have claimed a place in the community that I've always felt akin to. I have supported the GLBT community, but I feel now that I claim a place, that I really belong in that community whereas before I sort of viewed myself as a straight person who was attracted to women, but was very supportive of issues of diversity, so that feels different to me. I feel a real sense of belonging, and in the recent years, having met people more and more each year who are bisexual (because at first I was the only person I knew who was bisexual) and of course there still are plenty of people out there who'd have me believe if I'm going to be in a relationship with a woman, I'm truly lesbian, and when I'm in a relationship with a man I was heterosexual, so there's a sense of grounding. I think also that, professionally—I'm a speech and language pathologist, and having been outed at my state convention two years ago when I was president elect—fortunately I didn't find this out until after the convention was over; I think it would have been a difficult situation to manage. But I was outed as a lesbian so that has been really a call to action in terms of my personal development. How do I want to handle this? Do I want to handle this? Do I want to say anything to the people, who talk to one of my best friends about my sexuality, who obviously were not close enough friends of mine to talk to me about it—how did I want to handle it? And I talked to several friends; I talked to a psychologist. And now, two years later when I'm past president of the convention, I am choosing (as part of a lecture that I'm giving in a few weeks at the state convention about the role of spirituality in healing persons with voice and language disorders)—I'm going to talk about, just as we want to be open to persons of all different religions, including pagan, who are spiritual persons even though they don't believe in a deity—so in our bylaws it says as speech and language pathologists that we want to be open to working with people from all different cultures, different sexual identities. And I will use the opportunity to talk of my own experience as a bisexual person, how I have been misperceived by others, how assumptions have been made for me, so . . .

INTERVIEWER: That's pretty scary stuff.

ANITA: Yeah, it's a big risk. But I've been thinking about it for a long time, and I feel ready to do it, and I'm really excited about it.

INTERVIEWER: Why?

ANITA: To me it's a choice. For some people it's not a choice, but for me it's a choice: I could pretend. I could pass as someone who is straight. I could, if I wanted to, present myself as a person who looked very butch.

That doesn't have to be my look, but in the way that I look and what I do professionally, I feel like it's an incredible opportunity to educate. And, you know, I've lectured about my profession periodically my whole life (I've had undergraduate and graduate students). Now I have an opportunity to speak out within what I think is an appropriate context, educational context, talk about bisexuality, and reach however many people are there, to reach them.

INTERVIEWER: Would you have done this six years ago?

ANITA: No way. You know, I have been looking—ever since the outing two years ago—I've been looking for the appropriate venue. I chose not to write about it in my presidential column that was in the association's newsletter. I wanted to be in a situation where it seemed natural.

INTERVIEWER: Do you feel connected to a bisexual community? Is that community that you're feeling? And what does that community look like to you?

ANITA: It's feeling more and more so. You know, at first (this is the third BECAUSE Conference I've attended)—and two years ago I sort of, I don't know what I thought, that there were going to be people who looked just like me or something; it was very weird. But now—and however much is just my own day-to-day living with myself and seeing more people that I've met at the conferences—I do feel connected through this conference and through some of the people that I've met, and I want to know people who are bisexual. And what I'm finding out is that we're just as diverse a community as is each community—each community of diversity, each community of religion, each community of nationality— in all the ways that people differ, so do we. And we just happen to have an interest or the same values in common.

INTERVIEWER: What are they?

ANITA: Well, I think there is an interest in education, an interest in communication. There's an interest in self-development and an interest in personal growth.

INTERVIEWER: Is there a movement—is there a bisexual movement?

ANITA: I think there is—I saw it—and I think it was because of my participation last year in the conference. I saw how much is going on nationally. Even though I had read about it, I felt more a part of it last year; I feel an even greater part of it this year. And I feel—especially, as I'm, you know, this is my last year in the presidency role with my state professional organization—I feel like okay, this is where I want to go next, this is where I want to put my extra time in terms of volunteerism: involvement with the bisexual projects that are local.

INTERVIEWER: So what are we working toward? What's the ideal situation?

ANITA: Well, for me the ideal situation would be that nobody cares, you know. It doesn't matter to anybody who I am or who I love, and I guess, ultimately, that's my goal, that's what I'd like to see worked toward.

INTERVIEWER: What's the barriers between then and now? What do we have to overcome?

ANITA: A lot of prejudice. A lot of prejudice that is within our own family of the GLBT community. I still feel prejudice from others that if I love a woman, I should be calling myself a lesbian.

INTERVIEWER: Why should you be calling yourself a lesbian if you love a woman?

ANITA: Well, exactly. Why should I?

INTERVIEWER: Well, why?

ANITA: Well, because that's who women are who love women—that's what has been said to me. And as one man said to me at a national twelve-step conference a number of years ago, "I don't really believe there's anything like bisexuality anyway." You know, like he should know me. I mean, that's what's so amazing is that we assume that we know, that someone would assume that he or she knows me better than I know myself. I mean, that's just bizarre to me.

INTERVIEWER: Anything else you want to have on record in history?

ANITA: Just that I'm grateful for all the people that have been in our organizations before I even knew they existed, who've done so much groundwork: Robyn Ochs, Fritz Klein, so many names that I can't name. I am thankful locally for Marge Charmoli, and Scott Bartell, and Gary Lingen all the people who have been out there, Bill Burleson, Heidi who works with Bill in the support group, these are people who are putting their time and energy where their heart and soul are. They inspire me to move forward now that I'm ready.

KATHLEEN

KATHLEEN: My name is Kathleen, and I'm thirty-nine. I live in Minneapolis, and I've identified as bisexual most of the time since, well, about twenty years ago, since I was nineteen.

INTERVIEWER: So you came out to yourself when you were nineteen?

KATHLEEN: I came out to myself twenty years ago when I was nineteen. I went to a Halloween party and realized afterward that a woman was interested in me, and I was oblivious. My roommate was telling me, "Oh, this woman, she was really attracted to you, and didn't you get any of these hints?" And I was like, "No, I didn't." I hadn't ever thought about a woman being interested in me, and when I realized that, I thought that was kind of interesting that a woman might be interested in me, and I was living in California at the time, and I don't know. It just sort of entered my head as something that was a possibility. It was really scary at first. It was like, this isn't something I've ever thought of as a possibility for me. So it was scary, but once I finally met somebody that I wanted to date, then it was fun, then it was exciting. It was still like not something that I ever thought of as a possibility for me though.

INTERVIEWER: Why not?

KATHLEEN: I guess I just thought I would get married and have kids and have a house and never tell my family any of this. I was brought up Catholic, so there was all of this repression and not okay to be sexual at all, much less date women. It was always the monogamy and marriage rule, you know, and be a virgin till you're married, and . . .

INTERVIEWER: How has being bisexual changed your life?

KATHLEEN: Well, I did, ultimately, decide to get married. I was married for thirteen years, and now I'm going through a divorce, and . . .

INTERVIEWER: To a man?

KATHLEEN: Yeah, I was married to a man for thirteen years, and he knew that I was bisexual when shortly after we met, I told him. We dated for five years before we got married, so I was with him for most of my adult life. But how it's changed my life, I guess, is I never intended to get married and get divorced. I thought if I would get married, I would just stay married. I think that there's just more to me than just being the stay at home, be the good wife, be a mom, keep the house kind of person. Now I'm becoming more involved in being more of an activist. I'm one of the leaders of the BGL group at my college. I went back to school to be a teacher. I feel like I'm more vocal now, and I'm stronger than I was before. I think when I got married, it partly was a reaction to not wanting to be a lesbian. So I was never really out to a lot of people. There were always a few people that knew, but I was never really out to a lot of people. Now I'm coming out to more and more people.

INTERVIEWER: How does that feel?

KATHLEEN: It's still scary because I want to be a teacher, and I don't want it to affect my ability to have a job. But it feels good to be able to be myself in more of my life. I did finally come out to my family last year. More and more people are starting to be aware of me either as someone who dates women or as a bisexual.

INTERVIEWER: Are there other important aspects of your identity?

KATHLEEN: I'm a mom. I'm a student and a teacher. I feel I'm a somewhat spiritual person. Those are important aspects of my identity as well.

INTERVIEWER: How are they wrapped up in being a bisexual?

KATHLEEN: Well, being a single mom and being bisexual can be a little complicated. Just trying to date and to be a mom is complicated. Also there's the whole, the lesbians don't want me if I date men, and the men don't want me if I'm a lesbian. And you know, so the whole thing of whether or not to say I'm bisexual or just to not say or just to date who I want to date and not really deal with a whole lot. It's all kind of . . .

INTERVIEWER: Are you a lesbian?

KATHLEEN: I kind of go—more often I go by queer; I'll identify as queer. But the more that I've gotten to know more bisexual people who are comfortable with that, I've been more comfortable. Although, I've been in counseling and I've identified myself as bisexual in counseling for twenty years. So there I felt comfortable just saying it as a simple and very truthful description of me. And I think that since I came out to myself, I've been more attracted to women than to men. But I've dated more men, and it just was . . .

INTERVIEWER: Why was that?

KATHLEEN: Well, it's easier. You just open the door and there the guys are. It's harder to find women to date. It's not usually hard to find men to date. Men and women can generally look at each other and know if they're attracted or not. Women can look at each other and first have to figure out if they date women and then, do they have a partner?—and you know, it seems to take a little bit longer to get to that same point.

INTERVIEWER: Do you feel connected to a bisexual community?

KATHLEEN: Not so much. I want to. And partly I'm still going through this divorce. My husband just left two years ago, so I'm just starting to get involved in things. I met some people at a bi community picnic last year, and this is the first time I've come to a conference like this.

INTERVIEWER: Do you like it?

KATHLEEN: Yeah, I've met some interesting people so far. Kind of getting over the shyness factor—just going up and say, "Hi." And kind of knowing that other people are bi as opposed to some other conferences I've been to where it was more of a gay-identified crowd and not necessarily bi.

INTERVIEWER: What's the big difference? Why does it matter so much?

KATHLEEN: You know, I didn't really think about it a lot until I got involved with an organization on campus. . . . I started to realize that there were women who they didn't mind being my friends, but they just did not get it. "How could you be bisexual? How could you want to date men? What's the attraction?" You know, for me, I don't see gender as an issue when I fall for someone. When I'm attracted to someone, I'm attracted to a person for a lot of different reasons, and whether they're male or female or somewhere in the middle doesn't really factor into it for me. And that's partly to why I'm becoming more comfortable with identifying as bisexual, because I feel like I've had to defend it a little.

INTERVIEWER: What brought you here?

KATHLEEN: Partly to go to some of the conference meetings. I have a friend that I thought might be here, and I did run into him, so that was cool. I didn't come last night. I decided to just come for today. I still have the whole issue with my child and spending time with her, and I figured I could take one day out. And I have enjoyed the conference sessions that I've gone to, met a few new people.

INTERVIEWER: You didn't feel like you could bring her?

KATHLEEN: I didn't sign up for the child care ahead of time, and I didn't know if that would be okay or not. And it's her time to spend with her dad right now, so that worked out.

INTERVIEWER: We sort of already touched on this, but describe an ideal situation for you. Where would you like to be in your life?

KATHLEEN: Well, I want a job. [laugh] No, I know what you mean. I'd like to have a relationship where it didn't matter if the person I was with was male or female; it mattered more that we were compatible and got along and were raising our family together, and I don't know. I mean, I think I want to be in a monogamous relationship again. I think that was comfortable for me. I'm meeting more people who have different ideas about how they want to be, whether they want open relationships or they want poly relationships, and I think I'm more of a monogamous kind of a person. An ideal situation would be: everyone in my neighborhood could know that I was bisexual and it wouldn't matter. It wouldn't matter if I hung rainbow flags out my window or not. My daughter wouldn't be teased about her mom being gay or bisexual.

INTERVIEWER: What are some of the challenges that are going to prevent you from getting there?

KATHLEEN: Well, part of it is the things that go on at school. And I am vocal, and I do go and tell—there is a safe staff in school, and I will go and tell them. And kids say there is a gay crowd at school, and I go and talk to them about that and talk to them about the kids that say "gay" as a cuss word, and it's bad. I talk to my daughter about it. And I think that the more she knows who I am and what I'm about—it's better for her. You know, I've asked her if she thinks she's gay, and she says, "No, I'm not old enough to be gay." So I thought that was very nice.

INTERVIEWER: How old is she?

KATHLEEN: She's six. And she said I'm almost gay, and I thought she understood what bisexuality was. And she said, "Mom, you're almost gay."

This was after the Rainbow Families Conference. And I said, "What do you mean by that?" And she said, "You're not actually married to another woman, you just date them."

INTERVIEWER: Anything else I didn't ask you about you'd like to talk about?

KATHLEEN: Sometimes I wish that people could look beyond the orientation issue a little bit and just see each other as people, and you know, I think some people do. You do end up meeting people, hooking up with them, and you might decide to date or not date, but why can't you just be friends first and see where it goes? Why does it always have to be, "Well, how do you identify?" You know, I've gone to lesbian events, dances and things identified as women-only events, and the first question is, "Well, are you lesbian or bisexual?" And it's like, "It depends." It's like, "Do you want to go out with me? If you want to go out with me maybe I'll be lesbian, maybe I'll tell you later. If you have a partner, then maybe I'll tell you I'm bisexual. Why? What does it matter?" I don't think it should matter. My daughter says it doesn't matter if you're black or if you're gay. What matters is your friendliness. That's what I think, too. I think what matters should be your friendliness.

DAVID

DAVID: I'm David. I'm twenty-nine. I'm living in Minneapolis. I came out bi when I was twenty-one. "Came out" was more like just realizing. I was coming out of a relationship with a woman and looking at the friends who were most supportive of me and who listened to me. And this guy was one of them. And I found that for some reason my fantasies were going toward sort of sucking his cock. It's like, "Wow, gosh, okay, no big deal." And then the word, the word, the word for this is bisexual, sure. Great. And there it was. And I took it, and I've been carrying it ever since. Even though I'm not in significant relationships at any time in my life, and basically I'm asexual, I consider myself as bisexual identified based on what my attractions are.

INTERVIEWER: So you feel like the word bisexual should mean that you are sexually active?

DAVID: No, I don't. I just think it means that I'm attracted to men and attracted to women, and kind of looking forward, if my life worked the way I wanted it to, I would have a relationship with a man and a woman. And that's what seems natural to me, although I realize that logistically it's a pretty complicated thing.

INTERVIEWER: Are there other important aspects of your identity?

DAVID: Yeah, poly. I want to have at least a man and a woman in my life. I don't consider myself monogamous. I consider myself a top-bottom switch in S and M play, sado-masochism. To me it's about alternative sensations. I don't like the word "pain." I don't enjoy pain in my play scenes, I enjoy sensations that are delivered with positive intent, and they may be sensations that other people would call painful, they may be sensations that if they were not delivered with loving intent, would be painful. And being top and bottom means I like to be the giver and the receiver. But I don't really like dominance and submission because personally, because I think that puts power issues in the relationship that I don't want in my relationships.

INTERVIEWER: Is bisexuality about power?

DAVID: Bisexuality, for me, is just about loving. And sex, of course. That's what it's about.

INTERVIEWER: How do the different aspects of your personality relate to being bisexual?

DAVID: It's about allowing myself more freedom, about not having to choose, not having to say, "This is what I am forever—although I choose the label bisexual for quote, unquote, forever for now because it seems to work for me. And I think that that is how I am somehow in my core. I also consider myself a spiritual being. I identify as male, but that's basically because of the birth diagnosis and the body I live in, and it's not important to me otherwise.

INTERVIEWER: How has being bisexual changed you life?

DAVID: I am more, I think, more true to me than I used to be. I am more aware of who I am. It's not that I lived lies, but I realized that there's more to me than I used to realize there was, and I'm pretty happy about that.

INTERVIEWER: Do you see things differently because of being bisexual?

DAVID: Um-hmm. Unfortunately, I would say the person was political. I react to injustice more strongly now than I did before I identified as bisexual.

INTERVIEWER: You say "unfortunately"?

DAVID: Unfortunately because I'd rather just get on with living my life, and not have to deal with the politics. It gets really tiring; it really does. Sometimes I wish I could just pass and keep my mouth shut. But I can't do that. At this point in my life I cannot allow myself to do that. I would like that—I would like to be able to sometimes just let the war rage outside, let the wind blow, let the snow blow, and be inside where it's comfortable and warm. And there are other times when I'd rather be out playing in the snow.

INTERVIEWER: Do you feel connected to a bisexual community?

DAVID: Yeah, I have a bunch of friends out there who are bisexual. I am, as an activist, definitely involved in trying to make this community grow. I wish it were bigger; I wish it were more of a community. Again, I wish there was less work involved in it. I wish it were like I could go into a café and know that there can be a lot of bisexual people there who can relate to the life that I live. I can find that in gay space, but it's not the same somehow. So I want to have that bi space.

INTERVIEWER: You say this isn't yet community. What do you mean?

DAVID: Well, because right now it feels pretty event driven. I mean the BECAUSE Conference—it's a cabaret that happens to support the BECAUSE Conference, or it's a picnic that happens during summer, or it's meetings that happen to plan things to make them happen, and gosh, you know, it'd be just nice if there were more of, like, "I'll call up so and so, and so and so, and so and so, and so and so," and it'll just happen, it'll just be, we'll all kind of know.

INTERVIEWER: You describe yourself as an activist. Why?

DAVID: Why am I being an activist? Because I believe it has to be done.

INTERVIEWER: Why?

DAVID: Well, that's a good question. There's a nifty little phrase that Rabbi Hillel said, "If not me, who? If not now, when? If I am only for myself, what am I? If I am not for me, who will be for me?"* I may be messing it up a bit, but that's the basic idea. So, someone's got to do it. And I feel compelled. I also so believe that in some way this will be returned to me, Karmicly speaking if you want to call it that or whatever. I believe my life will be better for this. And I don't know, I just believe that . . .

INTERVIEWER: How would it be better?

DAVID: More ease. And I take pleasure from seeing other people out there who are happy. To see a more fluid bisexual community, to see more people being able to walk out of a space and no one stares. Just seeing more gay people on the street, on the street being happy. I'm working as an activist for everyone's rights to live and love as they want: gay, straight, lesbian, bisexual, transgender, other, whatever.

INTERVIEWER: So what challenges lie ahead for the community, do you think?

DAVID: More work. Hopefully less personal stuff where if this issue isn't being dealt with exactly the way I need it to be dealt with, I will take everything I've done away from the table.

INTERVIEWER: So is this going on?

---

*Rabbi Hillel's original quote was as follows: "If I am not for myself, then who will be for me? And if I am only for myself, what am I? And if not now, when?"

DAVID: Oh, yeah. I won't get into specifics. But I know it's going on. More, just, more people. Get more people out there who know about this possibility to be bi, to identify bi, and to live by that and to have people feel free to label themselves if they want to, the way they want to label themselves. I think that if this bi option exists, some of those people say, "Well, maybe on occasion I want to be gay, but I can't really stand that label," then that makes it easier for them to fluidly be who they are sexually.

INTERVIEWER: Anything else you want to say?

DAVID: I'm very hopeful, I really am. I think that—I have high hopes, moderately high expectations. And you know, there are a couple of kids here I'll call them kids; they're in high school. It's a different world. People view bisexuality differently than they did ten, fifteen, twenty years ago, and I think that—I hope—what I'm doing now is helping make that happen.

Appendix C

Resources and Further Reading

THE INTERNET

As discussed in Chapter 10, for bisexuals seeking connection, the Internet is a big part of the present and promises to be an even bigger part of the future. Therefore, a good starting point in a search for the bisexual community is right at the home computer or, if need be, at the public library's computers. Check out the following Web sites.

BISEXUAL FOUNDATION <www.bisexual.org>

Comments: This Web site for the Bisexual Foundation was started by Dr. Fritz Klein. The site has a nearly unabridged list of all the bi groups in the United States plus groups throughout the world. To find out if a town has an active bi organization or support group, this is where to look. Also, this Web site is great for seeking events such as conferences.

THE BISEXUAL RESOURCE CENTER <www.biresource.org>

Comments: This is the Web site for the Bisexual Resource Center. It features great links to other Web pages and, best of all, their informational brochures. The Bisexual Resource Center publishes about twenty pamphlets about various topics such as safer sex, coming out, and bi community history, and most are in a downloadable form. This site also offers the *Bisexual Resource Guide* for sale. Edited by Robyn Ochs, it is now in its fourth edition.

ALL THINGS BI <www.allthingsbi.com>

Comments: Speaking of greats links, the All Things Bi Web site provides a huge list of resources and information about bisexuality. Perhaps more social rather than activist oriented, one can find organizational Web pages, personal pages, Yahoo groups, and just about anything else that can be imagined and probably some that cannot.

BOOKS

Nonfiction

A mini-explosion of books about bisexuality erupted in the 1990s. Most fall into two categories: academic research and compilations of essays. Non-academics should beware of just ordering a book off the Internet, because it might mean wading through what was probably somebody's doctoral dissertation. Friendlier are the essay compilations. Some are better than others, but all offer an insider view of the bisexual community. The following are four suggestions for good places to start.

HUTCHINS, LORAINE AND KAAHUMANU, LANI (Eds.) (1991). *Bi any other name: Bisexual people speak out.* Los Angeles, CA: Alyson Publications.

Comments: The list of bisexual literature is replete with collections of essays, but one of the first and still perhaps the best is *Bi Any Other Name.* Edited by two bi activists, it covers a gambit of topics such as coming out and spirituality. Perhaps more interesting as a look at the activist bisexual community rather than the greater number of people who identify as bisexual, this book has served to define the issues of the community in the same way the *Bisexual Option* has defined orientation.

KLEIN, FRITZ (1993). *The bisexual option,* Second edition. Binghamton, NY: The Haworth Press.

Comments: This is the seminal book about bisexuality. *The Bisexual Option* has shaped the discussion about human sexuality since it first published in 1978, and it remains as relevant as ever. Dr. Klein is an academic and explores bisexuality from a psychological point of view, but fortunately his work is lay reader friendly. Using a new model of sexuality, called the Klein Sexual Orientation Grid, he explores the great diversity of human sexuality.

OCHS, ROBYN (Ed.) (2001). *The bisexual resource guide,* Fourth edition. Boston: Bisexual Resource Center.

Comments: Published by the Bisexual Resource Center in Boston, the *Bisexual Resource Guide* lists 352 bi groups and 2,129 bi-inclusive groups in 66 countries, plus essays, film guides, photos; heck, everything! This is an outstanding volunteer effort led by Robyn Ochs and her team of contributors from all over the world.

TUCKER, NAOMI, HIGHLEYMAN, LIZ, and KAPLAN, REBECCA (Eds.) (1995). *Bisexual politics: Theories, queries, and visions.* Binghamton, NY: Harrington Park Press.

Comments: Like *Bi any Other Name,* this collection of essays is an excellent look at the established and activist bisexual community. Well organized and complete, it offers excellent information about bisexual community history and queer politics in general. As time passes, this book becomes increasingly important for its insider documentation of bisexual community paradigms in 1995.

WEINBERG, MARTIN S., WILLIAMS, COLIN J., and PRYOR, DOUGLAS W. (1995). *Dual attraction: Understanding bisexuality,* Reprint edition. New York: Oxford University Press.

Comments: In the early 1980s, the authors explored in depth the Bisexual Center of San Francisco. Their book is still the one true sociological study of a segment of the bisexual community. Complete with a large amount of data, it serves as a much-needed record of this unique group in a unique time in history.

Notes

Introduction

1. Kenji Yoshino, The epistemic contract of bisexual erasure, *Stanford Law Review,* 52(2)(January 2000), p. 353.

Chapter 2

1. Joseph P. Stokes and Robin L Miller, Toward an understanding of behaviorally bisexual men: The influence of context and culture, *Canadian Journal of Human Sexuality,* 7(2)(Summer 1998), p. 101.

2. Tamara Jones, A carefully considered rush to the altar: Lesbian pair wed after 7 years together, *Washington Post,* May 18, 2004, p. A1.

3. Bruce Vilanch, A beautiful mind game, *Advocate,* Issue 857(February 19, 2002), p. 43.

4. John Leland and Steve Rhodes, Bisexuality, *Newsweek,* 126(3)(July 17, 1995), p. 44.

5. Janna L. Horowitz and Michael D. Newcomb, Bisexuality, not homosexuality: Counseling issues and treatment approaches, *Journal of College Counseling,* 2(2)(Fall 1999), p. 148.

6. Anne H. Faulkner and Kevin Cranston, Correlates of same-sex sexual behavior in a random sample of Massachusetts high school students, *American Journal of Public Health,* 88(2)(February 1998), p. 262.

7. Horowitz and Newcomb, 1999, p. 148.

8. *See* Robyn Ochs, Biphobia: It goes more than both ways, in Beth Firestein (Ed.), *Bisexuality: The psychology and politics of an invisible minority* (Thousand Oaks, CA: Sage, 1996), pp. 217-239.

9. Stokes and Miller, 1998, p. 101.

10. Horowitz and Newcomb, 1999, p. 148.

11. Stokes and Miller, 1998, p. 101.

Chapter 3

1. Microsoft Corporation, Bonobo, *Microsoft encarta encyclopedia 2001* (1993-2000).

2. Gilbert Herdt, *Same sex, different culture* (Boulder, CO: Westview Press, 1997), pp. 66-76.

3. Franxcis Mark Mondimore, *A natural history of homosexuality* (Baltimore, MD: Johns Hopkins University Press, 1996), pp. 10-11.

4. Ibid.

5. Herdt, 1997, pp. 66-76.

6. R. Jean Cadigan, Woman-to-woman marriage: Practices and benefits in Sub-Saharan Africa, *Journal of Comparative Family Studies,* 29(Spring 1998), p. 89.

7. Ibid.

8. Herdt, 1997, pp. 112-117.

9. M. Reynolds, Kandahar's lightly veiled homosexual habits, *Los Angeles Times* (April 3, 2002), p. A5.

10. Paula Rodriguez Rust, Managing multiple identities: Diversity among bisexual women and men, in Beth A. Firestein (Ed.), *Bisexuality: The psychology and politics of an invisible minority* (Thousand Oaks, CA: Sage Publications, 1996), pp. 53-83.

11. Mondimore, 1996, pp. 10-11.

12. Ibid., p. 61.

13. On writ of certiorari to the Court of Appeals of Texas, Fourteenth District, brief of professors of history, George Chauncey, Nancy F. Cott, John D'Emilio, Estelle B. Freedman, Thomas C. Holt, John Howard, Lynn Hunt, Mark D. Jordan, Elizabeth Lapovsky Kennedy, and Linda P. Kerber, as Amici Curiae in support of petitioners, Roy T. Englert, Jr., counsel of record Alan Untereiner, Sherri Lynn Wolson Robbins, Russell, Englert, Orseck and Untereiner Llp, Washington, DC, Supreme Court of the United States, *John Geddes Lawrence and Tyron Garner, Petitioners, v. State of Texas, Respondent.*

14. Herdt, 1997.

15. Colin Spencer, *Homosexuality in history* (Orlando, FL: Harcourt Brace and Company, 1995), pp. 320-321.

16. Rust, 1996, p. 59.

17. Joseph P. Stokes and Robin L. Miller, Toward an understanding of behaviorally bisexual men: The influence of context and culture, *Canadian Journal of Human Sexuality,* 7(2)(Summer 1998), p. 101.

18. A.C. Kinsey, W.B. Pomeroy, and C.E. Martin, *Sexual behavior in the human male* (Philadelphia: W.B. Saunders, 1948); A.C. Kinsey, W.B. Pomeroy, C.E. Martin, and P.H. Gebhard, *Sexual behavior in the human female* (Philadelphia: W.B. Saunders, 1953).

19. Kinsey, Pomeroy, and Martin, 1948, p. 639.

20. Fritz Klein, *The bisexual option,* Second edition (Binghamton, NY: The Haworth Press, 1993).

21. M.D. Storms, Sexual orientation and self perception, in P. Pliner, K.R. Blanstein, I.M. Spigel, T. Alloway, and L. Krames (Eds.), *Perception of emotion in self and others: Advances in the study of communication and affect,* Volume 5 (New York: Plenum, 1978), pp. 165-180.

22. Stokes and Miller, 1998, p. 101.

23. Janna L. Horowitz and Michael D. Newcomb, Bisexuality, not homosexuality: Counseling issues and treatment approaches, *Journal of College Counseling,* 2(2)(Fall 1999), p. 148.

24. Beth A. Firestein, Introduction, in Beth A. Firestein (Ed.), *Bisexuality: The psychology and politics of an invisible minority* (Thousand Oaks, CA: Sage Publications, 1996), xix-xx.

25. Allison Abner, Bisexuality out of the closet, *Essence,* 23(6)(October 1992), p. 61.

26. Abner, 1992, p. 61.

27. Elizabeth B. Smiley, Counseling bisexual clients, *Journal of Mental Health Counseling,* 19(4)(October 1997), p. 373.

28. Kenji Yoshino, The epistemic contract of bisexual erasure, *Stanford Law Review,* 52(2)(January 2000), p. 353.

29. *Oxford English dictionary* (Oxford, UK: Oxford University Press, 1989).

30. L. Remez, As many lesbians have had sex with men, taking a full sexual history is important, *Family Planning Perspectives,* 32(2)(March/April 2000), p. 97.

31. Debbie Block-Schwenk, Musings on my poly lives, *BiWomen Newsletter* (Boston Bisexual Women's Network), 19(5) (October/November), p. 1.

32. Kayley Vernallis, Bisexual monogamy: Twice the temptation but half the fun? *Journal of Philosophy,* 30(3)(Winter 1999), p. 45.

33. B. Grant Hayes, Working with the bisexual client: How far have we progressed? *Journal of Humanistic Counseling, Education and Development,* 40(1) (Spring 2001), p. 11.

34. David J. McKirnan and Joseph P. Stokes, Bisexually active men: Social characteristics and sexual behavior, *Journal of Sex Research,* 32(1)(1995), p. 65.

35. Janet Lever and Sally Carson, Behavior patterns and sexual identity of bisexual males, *Journal of Sex Research,* 29(2)(May 1992), p. 141.

36. Christopher Bagley and Pierre Tremblay, Kinsey corroborated, *Gay and Lesbian Review,* 7(2)(Spring 2000), p. 17.

37. J. Billy, K. Tanfer, W. Grady, and D. Klepinger, The sexual behavior of men in the United States, *Family Planning Perspective,* 25(25)(1993), pp. 52-60.

38. Kinsey, Pomeroy, and Martin, 1948.

39. Kinsey et al., 1953.

40. Kinsey, Pomeroy, and Martin, 1948; Kinsey et al., 1953.

41. R.T. Michael, J.H. Gagnon, E.O. Laumann, and G. Kolata, *Sex in America: A definitive survey* (Boston: Little, Brown and Company, 1994), pp. 174-175.

42. Ibid.

43. M. Klitsch, Monogamy is the rule, many partners the exception among most Americans, first U.S. sex survey finds, *Family Planning Perspectives,* 27(1)(January/February 1995), p. 37.

44. Samuel S. Janus and Cynthia L. Janus, *The Janus report* (New York: John Wiley and Sons Inc., 1993), p. 70.

45. Kinsey, Pomeroy, and Martin, 1948.

46. Michael et al., 1994.

47. Beth Firestein, The bisexual challenge: Is the issue bisexuality, or is it lesbianism? *Journal of Sex Research,* 34(1)(1997), p. 107.

Chapter 4

1. Sharon A. Deacon, Laura Reinke, and Dawn Viers, Cognitive-behavioral therapy for bisexual couples: Expanding the realms of therapy, *The American Journal of Family Therapy,* 24(3)(Fall 1996), p. 293.

2. Janet Lever and Sally Carson, Behavior patterns and sexual identity of bisexual males, *Journal of Sex Research,* 29(2)(May 1992), p. 141.
3. J. Gagnon, Disease and desire, *Daedalus,* 118(1989), pp. 46-77.
4. Deacon, Reinke, and Viers, 1996, p. 242.
5. The Polyamory Society, What is polyamory? (2004), available at <www.polyamorysociety.org>.

Chapter 5

1. Neal Justin, Kiss the girls, *Minneapolis* (MN) *Star Tribune* (February 6, 2003), p. 1E.
2. Letitia Anne Peplau and Linda D. Garnets, A new paradigm for understanding women's sexuality and sexual orientation, *Journal of Social Issues,* 56(2)(2000), p. 332.
3. Carolyn J. Dean, *Sexuality and modern Western culture* (New York: Twayne Publishers, 1996), pp. 26, 29.
4. Amanda Udis-Kessler, Identity politics: A history of the bisexual movement. In Naomi Tucker (Ed.), *Bisexual politics: Theories, queries, and visions* (Binghamton, NY: Harrington Park Press, 1995), p. 20.
5. Corrinne Bedecarre, Swear by the moon, *Hypatia,* 2(3)(1997), p. 195.
6. Ibid., p. 190.

Chapter 6

1. R. Ettner, *Gender loving care: A guide to counseling gender-variant clients* (New York: Norton, 1999).
2. R. Jean Cadigan, Woman-to-woman marriage: Practices and benefits in Sub-Saharan Africa, *Journal of Comparative Family Studies,* 29(Spring 1998), p. 89.
3. Gender Education and Advocacy, Gender variance: A primer (2001), available at <www.gender.org>.
4. A.E. Eyler and K. Wright, Gender identification and sexual orientation among genetic females with gender-blended self-perception in childhood and adolescence, *The International Journal of Transgenderism,* 1(1)(July-September 1997), available at <www.symposium.com/ijt/ijtc0102.htm>.
5. Ibid.
6. Gender Education and Advocacy, 2001.
7. Lynne Carroll and Paula J. Gilroy, Transgender issues in counselor preparation, *Counselor Education and Supervision,* 41(March 2002), pp. 233-242.
8. Ettner, 1999.
9. Lynne Carroll, Paula J. Gilroy, and Jo Ryan, Counseling transgendered, transsexual, and gender-variant clients, *Journal of Counseling and Development,* 80(2)(Spring 2002), pp. 131-139.
10. Carroll and Gilroy, 2002.
11. Gender Education and Advocacy, 2001.
12. Carroll, Gilroy, and Ryan, 2002.
13. Corrinne Bedecarre, Swear by the moon, *Hypatia,* 2(3)(1997), p. 191.

Chapter 7

1. Samuel S. Janus and Cynthia L. Janus, *The Janus report* (New York: John Wiley and Sons Inc., 1993), p. 196.
2. Janna L. Horowitz and Michael D. Newcomb, Bisexuality, not homosexuality: Counseling issues and treatment approaches, *Journal of College Counseling,* 2(2)(Fall 1999), p. 148.
3. Kayley Vernallis, Bisexual monogamy: Twice the temptation but half the fun? *Journal of Philosophy,* 30(3)(Winter 1999), p. 360.
4. Ibid., p 359.
5. Ibid., p. 351.
6. Elizabeth B. Smiley, Counseling bisexual clients, *Journal of Mental Health Counseling,* 19(4)(October 1997), p. 373.
7. Horowitz and Newcomb, 1999, p. 148.
8. M.S. Weinberg, C.J. Williams, and D.W. Pryor, *Dual attraction: Understanding bisexuality* (New York: Oxford University Press, 1994).
9. Taimur Malik, Bisexual community needs assessment, unpublished, Outfront Minnesota, 2001.
10. The Polyamory Society, What is polyamory? (2004), available at <www.polyamorysociety.org>.

Chapter 8

1. All risk statistics are as reported by Liz Highleyman, Sexual transmission in the era of new treatments, *Bulletin of Experimental Treatments,* San Francisco AIDS Foundation (Summer 1999), p. 12.
2. Diane Richardson, The social construction of immunity: HIV risk perception and prevention among lesbians and bisexual women, *Culture, Health and Sexuality,* 2(1)(2000), p. 38.
3. Centers for Disease Control and Prevention (CDC), U.S. HIV and AIDS cases reported through December 2001, *The HIV/AIDS Surveillance Report,* 13(2) (2001), pp. 1-44.
4. Lynda Doll, Ted Myers, M. Kennedy, and D. Allman, Bisexuality and HIV risk: Experiences in Canada and the United States, *Annual Review of Sex Research,* 8(1997), p. 102.
5. Ibid.
6. Ibid.
7. Joseph P. Stokes and Robin L. Miller, Toward an understanding of behaviorally bisexual men: The influence of context and culture, *Canadian Journal of Human Sexuality,* 7(2)(Summer 1998), p. 101.
8. Doll et al., 1997, p. 102.
9. David J. McKirnan and Joseph P. Stokes, Bisexually active men: Social characteristics and sexual behavior, *Journal of Sex Research,* 32(1)(1995), p. 65.
10. Robert W. Wood, Leigh E. Krueger, and Tsilke C. Pearlman, HIV transmission: Women's risk from bisexual men, *American Journal of Public Health,* 83(12) (1993), pp. 1757-1759.
11. Doll et al., 1997, p. 102.

252   *BI AMERICA: MYTHS, TRUTHS, AND STRUGGLES*

12. Ibid.
13. B. Bower, Risky sex and AIDS, *Science News,* 140(9)(August 31, 1991), p. 141.
14. Chris Lombardi, Lesbians face unique set of AIDS risks, *Women's E News* (March 13, 2003), available at <www.womensenews.org>.
15. Ibid.
16. Centers for Disease Control and Prevention (CDC), HIV/AIDS and U.S. women who have sex with women (WSW) fact sheet (2003), available at <www.cdc.gov>.
17. Richardson, 2000, p. 40.
18. Ibid.
19. Helena A. Kwakwa and M. W. Ghobrial, Female to female transmission of human immunodeficiency virus, *Clinical Infectious Diseases,* 36(2003), p. e40.
20. Richardson, 2000, p. 35.
21. Kaiser Network, Daily HIV report: Risk behavior: Lesbians have similar risk of STDs as heterosexual women (October 25, 2000), available at <www.kaisernetwork.org>.
22. Kaiser Network. Daily HIV report: Lesbians and bisexual women at risk for sexually transmitted infections (October 19, 2001), available at <www.kaisernetwork.org>.

Chapter 9

1. Denise Penn, Bisexual visibility, *Lesbian News,* 27(3)(October 2001), p. 48.
2. Stephen Donaldson, The bisexual movement's beginnings in the '70s: A personal retrospective, in Naomi Tucker (Ed.), *Bisexual politics: Theories, queries, and visions.* (Binghamton, NY: Harrington Park Press, 1995), pp. 32-34.
3. Ibid., p. 34.
4. Merl Storr, Postmodern bisexuality, *Sexualities,* 2(1999), p. 309.
5. Donaldson, 1995, pp. 32-33.
6. Naomi Tucker, Bay Area bisexual history: An interview with David Lourea, in Naomi Tucker (Ed.), *Bisexual politics: Theories, queries, and visions* (Binghamton, NY: Harrington Park Press, 1995), p. 10.
7. BiNet USA, A brief history of the bisexual movement (n.d.), available at <www.binetusa.org>; Donaldson, 1995, pp. 42-43.
8. Bisexual chic: Anyone goes, *Newsweek,* 83(May 27, 1974), p. 90.
9. Danielle Raymond and Liz A. Highleyman, Brief timeline of bisexual activism in the United States, in Naomi Tucker (Ed.), *Bisexual politics: Theories, queries, and visions* (Binghamton, NY: Harrington Park Press, 1995), p. 334.
10. Tucker, 1995, p. 49.
11. M.S. Weinberg, C J. Williams, and D.W. Pryor, *Dual attraction: Understanding bisexuality* (New York: Oxford University Press, 1994).
12. Naomi Tucker, Liz A. Highleyman, and Rebecca Kaplan, *Bisexual politics: Theories, queries, and visions* (Binghamton, NY: Harrington Park Press, 1995), pp. 19-20, 26.
13. Raymond and Highleyman, 1995, p. 334.

14. Wayne M. Bryant, *Bisexual characters in film: From Anaïs to Zee* (Binghamton, NY: The Haworth Press, 1997).

15. Raymond and Highleyman, 1995, p. 334.

16. Loraine Hutchins and Lani Kaahumanu (Eds.), *Bi any other name: Bisexual people speak out* (Los Angeles, CA: Alyson Publications, 1991).

17. Tucker, Highleyman, and Kaplan, 1995.

18. Marjorie Garber, *Bisexuality and the eroticism of everyday life* (New York: Routledge, 1995).

19. Donaldson, 1995, p. 26.

Chapter 10

1. Cheryl Dobinson, Beyond bisexuality, *Herizons,* 13(2)(Summer 1999), p. 27.

2. Stephen Donaldson, The bisexual movement's beginnings in the '70s: A personal retrospective, in Naomi Tucker (Ed.), *Bisexual politics: Theories, queries, and visions* (Binghamton, NY: Harrington Park Press, 1995), p. 37.

3. Neal Justin, Kiss the girls, *Minneapolis* (MN) *Star Tribune* (February 6, 2003), p. 1E.

Chapter 11

1. Samuel S. Janus and Cynthia L. Janus, *The Janus report* (New York: John Wiley and Sons Inc., 1993), p. 70.

2. M. Reynolds, Kandahar's lightly veiled homosexual habits, *Los Angeles Times* (April 3, 2002), p. A5.

Bibliography

Abner, Allison (1992). Bisexuality out of the closet. *Essence,* 23(6)(October): 61.

Bagley, Christopher and Tremblay, Pierre (2002). Kinsey corroborated. *Gay and Lesbian Review,* 7(2)(Spring): 17-21.

Bedecarre, Corrinne (1997). Swear by the moon. *Hypatia,* 12(3): 189-196.

Billy, J., Tanfer, K., Grady, W., and Klepinger, D. (1993). The sexual behavior of men in the United States. *Family Planning Perspective,* 25(25): 52-60.

BiNetUSA (n.d.). A brief history of the bisexual movement. Available at <www. binetusa.org>.

Bisexual chic: Anyone goes (1974). *Newsweek,* 83(May 27): 90.

Block-Schwenk, Debbie (2001). Musings on my poly lives. *BiWomen Newsletter* (Boston Bisexual Women's Network), 19(5): 1, 4-5.

Bower, B. (1991). Risky sex and AIDS. *Science News,* 140(9)(August 31): 141.

Bryant, Wayne M. (1997). *Bisexual characters in film: From Anaïs to Zee.* Binghamton, NY: The Haworth Press.

Cadigan, R. Jean (1998). Woman-to-woman marriage: Practices and benefits in Sub-Saharan Africa. *Journal of Comparative Family Studies,* 29(1): 89-98.

Carroll, Lynne and Gilroy, Paula J. (2002). Transgender issues in counselor preparation. *Counselor Education and Supervision,* 41(March): 233-242.

Carroll, Lynne, Gilroy, Paula J., and Ryan, Jo (2002). Counseling transgendered, transsexual, and gender-variant clients. *Journal of Counseling and Development,* 80(2)(Spring): 131-139.

Centers for Disease Control and Prevention (CDC) (2001). U.S. HIV and AIDS cases reported through December 2001. *The HIV/AIDS Surveillance Report,* 13(2): 1-44.

Centers for Disease Control and Prevention (CDC) (2003). HIV/AIDS and U.S. women who have sex with women (WSW) fact sheet. Available at <www. cdc.gov>.

Deacon, Sharon A., Reinke, Laura, and Viers, Dawn (1996). Cognitive-behavioral therapy for bisexual couples: Expanding the realms of therapy. *The American Journal of Family Therapy,* 24(3)(Fall): 242-258.

Dean, Carolyn J. (1996). *Sexuality and modern Western culture.* New York: Twayne Publishers.

Dobinson, Cheryl (1999). Beyond bisexuality. *Herizons,* 13(2)(Summer): 27.

Doll, L., Myers, T., Kennedy, M., and Allman, D. (1997). Bisexuality and HIV risk: Experiences in Canada and the United States. *Annual Review of Sex Research,* 8: 102-147.

Donaldson, Stephen (1995). The bisexual movement's beginnings in the '70s: A personal retrospective. In Naomi Tucker (Ed.), *Bisexual politics: Theories, queries, and visions* (pp. 31-45). Binghamton, NY: Harrington Park Press.

Ettner, R. (1999). *Gender loving care: A guide to counseling gender-variant clients.* New York: Norton.

Eyler, A.E. and Wright, K. (1997). Gender identification and sexual orientation among genetic females with gender-blended self-perception in childhood and adolescence. *The International Journal of Transgenderism,* 1(1)(July-September). Available at <www.symposium.com/ijt/ijtc0102.htm>.

Faulkner, Anne H. and Cranston, Kevin (1998). Correlates of same-sex sexual behavior in a random sample of Massachusetts high school students. *American Journal of Public Health,* 88(2)(February): 262-266.

Firestein, Beth (Ed.) (1996). *Bisexuality: The psychology and politics of an invisible minority.* Thousand Oaks, CA: Sage Publications.

Firestein, Beth (1997). The bisexual challenge: Is the issue bisexuality, or is it lesbianism? *Journal of Sex Research,* 34(1): 107.

Gagnon, J. (1989). Disease and desire. *Daedalus,* 118: 47-77.

Gender Education and Advocacy (GEA) (2001). Gender variance: A primer. Available at <www.gender.org>.

Hayes, B. Grant (2001). Working with the bisexual client: How far have we progressed? *Journal of Humanistic Counseling, Education and Development,* 40(1) (Spring): 11-20.

Herdt, Gilbert (1997). *Same sex, different culture.* Boulder, CO: Westview Press.

Horowitz, Janna L. and Newcomb, Michael D. (1999). Bisexuality, not homosexuality: Counseling issues and treatment approaches. *Journal of College Counseling,* 2(2)(Fall): 143-163.

Janus, Samuel S. and Janus, Cynthia L. (1993). *The Janus report.* New York: John Wiley and Sons Inc.

Justin, Neal (2003). Kiss the girls. *Minneapolis* (MN) *Star Tribune,* February 6, p. IE.

Kaiser Network (2000). Daily HIV report: Risk behavior: Lesbians have similar risk of STDs as heterosexual women, October 25. Available at <www.kaisernetwork. org>.

Kaiser Network (2001). Daily HIV report: Lesbians and bisexual women at risk for sexually transmitted infections, October 19. Available at <www.kaisernetwork. org>.

Kinsey, A.C., Pomeroy, W.B., and Martin, C.E. (1948). *Sexual behavior in the human male.* Philadelphia: W.B. Saunders.

Kinsey, A.C., Pomeroy, W.B., Martin, C.E., and Gebhard, P.H. (1953). *Sexual behavior in the human female.* Philadelphia: W.B. Saunders.

Klein, Fritz (1993). *The bisexual option,* Second edition. Binghamton, NY: The Haworth Press.

Klitsch, M. (1995). Monogamy is the rule, many partners the exception among most Americans, first U.S. sex survey finds. *Family Planning Perspectives,* 27(1) (January/February): 37.

Kwakwa, Helena A. and Ghobrial, M.W. (2003). Female to female transmission of human immunodeficiency virus. *Clinical Infectious Disease,* 35: 40-41.

Leland, John and Rhodes, Steve (1995). Bisexuality. *Newsweek,* 126(3)(July 17): 44-50.

Lever, Janet and Carson, Sally (1992). Behavior patterns and sexual identity of bisexual males. *Journal of Sex Research,* 29(2)(May): 141-167.

Lombardi, Chris (2003). Lesbians face unique set of AIDS risks. *Women's E News,* March 13. Available at <www.womensenews.org>.

Malik, Taimur (2001). Bisexual community needs assessment. Unpublished, Outfront Minnesota.

McKirnan, David J. and Stokes, Joseph P. (1995). Bisexually active men: Social characteristics and sexual behavior. *Journal of Sex Research,* 32(1): 65-76.

Michael, R.T., Gagnon, J.H., Laumann, E.O., and Kolata, G. (1994). *Sex in America: A definitive survey.* Boston: Little, Brown and Company.

Mondimore, Franxcis Mark (1996). *A natural history of homosexuality.* Baltimore, MD: Johns Hopkins University Press.

Penn, Denise (2001). Bisexual visibility. *Lesbian News,* 27(3)(October): 48.

Peplau, Letitia Anne and Garnets, Linda D. (2000). A new paradigm for understanding women's sexuality and sexual orientation. *Journal of Social Issues,* 56(2): 329-350.

The Polyamory Society (2004). What is polyamory? Available at <www.polyamorysociety.org>.

Raymond, Danielle and Highleyman, Liz A. (1995). Brief timeline of bisexual activism in the United States. In Naomi Tucker (Ed.), *Bisexual politics: Theories, queries, and visions* (pp. 333-338). Binghamton, NY: Harrington Park Press.

Remez, L. (2000). As many lesbians have had sex with men, taking a full sexual history is important. *Family Planning Perspectives,* 32(2)(March/April): 97-98.

Reynolds, M. (2002). Kandahar's lightly veiled homosexual habits. *Los Angeles Times,* April 3, p. A5.

Richardson, Diane (2000). The social construction of immunity: HIV risk perception and prevention among lesbians and bisexual women. *Culture, Health and Sexuality,* 2(1): 33-49.

Rust, P.C. (1996). Managing multiple identities: Diversity among bisexual women and men. In Beth A. Firestein (Ed.), *Bisexuality: The psychology and politics of an invisible minority* (pp. 53-83). Thousand Oaks, CA: Sage Publications.

Smiley, Elizabeth B. (1997). Counseling bisexual clients. *Journal of Mental Health Counseling,* 19(4)(October): 373-382.

Spencer, Colin (1995). *Homosexuality in history.* Orlando, FL: Harcourt Brace and Company.

Stokes, Joseph P. and Miller, Robin L. (1998). Toward an understanding of behaviorally bisexual men: The influence of context and culture. *Canadian Journal of Human Sexuality,* 7(2)(Summer): 101-113.

Storms, M.D. (1978). Sexual orientation and self-perception. In P. Pliner, K.R. Blanstein, I.M. Spigel, T. Alloway, and L. Krames (Eds.), *Perception of emotion in self and others: Advances in the study of communication and affect,* Volume 5 (pp. 165-180). New York: Plenum.

Storr, Merl (1999). Postmodern bisexuality. *Sexualities,* 2: 209-226.

Tucker, Naomi (1995). Bay Area bisexual history: An interview with David Lourea. In Naomi Tucker (Ed.), *Bisexual politics: Theories, queries, and visions* (pp. 47-62). Binghamton, NY: Harrington Park Press.

Udis-Kessler, Amanda (1995). Identity politics: A history of the bisexual movement. In Naomi Tucker (Ed.), *Bisexual politics: Theories, queries, and visions* (pp. 17-30). Binghamton, NY: Harrington Park Press.

Vernallis, Kayley (1999). Bisexual monogamy: Twice the temptation but half the fun? *Journal of Philosophy,* 30(3)(Winter): 347-368.

Vilanch, Bruce (2002). A beautiful mind game. *Advocate,* Issue 857(February 19): 43.

Weinberg, M.S., Williams, C.J., and Pryor, D.W. (1994). *Dual attraction: Understanding bisexuality.* New York: Oxford University Press.

Wood, Robert W., Krueger, Leigh E., and Pearlman, Tsilke C. (1993). HIV transmission: Women's risk from bisexual men. *American Journal of Public Health,* 83(12): 1757-1759.

Yoshino, Kenji (2000). The epistemic contract of bisexual erasure. *Stanford Law Review,* 52(2)(January): 353-461.

Index

Page numbers followed by the letter "t" indicate tables.